D1596872

Group Agency

Group Agency

The Possibility, Design, and Status of Corporate Agents

Christian List
London School of Economics

and

Philip Pettit
Princeton University

OXFORD
UNIVERSITY PRESS

OXFORD
UNIVERSITY PRESS

Great Clarendon Street, Oxford ox2 6DP

Oxford University Press is a department of the University of Oxford.
It furthers the University's objective of excellence in research, scholarship,
and education by publishing worldwide in

Oxford New York

Auckland Cape Town Dar es Salaam Hong Kong Karachi
Kuala Lumpur Madrid Melbourne Mexico City Nairobi
New Delhi Shanghai Taipei Toronto

With offices in

Argentina Austria Brazil Chile Czech Republic France Greece
Guatemala Hungary Italy Japan Poland Portugal Singapore
South Korea Switzerland Thailand Turkey Ukraine Vietnam

Oxford is a registered trade mark of Oxford University Press
in the UK and in certain other countries

Published in the United States
by Oxford University Press Inc., New York

© Christian List and Philip Pettit 2011

The moral rights of the authors have been asserted
Database right Oxford University Press (maker)

First published 2011

All rights reserved. No part of this publication may be reproduced,
stored in a retrieval system, or transmitted, in any form or by any means,
without the prior permission in writing of Oxford University Press,
or as expressly permitted by law, or under terms agreed with the appropriate
reprographics rights organization. Enquiries concerning reproduction
outside the scope of the above should be sent to the Rights Department,
Oxford University Press, at the address above

You must not circulate this book in any other binding or cover
and you must impose this same condition on any acquirer

British Library Cataloguing in Publication Data

Data available

Library of Congress Cataloging in Publication Data

Data available

Typeset by SPI Publisher Services, Pondichery, India
Printed in Great Britain
on acid-free paper by
MPG Books Group, Bodmin and King's Lynn

ISBN 978–0–19–959156–5

Contents

Part III. The Normative Status of Group Agents

Preface

Can groups be unified rational agents over and above their individual members? In this book, we argue that they can, and identify conditions under which it is methodologically and normatively justified to view a collective as a single agent. We argue further that recognizing the existence of group agents leads us to reconceptualize some of the contours of the social world, from both positive and normative perspectives.

From a positive perspective, one can often achieve greater descriptive and explanatory parsimony by viewing a collective as a single agent, acting in pursuit of a single set of desires, in accordance with a single set of beliefs. Candidates for group agents include governments, commercial corporations, collegial courts, political parties, and expert panels, to give just a few examples. To defend the view that there are group agents, we must explain how the required agential unification can emerge at the collective level, despite the fact that individual group members have their own divergent sets of beliefs and desires as well as conflicts of interest. We suggest such an explanation and give an account of how a group must be organized in order to function as a single agent.

From a normative perspective, once we recognize the existence of group agents, we are able to assign responsibility to entities that were previously unacknowledged; we are able to extend the universe of persons in a way that allows us to track obligations, entitlements, and power relations in places where we did not previously see them; and we are able to clarify the nature of the conflicting demands on people's identities that may otherwise seem opaque.

In short, this book is intended to lay the foundations for a revised picture of the *loci* of agency in our complex social world. Crucially, our approach seeks to explain the possibility of group agency in a non-mysterious way. We reject the emergentist approaches that can be found in some of the older, heavily metaphysical accounts of group agency which had their origins in nineteenth-century and early twentieth-century continental traditions and which tended to elevate group agents above individuals, hailing them like transcendent realities that radiate into the minds of individuals. Instead, our approach is inspired and informed by recent developments in rational and social choice theory and other contemporary fields of philosophy and the social sciences, and so is compatible with the broadly individualistic foundations of those modern fields.

After a more detailed introduction, the book is divided into three parts. In the first part, we defend the logical possibility of group agents. In the second, we discuss several challenges that arise in the organizational design of group agents and suggest some general strategies for meeting those challenges. In the third and final part, we discuss the normative status of group agents, addressing issues such as their responsibility, person-hood, and role in processes of identification.

This book should be regarded as a piece of foundational research rather than empirical social science or applied political theory. The book is primarily meant to be a contribution to the philosophy of social science as well as to the foundations of political theory. We are unable to offer a fully developed social-scientific theory of group agency, with fully worked-out theoretical models and empirical tests. Neither are we able here to offer a full account of how group agents fit into the normative theories of politics that are being developed by political philosophers. Instead, we sketch what we take to be some of the core ingredients of a theory of group agency and its normative significance. We hope that this general picture proves to be persuasive and leads to further social-scientific and philosophical work on the many topics and questions that this volume does not address.

We have worked on some of the material in this book for ten years and have accumulated an enormous range of debts, joint and individual. It is impossible to name everyone who has helped us over that period – some people have been thanked in the various papers that the research has generated – but we would like to single out for mention a small number of people.

In developing the ideas presented in the book, we have benefited enormously from exchanges with colleagues in the institutional settings in which we have worked separately and often together. Having worked together in the Research School of Social Sciences at the Australian National University, and the University Center for Human Values at Princeton University, we would like to express our gratitude to both of those institutions for their intellectual and financial support. Our work has also benefited very much from the stimulating intellectual environment Christian List has enjoyed in the Choice Group and the Political Theory Group at the London School of Economics.

A number of individuals in those institutions and elsewhere have been particularly important interlocutors and collaborators on topics related to this book, including Richard Bradley, Geoffrey Brennan, Franz Dietrich, and Wlodek Rabinowicz, and we owe a lot to their friendship and wisdom. We are also greatly indebted to several people who have generously provided detailed comments on earlier drafts of this book or some of its chapters, including Rachael Briggs and her colleagues Alison Fernandes and Mark Jago in the epistemology reading group at Macquarie University, Bruce Chapman and two other, anonymous readers for Oxford University Press, Katrin Flikschuh, Natalie Gold, Lewis Kornhauser, Carlo Martini, Hilde Nagell, Kai Spiekermann, Laura Valentini, and several former students at the LSE and Princeton University, including Lara Buchak, Zsuzsanna Chappell, Krystalli Glyniadakis, and Cecile Hoareau.

In addition, we are grateful to a large number of people who in different ways have shaped our thinking on the present topic and galvanized our efforts over the years. Inevitably, we can provide only an incomplete list: Jason Alexander, David

Austen-Smith, Nick Baigent, Luc Bovens, Steven Brams, Michael Bratman, Johan van Benthem, John Dryzek, Christian Elsholtz, David Estlund, Tim Feddersen, John Ferejohn, Marc Fleurbaey, Margaret Gilbert, Alvin Goldman, Robert Goodin, Alan Hájek, Martin van Hees, Frank Hindriks, Ron Holzman, Robert Luskin, Victoria McGeer, Jane Mansbridge, Jose Marti, Peter Menzies, David Miller, Philippe Mongin, Klaus Nehring, Dan Osherson, Eric Pacuit, Marc Pauly, Rohit Parikh, Gabriella Pigozzi, Clemens Puppe, Ed Rock, Olivier Roy, David Runciman, Maurice Salles, David Schweikard, Quentin Skinner, Michael Smith, Katie Steele, Kim Sterelny, Richard Tuck, and Raimo Tuomela. We hope that we will not seem ungrateful to others not mentioned. As the authors of a book on group agency, we are acutely aware of how much we have benefited from the collective wisdom of the academic communities we have been fortunate to belong to.

Christian List also acknowledges financial support from the Nuffield Foundation and the Leverhulme Trust, and Philip Pettit similar support from the Center for Ethics at Harvard University.

Finally, and most importantly, we wish to thank Laura Valentini and Victoria McGeer as well as Klaus Jürgen List and Barbara List for their unfailing support and patience.

Introduction

Common sense and the social sciences represent many collections of human beings as if they were unitary agents, capable of performing like individuals. We speak in ordinary life of what Greenpeace or Amnesty International intends, what the Catholic Church holds sacred, what the medical profession wants, what generation X values, and what the financial markets expect. Similarly, social scientists speak of the utility functions commercial corporations maximize, the national interests states pursue, and the agenda a political elite seeks to further.

How should we interpret such talk? The bodies referred to are clearly groups, not individuals. But how should we analyze the ascription of attitudes, intentions, or agency to them? Should we understand it literally, taking it to impute a group agency that replicates the agency of individuals; and if so, should we endorse this imputation or treat it as an error? Or should we understand the language metaphorically or figuratively, taking it to suggest that while groups can simulate agency, they cannot really replicate it? On the latter view, the reference to a group's attitudes, intentions, or agency might serve useful shorthand purposes but would not have any ontological significance; it would be a mere *façon de parler*.

These questions are of pressing importance for the study of social, political, and economic issues, positive as well as normative. Our answers to them will determine how we think social and economic science should proceed in explaining the behavior of firms, states, and churches, for example, and in tracing the effects of different institutional designs. And they will determine how we think legal and moral theory should conceptualize the rights and responsibilities of corporate bodies and the claims they can make on their members. The issue of group agency lies at the heart of social-scientific and economic methodology and of legal and political philosophy.

Despite their foundational place, however, the questions have received surprisingly little attention in recent philosophy and the methodology of the social sciences. There have certainly been fruitful efforts, as we shall see, to analyze what it is for two or more individuals to perform a joint action (e.g., Bratman 1987; Searle 1995; Tuomela 1995; Gilbert 2001; Bacharach 2006; Gold and Sugden 2007). But, with some exceptions mentioned later, these have not been complemented by equally wide-ranging studies of the capacity of several individuals, not just to perform a single action together, as even a casual grouping might do, but to establish a more enduring collective entity that can count as an agent in its own right. The constitution of an individual agent gives us a basis, other things being equal, to think about how he or she will behave in the future and to reason counterfactually about how he or she would respond to changed circumstances. There is no generally accepted account of how far groups can themselves constitute agents, allowing us in the same way to predict how they will behave in the future and to speculate about how they would respond in various hypothetical conditions.

This book develops a theory of group agency, and explores its implications for the organizational design of corporate entities and for the normative status they ought to be accorded. Part I of the book argues for the possibility of group agents, drawing on work on the aggregation of judgments with which we have been jointly and separately associated. Part II looks at the extent to which group agents can be designed to satisfy various organizational desiderata: the epistemic reliability of a group's judgments; the incentive compatibility of its organizational requirements; and its responsiveness to the needs and rights of members. Part III explores the degree to which a group agent can be held responsible in its own right; its standing as a legal person; and the way it requires members to identify with it as a body they constitute.

While the theory we develop fills a gap in the contemporary literature, it draws on work in a variety of fields. This includes the research mentioned on joint action but also work in the theory of rational agency and intentionality, in social choice theory and the theory of judgment aggregation, in social ontology and the sociology of collectives and systems, in the constructivist theory of the state, and in the many studies of collective responsibility and legal personhood.[1] Although the book takes a distinctive approach, not always building explicitly on this work, our intellectual debt to those earlier contributions should be evident.

In this introduction, we pursue three topics. We look at how our approach maintains the reality of group agents, breaking with an 'eliminativist' tendency in recent thought; we show how it fits into the broader history of social and political thought about groups; and we illustrate the way in which it provides a novel perspective on issues in social and economic science and in legal and political theory.

For realism about group agents

Without doubt, some talk of group agents is just a metaphorical shorthand. Referring to what the market expects is just a handy way of describing the expectations behind individual investments. And, notwithstanding the rhetoric of politicians, referring to what the electorate has decided directs us only to a pattern in individual votes. There is no market or electorate that holds attitudes as an individual does. To suggest that there was would be to multiply entities unnecessarily, in violation of Occam's razor principle. Everything that needs to be accounted for is already itemized exhaustively in speaking of the dispositions and behavior of individual investors and voters.

The fact that some talk of group agents is certainly metaphorical has led many social theorists and philosophers to deny the reality of group agents altogether. Anthony Quinton (1975, p. 17) provides a good example of this attitude:

We do, of course, speak freely of the mental properties and acts of a group in the way we do of individual people. Groups are said to have beliefs, emotions, and attitudes and to take decisions and make promises. But these ways of speaking are plainly metaphorical. To ascribe mental predicates to a group is always an indirect way of ascribing such predicates to its members ... To say that the industrial working class is determined to resist anti-trade union laws is to say that all or most industrial workers are so minded.

According to this 'eliminativism' about group agents, there are only individual agents like Christian, Philip, and other people; when such individuals cooperate in groups, they do not bring novel agents into existence. Anything ascribed to a group, so the line goes, can be re-expressed by reference to its members. To think that firms and states are genuine corporate agents that act on the basis of collective attitudes would be to mistake metaphorical shorthand for literal characterization.

Quinton's account is not the only form the denial of group agents can take. Another suggests that talk of group agents is sometimes intended to be literal, contrary to what Quinton claims, but that it is misconceived; there are no such entities out there. In what follows, we abstract from this difference and describe any non-realist view of group agents as 'eliminativist'. We could also re-describe such a view more positively as 'singularism', using a term introduced by Margaret Gilbert (1989). Singularism asserts that there are only individual agents and that any talk of group agents is either metaphorical or wrong.

Eliminativism about group agents seems supported by a methodological conviction at the heart of much of economics and the social sciences over the past fifty years or so. This is the methodological individualism of the philosopher Karl Popper, the economist Friedrich Hayek, and many others for whom it became an orthodoxy. As we understand it here, it is the view that good explanations of social phenomena should not postulate any social forces other than those that derive from the agency of individuals: that is, from their psychologically explicable responses to one another and to their natural and social environment.

Individualism is to the social sciences and economics what physicalism is to biology and psychology. Physicalism is the view that biological explanations should not appeal to any physically or chemically mysterious life-force – a *vis vitalis*, as it was once called – and that psychological explanations should not appeal to any physically or biologically mysterious source of mentality – anything like Descartes's *res cogitans*. Similarly, individualism says that economic and social explanations should resist any appeal to psychologically mysterious social forces (Pettit 1993). What counts as psychologically mysterious may require further explication, of course, but we abstract from that issue here, taking it to be something that research in psychology can adjudicate.

Eliminativism about group agents seems to go naturally with methodological individualism. If eliminativism is true, the behavior of groups involves no mysterious forces, and this may well have bolstered eliminativism's philosophical appeal. But while eliminativism, if correct, would suffice to give a non-mysterious account of a group's behavior, it is by no means necessary for that purpose. In other words, while eliminativism entails individualism, individualism need not entail eliminativism; it may also be consistent with certain forms of non-eliminativism, as indeed we argue it is.

Something close to an eliminativist view is implicit in most legal and economic analyses of corporate bodies, particularly of commercial firms. There are many accounts of why economically rational individuals will choose corporate organization over looser market relationships, but most represent incorporation as little more than a source of denser contractual ties than the market provides. While incorporation certainly has the effect of creating such binding ties, few accounts raise the possibility that, unlike the market, incorporation might, in addition, establish a novel, collective agent. On the standard analysis, as one commentator puts it, the notion of the firm is just 'a collective noun for the web of contracts that link the various participants' (Grantham 1998, p. 579).

The view defended in this book rejects eliminativism and any variant that denies the reality or significance of group agents. Some talk of group agents may be metaphorical, to be sure, and some may misconceive reality. But often the ascription of agency to groups expresses a correct and important observation, both in common and in scientific discourse: a correct observation, because there really are group agents; and an important one, because to overlook their presence would be to miss out on a significant aspect of the social world.

These are strong claims, as should become clear, but for all their strength, they do not undermine methodological individualism; they do not introduce any psychologically mysterious forces. As the agency of individual human beings depends wholly on the configuration and functioning of biological subsystems, so the agency of group agents depends wholly on the organization and behavior of individual members. Despite being non-eliminativist, this picture conforms entirely with methodological individualism.

We defend these claims in the first part of the book. Beginning with a discussion of individual agents, we identify the conditions that any system, whether an individual or a group, must satisfy to count as an agent. We show how a group can be organized to satisfy them and thereby to become quite literally an agent. The recognition that such a group is an agent then allows us better to understand and explain its actions, its relationships with other agents, and the responses it evokes in individual members and non-members.

In particular, we show that, despite the absence of any mysterious new forces, the presence of group agents is an important feature of the social world. It is important for two reasons, one negative, the other positive. The negative reason is that, on our analysis, talk of group agents cannot be dispensed with in favor of talk about individual agents. And the positive is that, by thinking in terms of group agents, we are equipped to relate to the social world in a distinctive way.

The argument for the negative claim is elaborated in the second and third chapters. Drawing on recent work in the theory of judgment aggregation, we show that the attitudes – beliefs and desires – we need to ascribe to any group that meets the conditions of agency are not readily reducible to the attitudes of individuals. A group agent, like an individual, has to satisfy certain minimal requirements of consistency, and to avoid breaching them, it may be constrained to form attitudes on some issues that depart from the attitudes of its members. In the limit, it may even have to form an attitude on some issue that all its members individually reject. Since the ascription of attitudes is needed to make sense of such a group's behavior, the lack of an easy translation of group-level attitudes into individual-level ones requires us to recognize the existence of group agents in making an inventory of the social world.

This point is worth stressing, since we can easily imagine cases where there is nothing wrong in postulating the existence of certain entities, but there would be little gained by doing so. Imagine a simple language that allows us to refer to concrete physical objects but not to abstract properties. We can compare any two objects, for instance, by saying whether one weighs the same as the other, but we cannot speak of 'weight' as an abstract property. Now suppose we extend this language by defining an object's weight, abstractly, as the equivalence class the object falls into with respect to the relation 'weighs the same as': two objects have the same weight if and only if they weigh the same. It is then perfectly possible to postulate the existence of weights, and doing so may be expressively useful. But because this abstract language can be easily translated back into the earlier concrete one, the postulation of weights has little ontological significance. Any insights gained from it would be translatable into the original, simpler language.

Although abstract weights are just as real as concrete objects, then, the failure to recognize them would not lead us to miss out on anything in the physical world. On the picture defended in this book, things are very different with group agents. These agents relate to their members in such a complex manner that talk of them is not readily reducible to talk about the members. Not only does that negative claim hold true. Our complementary positive claim, supported by the overall thrust of the book, is that this explanatory ascription of agency to groups opens up a distinctive way of relating to and interacting with such groups, as is implicit in the role that talk of group agents plays in ordinary as well as social-scientific discourse.

Once we recognize a collective entity as an agent, we can interact with it, criticize it, and make demands on it, in a manner not possible with a non-agential system.[2] And we can relate to it in this way without having to look at everything that happens at the individual level. The primary center of agency in such a case – and the primary target of criticism or contestation – is the group, not any individual. At the time at which we are completing this introduction, for example, BP, a multinational corporation, has come under attack for causing a massive oil spill in the Gulf of Mexico. The entire politics of this affair, especially the way in which everyone, from affected residents to criminal investigators, tends to relate to BP, would be impossible to make sense of without ascribing agency to BP. If we viewed the world through an eliminativist lens, this mode of explanation and interaction would be unavailable.

The shift in perspective opened up by the recognition of group agents is parallel to the one opened up, according to many physicalists, when we move from thinking of an apparatus as an electronic device to recognizing it as a computer programed to play chess; or when we move from thinking of an organism as a purely biological system to viewing it as an intentional agent that forms and acts on certain beliefs and desires in a more or less rational way. In short, it parallels the move from taking a 'physical stance' towards a given system to taking an 'intentional stance' (Dennett 1979). Here, too, the new perspective enables us to see higher-level regularities that can guide us in thinking about the outputs likely to result from various inputs, and in determining how we should respond to the system in question, often in abstraction from much of what happens at the lower level.

Given that talk of group agents is not readily translatable into individualistic terms, and given that it supports a distinct way of understanding and relating to the social world, we can think of such entities as autonomous realities. Although their agency depends on the organization and behavior of individual members, as individualism requires, they display patterns of collective behavior that will be lost on us if we keep our gaze fixed at the individual level. And to lose sight of those patterns is to lose an important source of guidance as participants in the social world.

Eliminativism denies the existence and importance of group agents, and our aim is to replace it by a theory according to which some group agents not only exist but also have the importance and autonomy just underlined. Our theory maintains this realist view of group agents without compromising the individualist claim that no psychologically mysterious forces should be invoked in giving an account of the social world. Many physicalists recognize that there are animal and human minds, and consider this recognition important for our understanding of the world, but deny that this requires any physically mysterious stuff or force − anything like Descartes's *res cogitans* mentioned above. Under the approach defended in this book, individualists can similarly hold that there are group agents, and that this recognition is important for a proper understanding of the social world, and yet deny that this requires any psychologically mysterious element. In virtue of our claim that group agents not only exist but that talk about them is not readily reducible to talk about individual agents, we may describe our account as not just a realist but a non-redundant realist theory. The position it occupies in relation to the other approaches discussed in this section is summarized in the following tree.

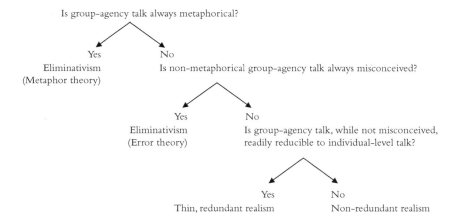

The historical novelty of our form of group-agent realism

How does our approach relate to classical realist or non-eliminativist approaches to thinking about group agents? We can identify two broadly different approaches in the history of realist thought over the last few centuries, and an interesting feature of our approach is that it breaks with both.

According to one approach, group agents exist when a collection of people each authorize an independent voice as speaking for them in this or that domain, committing themselves to be bound by it just as an individual is bound by what he or she affirms or promises. According to the other, group agents exist only when something much richer transpires; only, in an organic metaphor, when a collection of people are animated by a common purpose and mentality. We call the first approach the 'authorization theory' of group agency, the second the 'animation theory'.

The authorization theory was first explicitly formulated by Thomas Hobbes, most famously in Chapter 16 of his 1651 treatise, *Leviathan* (1994). He distinguished three ways a multitude or collection of individuals might form a group agent, particularly a state or commonwealth (Pettit 2008b, Ch. 5). The individuals might authorize one person to speak for them on every relevant question, binding themselves by such a monarch's words. Alternatively, they might authorize the voice of the majority on any issue, organizing themselves in what Hobbes described as a democratic manner. Or they might authorize a smaller group – say, an aristocracy that operates internally like a democracy – to speak for them on a majoritarian basis. No matter what form a group agent takes, on this account, it exists just in virtue of a process whereby individuals offload responsibility onto something independent: a natural person or a democratic or aristocratic majoritarian process.

We think this account of group agency is inadequate. Although some group agents may exist by virtue of the authorization of an individual spokesperson, this case is degenerate, since everything the recognition of such a group agent entails is already expressible in an individual-level language. Group agents of this kind are not very different from the abstract weights in our earlier example and, perhaps for that reason, they are often cast as less than fully real.[3] Rather than speaking of a group or corporate agent, we might as well speak of a corporately empowered individual: an individual – in the political case, a sovereign – capable of calling on those pledged to provide support. The realism appropriate in relation to this kind of group agent is a thin and relatively redundant one, compared to the non-redundant realism we defend more generally.

But what about group agents that exist by virtue of the authorization of a majoritarian process, whether across the membership as a whole or within an authorized subgroup? Aren't such entities group agents in a less redundant sense than those that reflect the will of a single spokesperson? We argue that they are not, because there is a different and surprisingly strong obstacle to the possibility of majoritarian group agents. This obstacle, discussed in Chapter 2, is that the voice of the majority cannot be relied upon to produce consistent, robustly implementable attitudes or decisions, even when there is nothing wrong with the attitudes of members. The 'discursive dilemma' explored in that chapter shows that even perfectly consistent individuals can deliver inconsistent majority votes on connected issues. Thus a collection of people committed to act on majority opinion across a variety of issues may find itself committed to conflicting courses of action. Such a collection, as we show, could not generally satisfy the conditions for agency.

But things are even more complicated than this suggests. As shown in Chapters 2 and 3, majority rule is not the only form of organization that fails to offer an independent, implementable voice individuals might authorize. It turns out that no plausible, equally simple process can provide such guidance, where the collective attitude on each issue is determined as a straightforward function of the individual attitudes on it. What we describe as the 'discursive dilemma' is just an illustration of a more general difficulty. And that difficulty arises with any plausible, issue-by-issue method of aggregation, majoritarian or otherwise, that is designed to deliver a suitable collective output on each issue from individual inputs. This observation has become ever more salient with the development of the theory of judgment aggregation.[4]

The lesson, broadly stated, is clear. If a group agent is to display the rationality that agency requires, its attitudes cannot be a majoritarian or other equally simple function of the attitudes of its members. The group agent has to establish and evolve a mind that is not just a majoritarian or similar reflection of its members' minds; in effect, it has to develop a mind of its own.[5] This gives rise to the kind of autonomy that we ascribe to group agents.

Following Hobbes, the authorization theory was endorsed at the end of the seventeenth century by John Locke, and at the end of the eighteenth by Jean-Jacques Rousseau. The rival, animation theory appeared only later, in the final decades of the nineteenth century and the early decades of the twentieth. It may have been inspired by the work of Hegel and other social philosophers, but it was most explicitly formulated by legal historians such as Otto von Gierke in Germany and Frederick Maitland in England (Runciman 1997). Drawing on research on medieval and later legal theory, these thinkers argued that group agents are emergent entities over and above the individuals who compose them; they embraced an emergentism that was starkly opposed to the eliminativism discussed in the last section.

We describe the emergentist approach as an 'animation theory', since its metaphors have a similar provenance to the ones deployed in the vitalist approach to life. Biological vitalists treat life as the product of a mysterious *vis vitalis*, denying that it is the precipitate of suitably complex chemical arrangements. Animation theorists treat group agency as the product of an equally mysterious, organicist force. Thus, Sir Ernest Barker (1950, p. 61), writing in this tradition, postulated 'the pulsation of a common purpose which surges, as it were, from above, into the mind and behaviour of members'.

Like the authorization account, this theory treats talk of group agents literally and seriously, thereby embracing realism about such entities. But where the earlier account treats such talk as a way of speaking about simple acts of coordination among individuals – their authorization of a shared voice for certain purposes – the animation theory takes it to refer to entities that coordination alone could not explain, at least not if its organicist metaphors are to be taken seriously. The view implicit in these metaphors suggests that it is possible, in a philosophical thought experiment, to replicate all the properties and relations we find among the individual members of a group agent without replicating the group agent itself. For the group agent to exist, so it is suggested, there must be something extra present: a force like the common purpose that Barker imagines surging from above.

The animation theory of group agency became fashionable in the early twentieth century, often giving rise to an enthusiastic rhetoric about the independent reality of associations, organizations, and states. It inspired several progressive political and legal developments, including the guild socialism supported by G. D. H. Cole, the political pluralism advocated by Harold Laski, and a pro-democratic movement in the American jurisprudence of organizations and organizational responsibility (Nicholls 1975; Vincent 1987, Ch. 5; Hager 1989; Runciman 1997). As fascism took over in Europe, however, it also became associated with a totalitarian image of society, and this may have led to its ultimate demise.

Independently of its political associations, the approach is objectionable on metaphysical grounds. It offends against methodological individualism in suggesting that group agency requires something above and beyond the emergence of coordinated, psychologically intelligible dispositions in individual members. This is metaphysically incredible. Whatever plausibility the idea of a chemically mysterious *vis vitalis* may have had in the theory of life, or a physically mysterious *res cogitans* in the theory of mind, it is hard to make sense of the idea that group agency requires not just the coordination of individual members but also the presence of a mysterious, individualistically inaccessible force.

It may have been the salience of the animation theory, especially given its association with fascism, that accounted for the rise of the eliminativist view of group agents in the twentieth century. If the reality of group agents seemed to require the animation of collections by an unexplained force, then it is understandable that many thinkers preferred to deny the existence of group agents altogether. They might have explored the earlier, authorization theory developed by Hobbes, but, perhaps because of worries about majoritarianism, most seem to have opted for eliminativism instead. The eliminativist approach was embraced especially strongly in libertarian politics, where it may have played the symbolic role of raising doubts about any policies that targeted collective entities – classes, cultures, society as a whole – rather than individuals. It was famously – or perhaps notoriously – expressed by Margaret Thatcher, Prime Minister of Great Britain, when she declared that there is 'no such thing as society'.[6]

Where the authorization theory casts group agents as credible but relatively redundant entities, on a par with the weights of our toy example, the animation theory casts them as entities of a non-redundant but incredible kind. The theory adopted in this book combines the merits of both approaches, while avoiding their shortcomings. It renders group agents credible, by showing how various forms of coordination can give rise to such agents. But it also renders them non-redundant for our understanding of the social world, by showing that the coordination required is far from straightforward. The coordination necessary implies, as we have pointed out, that on some matters the attitudes embraced by a group agent are not a systematic function of the attitudes of members. In the limit, a group that satisfies plausible conditions for agency may have to embrace an attitude or intention that is rejected by all its members individually. This point will be fully developed in the chapters to come.

In sum, the authorization theory supports only a thin realism about group agents under which group-agency talk is more or less redundant, but respects methodological individualism, whereas the animation theory offers a much thicker realism under which group-agency talk is as non-redundant as such talk could be, but invokes a mysterious, non-individualistic force. Our theory, by contrast, supports a realism under which group-agency talk is non-redundant, while remaining faithful to methodological individualism. Table 1 summarizes the positions.

While the view defended in this book breaks with both the authorization and animation approaches, it fits better with a view of corporate bodies found in medieval thinkers, particularly in legal thinkers of the fourteenth century like Bartolus of

Table 1: Realism about group agents

Realist theories	Redundant or non-redundant group-agency talk?	Methodologically individualistic or not?
Authorization theory	Redundant	Individualistic
Animation theory	Non-redundant	Non-individualistic
Our theory	Non-redundant	Individualistic

Sassoferrato and Baldus de Ubaldis (Woolf 1913; Canning 1987; Kantorowicz 1997). As we will mention in later chapters, it appears to have been medieval lawyers who first fashioned the idea of the legal person, using the resources of Roman law (Duff 1938). They argued that being able to have and assert rights of ownership and contract, and being susceptible to having such rights asserted against them, bodies like guilds, monasteries, and towns had the character of legal persons and agents. This early corporate thinking was the inspiration for Gierke's and Maitland's approach to group agents but, from our perspective, it looks far more congenial than the animation theory the later organicist language suggested. We would be happy to think that our theory is continuous with that earlier strand of thought about group agents.

Our theory also fits well with some pictures of group agency developed or assumed in more recent work in philosophy and the social sciences. It is congruent, for example, with the picture of group agency in Peter French's work on corporate responsibility (1984); in James Coleman's sociology of corporate power (1974; 1990); in Carol Rovane's philosophy of personal identity (1997); and in the work of John Braithwaite and his co-authors on corporate regulation (e.g., Braithwaite and Drahos 2000). And, as we discovered while finalizing this book, it is also in the spirit of a theory outlined in the late 1940s by E. T. Mitchell (1946) but not much taken up in subsequent work. We follow a somewhat different track from these thinkers in developing and defending our view of group agency and consequently refer to their work only occasionally. But they will not see the destination to which the track leads as unknown or unclaimed territory.

Methodological implications, positive and normative

In concluding this introduction, we should explain why we think the theory of group agency is central to positive social science and normative social and political theory. These subjects focus on issues in several domains, from the economic to the sociological, from the legal to the political. From a positive perspective, they are concerned with social explanation, prediction, and design; from a normative one, with questions in political philosophy, welfare economics, normative jurisprudence, and the evaluation of policy.

To appreciate the positive, as opposed to normative, issues a theory of group agency can illuminate, we must recognize the methodological significance of detecting when agency is present, and when not. Consider, once again, the significance of seeing an organism, perhaps a human being or a simpler animal, as an agent. Recall the difference between viewing the organism from within the intentional or agential stance and viewing it from within a physical or mechanical stance (Dennett 1979; 1981; Pettit 2002, Pt. 2, Ch. 1). Prior to seeing the organism as an agent, we may be able to make good biological sense of its behavior, identifying the role of neural and other stimuli in evoking various responses, and seeing the background conditions required for these responses to materialize. This grasp of the organism's workings will give us an explanatory and predictive understanding of how the organism responds to its environment, which will, in turn, facilitate physical and neural interventions. It will allow us to understand, for instance, that particular neural inputs lead to particular responses or that the suppression of some element in the organism's make-up promotes or impedes certain regularities in its behavior. Neurosurgery involves taking this stance towards a patient, at least during an operation.

But even if we have this neurobiological understanding of the organism, we will still suffer a significant epistemic blindness if we fail to recognize that the organism is an agent. Recognizing it as an agent will require detecting certain higher-level relations between its responses, actions, and environment. These will support the claim that the organism has goals that it seeks to realize through its actions, keeping track of relevant changes in the environment. That is, the organism acts for the satisfaction of its goals according to its representation of the environment. Cognitive psychologists and social scientists view human beings through this lens, and many behavioral ecologists take a similar stance towards any sufficiently complex animals they study.

Once we view an organism as an agent, we achieve a new understanding over and above the neurobiological one. Its importance becomes evident in the possibilities of interaction the agential or intentional stance makes possible. As intentional agents ourselves, we know how to interact with other intentional agents. We know, as it is sometimes said, what buttons to press. Or at least we have a better sense of the buttons available than a purely biological understanding can provide. Having identified the organism as an agent, we can interact with it effectively and profitably. If it is a human being, in particular, we can draw on the rich forms of communication possible in human social interactions.

A simpler analogy underlines this point. Suppose, as mentioned earlier, we are trying to understand an electronic device and come to recognize that it is not just a system with certain electronic properties; it is a computer designed to play chess. The intentional stance we thereby take towards the device opens up new ways of understanding and interacting with it. From within this stance, we can understand the device's responses, which we now identify as moves, in quite a different manner from how we understood them before. We can interact with the device by playing chess with it, something impossible if we interacted with it only on the basis of an electronic understanding.[7]

These observations illustrate the importance of recognizing when agency is present and when not. And just as they support this lesson in the individual case, so they support it in the collective one. Standard accounts, as we have noted, view commercial firms and competitive markets as more or less parallel ways of coordinating individual behavior. But markets are not group agents: participants act only for their own advantage, however significant their aggregate effects on pricing may be, and there is no further center of agency beyond the individual level. Firms, by contrast, are group agents on our account. And since we can rely on any agent to adjust and act in a systematic, purposeful way, we can interact with firms in ways impossible with a market. Generally, we can resent and protest against a group agent's actions, whether on the basis of its own endorsed goals or on the basis of goals we think it should endorse. We can threaten it with penalties if it does not improve its behavior. And we can go to law to enforce such penalties. In short, we can deal with a group agent as if it were an individual person.

Not only that. Daniel Dennett (1979; 1981) has long argued that, apart from the physical stance in which we understand a system mechanically, and the intentional one in which we interpret it as an agent, there is also a third perspective, which he calls the 'design stance'. In the design stance, we identify aspects of a system's make-up that limit its proper functioning as an agent – in the individual case, *idées fixes*, blindspots, obsessions, and the like. A theory that enables us to recognize when there are group agents and when not also allows us to adopt a design stance towards the group agents we recognize. The history and organization of a group agent often leave it susceptible to certain forms of malfunction and underperformance, and an important task is to identify these and to find ways they may be rectified. The second part of the book addresses issues of this kind, looking at how group agents can be designed to satisfy various organizational desiderata, ranging from the epistemic reliability of their judgments to the responsiveness of their actions to the needs and rights of their members.

There are two, sometimes competing preferences in the methodology of social science, and of science more generally. One is the mechanism-centered preference for explanations that identify the most basic factors at work in any given area of investigation. The other is the control-centered preference for explanations that direct us to the contextually most useful ways of predicting and intervening in what happens in that area. It should be clear from the foregoing that we are committed to the control-centered preference, believing that it is scientifically useful to identify the variables and laws that best facilitate intervention in any given area, even if they are not the most fundamental ones at work. We have each defended that methodological preference elsewhere (Pettit 1993, Ch. 5; List and Menzies 2009).

Even cursory reflection should indicate the potential interest of a control-centered theory of group agency in the social sciences. In thinking about firms, our theory would license economists to look at the aims and strategies of a corporation as if it were an individual agent, abstracting largely from the individual dispositions of its members. And it would support the adoption of a design stance, leading social scientists to explore how a firm's organization may shape its options and choices and to find ways in which any resulting difficulties might be overcome. These, in turn, are important questions in the theory of mechanism design (for a survey, see Royal-Swedish-Academy-of-Sciences 2007).

Equally, in accounting for the behavior of states, our theory would allow political scientists and international-relations theorists to treat a state as an integrated agent, with its own goals and strategies. And it would prompt them to explore how variations in institutional design, such as differences between democratic and non-democratic states, or between parliamentary and presidential democracies, can affect a state's agential performance, thereby speaking to some central questions in political science.

Within positive social science, the theory of group agency can finally be related to more formal approaches as well, such as decision theory, game theory, and social choice theory. Decision theory offers an account of a single agent's rational decision making. Game theory focuses on how several rational agents interact in situations of interdependent decision making. And social choice theory explores the different ways in which the attitudes of individual agents may be related to those of groups. But the theories themselves do not tell us who the rational agents are to which they apply. Do decision theory and game theory, for instance, apply to what group agents do? Should we think of the result of the aggregation of individual preferences, as studied in social choice theory, as the preferences of a group agent, or merely as some kind of summary statistic akin to an opinion poll? We cannot even begin to make sense of these questions without an independent theory of group agency.

These comments should underline the importance of a theory of group agency from a positive, social-scientific perspective, whether focused on explanation, prediction, or design, and whether formally oriented or not. But the theory we defend is also relevant to social and political theory of a normative kind. Among other things, the emphasis in such normative endeavors is on providing an account of the values and ideals that ought to prevail in any given area; identifying the agents who play a role in realizing those ideals; pinpointing the conditions under which these agents can be held responsible for what they do; and suggesting sanctions for various failures in performance. When we pursue such normative analysis, it matters significantly how we conceptualize groups of people and whether we take them to constitute agents in their own right.

The basic normative question regarding group agents is whether it is desirable that such agents play a role in social life and, if so, how they should be organized: how far firms or churches should be regulated by the state or other organizations, for example, and how far the state should be restricted by its citizenry. Assuming that group agents do get established, a number of questions arise. What responsibilities and rights should they have in relation to their members, and to individual or corporate outsiders? When, if at all, is it appropriate to hold them responsible in their own right for not living up to what we expect of them or for failing to respect the rights of others? How should we respond to group agents that do badly or well? Are resentment and appreciation called for, as with individual agents? And if they are, what moral or legal sanctions – penalties or rewards – might be suitable and effective?

These abstract questions take a more concrete form as we look at the particular groups that count, under our theory, as group agents. Consider commercial firms again. Such entities have only come into existence in the last few hundred years, and it is only since the mid-nineteenth century that they have assumed their now familiar form. Under this form, a corporation can be set up by a mere act of registration; it can operate in different territories and change its type of business at will; it is financially liable only up to the limit of its corporate resources; it can own other corporations and exert control over how they do business; and, subject to certain antitrust restrictions, there is no limit to how far its wealth and influence can grow.

Commercial corporations raise a host of normative questions that can only be dealt with adequately from within a theory of group agency. Are the rights of corporations, as currently established in most legal regimes, normatively desirable from the perspective of individuals? Do they distribute control over corporate bodies appropriately between the various stakeholders: directors, workers, shareholders, and the public at large? Should corporations be allowed to participate in the political process, providing campaign finance for political parties, for example? Should they be taxed independently of the taxation imposed on shareholders? Should they be held responsible in criminal law over and above the responsibility of offending employees, and if so, what sanctions should be employed against them? And should corporations be able to claim protection as persons, as they can do under the fourteenth amendment to the US Constitution?

The abstract normative questions about group agents assume a second form in the context of the law and legal institutions. Should the law be regarded, as Ronald Dworkin (1986) suggests, as the voice of the people? If so, what institutions are required to ensure that the voice is consistent, interpretable, and action-guiding? Is a single sovereign required, as in traditional absolutist thinking and under British parliamentary sovereignty? Or can those constraints be met within a more standard, mixed constitution? Should we regard a legislature as a single corporate body, capable of supporting a consistent set of intentions? And how can the courts read off those intentions in interpreting statutes?[8] In particular, how far should the courts be guided by a concern for the integrity of the law in this interpretive process?

The general normative questions we have raised take the most familiar and perhaps most forceful form in the political context. Should the state be conceptualized and organized as a corporate agent or merely as an impersonal apparatus of coordination? If it is a corporate agent, what standards should it honor in its relations with its members, and with outsiders, corporate and individual? How do legislative, executive, judicial, and other agencies relate to the state and to one another, and how should they be controlled by the people? Is enough control guaranteed by the election of those who run the legislature and executive and who appoint the officials in other areas of government? Or does it require other institutional devices: for example, the recognition of conventional or constitutional standards and the individual-level contestability of government for the satisfaction of those standards? Given the difficulty of exit, is such control enough to guarantee the legitimacy of the state? Or must the state also deliver justice in other respects, both domestically and perhaps in relation to residents of other states? And further, what is required for a legitimate global order among states?

These questions illustrate the open-ended range of normative issues to which the theory of group agency is relevant. There is no hope of addressing all these issues in a single book, or even in the entire body of work of a couple of authors. In the third part of the book, we cover only a few particularly salient normative questions about group agents. We look first at how far group agents are fit to be held responsible for what they do and how their responsibility relates to the responsibility of their members. Then we go on to the question of whether they are fit to be treated, not just as corporate agents, but as corporate persons, and to what extent this status gives them anything like the rights we assign to individual persons. Finally, we examine the ways in which individual members identify with the corporate agents they belong to and look at various questions concerning multiple identities.

Our discussions in the second and third parts of the book exemplify how the theory of group agency is relevant to positive and normative questions about the social world. Although we hope that these discussions are of interest in their own right, their primary purpose is to direct attention to how the theory we defend can be carried forward in social and economic science, and in legal and political theory. If this book proves useful, it will be as a pilot project, not as the final statement of any unchallengeable findings.

PART I

The Logical Possibility of Group Agents

1

The Conditions of Agency

The aim of the first part of this book is to defend the logical possibility of group agents. To do so, we introduce basic conditions of agency, investigate how individual inputs can be aggregated into group-level outputs, and explore different possible structures of a group agent. The three chapters in this first part are devoted in turn to these issues.

In this first chapter, we introduce the basic conditions a system must meet if it is to be an agent, identify ways in which agency may become more complex, and present a conception of how a group of individuals can form a group agent. The discussion is divided into three sections. The first offers a basic account of agency; the second addresses some complications; and the third introduces the idea of a group agent.

1.1 A basic account of agency

The core idea

The best way to introduce the notion of agency is to imagine a simple system and to ask what we expect of it when we think of it as an agent. Imagine a small robotic device, then, that moves around an area the size of a table top. Suppose that scattered across this area are several cylindrical objects, some upright, some on their sides. Now think about how you will view the device if it scans the area with its bug-like eyes, then moves about and, using its prosthetic limbs, puts any cylinders lying on their side into an upright position. Think about how you will view it if it remains on alert after all the cylinders are upright and responds to any cylinder falling over by restoring it to its old position.

You may wonder about how the device is constructed and, playing engineer, take it apart to find out. But even if you do not take it apart, you will be struck by the complexity of its performance as an agent. It registers the locations and orientations of the cylinders as it scans the environment with its eyes. It brings to this representation of the environment a motivating specification of how it wants the environment to be; in this specification all cylinders are upright. And when it registers a gap between how things are and how it wants them to be, it processes that fact and takes action to realize the motivating specification. Three features of the robot stand out, then:

First feature. It has representational states that depict how things are in the environment.

Second feature. It has motivational states that specify how it requires things to be in the environment.

Third feature. It has the capacity to process its representational and motivational states, leading it to intervene suitably in the environment whenever that environment fails to match a motivating specification.

An 'agent', on our account, is a system with these features: it has representational states, motivational states, and a capacity to process them and to act on their basis. When processed appropriately, the representational states co-vary with certain variations in the environment: for example, with the changing positions of the cylinders. And the motivational states leave the agent at rest or trigger action, depending on whether the motivating specifications are realized or unrealized in the represented environment. Our robot, for example, acts to maintain the pattern of upright cylinders in a recalcitrant and changing world, where cylinders topple under various influences.

Feasible limits, favorable conditions

Suppose that on playing around with the robot – perhaps it is a leftover from a lost civilization – we discover that when it moves towards cylinders at the edge of its area it knocks them off the board rather than setting them upright. Do we say that it has a dual goal: to set upright the cylinders in the center and to get rid of those near the edge? Or that it has the single goal of setting them upright and just fails to do this with cylinders at the margins? Although the first response is possible, the second seems more reasonable, particularly if the robot's motions are the same in the center of the area and at the edge, so that there is no behavioral evidence of a different goal. The second response presupposes that an agent like the robot need not always be successful at satisfying its motivations according to its representations. It may be successful only within feasible limits: the physical limits, in this case, of the board on which it moves.

Suppose we find, to take another case, that if the lights are turned off, the robot fails to respond to cylinders falling over; or that it does not reliably set cylinders upright if we play around with the light, shining it directly onto its eyes. Do we conclude that it is only a very hit-and-miss agent, perhaps even a random device that sometimes looks like an agent but isn't really one? Surely not. We would be more inclined to think that it is an agent but that it operates properly only in favorable conditions: the presence of standard lighting, in this case.

This suggests a slight modification of our emerging conception of an agent, particularly its third feature. An agent is a system that has representational and motivational states such that in favorable conditions, within feasible limits, it acts for the satisfaction of its motivations according to its representations.

States and attitudes

We have spoken of representational states and representations, motivational states and motivations. What are these? Representational and motivational states, which we also call 'intentional states', are configurations in an agent's physical make-up that play a particular role or function in engaging with other such states and in producing action. A state is 'representational' if it plays the role of depicting the world, and 'motivational' if it plays the role of motivating action. Two states instantiate the same representation if they play the same representational role, and they instantiate the same motivation if they play the same motivational role, just as two objects instantiate the same weight if they weigh the same.

We make no assumptions about the precise physical nature of intentional states. They may be of a wide variety of kinds. They may be electronic or neural configurations of the agent, for example, depending on its robotic or animal nature. They may be localized in the agent's brain or central processing system or dispersed throughout its body. We only require that they be configurations of the agent − or perhaps configurations of the agent in context − that play the appropriate functional role.

How should we think of the representations or motivations instantiated by an agent's intentional states? We think of a representation or a motivation as a pair of things: an intentional attitude and an object towards which the attitude is held. The attitude can be either representational or motivational; the object encodes what is being depicted or specified in the representation or motivation. Although there is room for some theoretical maneuver here, we take the object to be a proposition. If the attitude towards it is representational, the proposition is depicted as being true; if the attitude is motivational, it is specified as one the agent is motivated to make true through its actions.[9] Our little robot, for example, may hold a representational attitude towards the proposition that one of the cylinders is on its side: it 'believes' this to be the case; and it may hold a motivational attitude towards the proposition that this cylinder is in an upright position: it 'desires' this to be the case − and subsequently makes it true through the action of putting the cylinder upright.

Propositions can be conceptualized in several ways. Philosophers usually think of propositions as sets of possible worlds.[10] In the formal model introduced in the next chapter, we represent them as sentences of a particular language.[11] But various ways of modeling propositions are compatible with our approach.

From limited to enhanced attitudinal scope

The robot that has served as our paradigmatic agent holds intentional attitudes only within a very limited scope. As we shall see later, its attitudes are also limited in sophistication; for example, they leave the robot incapable of reasoning.

The scope of the robot's attitudes is limited in two respects. The first concerns their extent and detail. The robot has only one motivation: to keep the cylinders upright; and it represents only very few features of these cylinders: their locations and orientations. Its attitudes do not extend to anything beyond the cylinders, nor to any features of them beyond their locations and orientations. The second limitation in scope has a triple character, spatial, temporal, and modal. The robot only ever becomes disposed to act on the local, present, actual context; its representations and motivations bear only on the actual here and now. Thus the robot responds only to immediate gaps between how it represents things as being and how it is motivated to make them be. It is a wholly reactive agent.

Most agents we are familiar with, even simple animals, transcend both kinds of limitations. First, their representations and motivations pertain to objects other than cylinders and to features of such objects other than whether they are upright or not. A more complex agent than our little robot – perhaps an upgraded robot – may register the colors as well as the orientations of the cylinders, for example, and be motivated, not just to keep the cylinders upright but also to group them according to color. Or it may register their sizes too and be motivated to arrange them according to size in each color grouping, say, the smaller ones to the left, the larger to the right. Such an agent may further be able to detect orientational changes in the cylinders by hearing them topple, or to identify their sizes by the motions required to set them upright – in effect, by touch.

Secondly, complex agents like human beings also form representations and motivations concerning things at a spatial and temporal remove or under variations in this or that contingency. Their minds have a reach in space, time, and modality that the simple robot's mind does not. One sign of this reach is that human beings form long-term plans or intentions (Bratman 1987). These are motivations that select specific actions to be taken at a future time or in another place or under such and such a contingency.

The effects of enhanced scope

When the scope of an agent's representational and motivational attitudes is enhanced, as in the case of an animal, a human being, or perhaps a more complex robot, this has two effects. First, it exposes the agent to more ways of failing than those envisaged earlier, when we imagined our robot knocking cylinders off the board or not seeing things clearly. Second, while an enhanced attitudinal scope may make it harder for an outside observer to identify the precise intentional states governing the agent's behavior, it makes it harder still to explain that behavior on any other basis. It makes intentional explanation at once more difficult and less dispensable.

The first of these effects is due to an inverse relation between the scope of an agent's attitudes and actions and its ease of performing well, that is, of representing the environment correctly and satisfying its motivations. The more complex an agent's representations, the more ways they can break down. While it may still be relatively easy for an agent to form correct representations about such simple matters as whether the cylinders on the table are upright, it is much harder to be correct about more complex ones such as causal relationships in the world. If the robot were to represent the physical trajectory of a cylinder's toppling, for example, then it would face a much higher risk of error. Similarly, the more complex an agent's motivations, the more numerous the possibilities of not realizing them. We all know that, while it is still comparatively easy to fulfill a simple plan such as to put upright an object that has fallen over, the logistics of a more complex plan, such as to implement all propositions describing an ambitious project, can be extremely challenging.

The greater likelihood of breakdowns in a complex agent, in turn, makes it harder for a third-person observer to recognize what its precise intentional attitudes are. Think about how much longer it would take to identify the attitudes of an upgraded robot that is sensitive to the colors and sizes as well as the positions of the cylinders. Or, to take a more extreme example, think of a complex political, economic, or military project, perhaps a failed one. Figuring out *ex post* what the relevant agents' intentions behind it were can be very difficult, often causing historians, criminal investigators, journalists, and social scientists big headaches. Intentional explanation can thus become quite interpretive, requiring us to get a sense not only of what representations and motivations to ascribe to an agent but also what favorable conditions and feasible limits to assume.

Nonetheless this is unlikely to drive us towards a non-intentional explanation, say, in terms of how the agent is engineered, because the second effect of enhanced attitudinal scope comes into play. With our original, simple robot we may easily find an engineering-style explanation of its moves, looking at the electronic inputs and outputs that determine what happens. According to such an engineering-style explanation, the robot is to be viewed as a mechanical or electronic automaton, like a combustion engine or a soft-drinks vending machine, not as an agent with representations and motivations, like a human being or a cat or dog. Even the possibility of such a mechanical or electronic explanation, however, does not show that the robot is not an agent, only that viewing it as an agent may not be the only – or the simplest or most useful – way to explain what it does. But with an increasingly complex agent, which forms complicated representations and motivations, the resort to the engineering stance becomes less feasible.[12] Any dog owner will be able to testify that the best way to make sense of what a dog does involves ascribing representations and motiv-ations to it – such as the belief that there is food in the kitchen and the desire to eat – rather than devising a complicated causal model of how the dog, viewed as a bio-physical automaton, reacts to various physical conditions.

Although intentional interpretation may be difficult, then, we often find it impos-sible to dispense with what Dennett (1987) has called the 'intentional stance'. To adopt this stance is to set aside non-intentional possibilities of explanation, to presuppose that the system under explanation is an agent, and to try to ascribe representations and motivations to it that make sense of its actions. The intentional stance comes naturally to us, as is evident from the way in which even young children spontaneously ascribe purposes and perceptions to simple geometrical figures chasing one another about a screen (Heider and Simmel 1944). No doubt because we are a social species for whom mutual agential understanding is crucial, we are permanently poised to assume the intentional stance.

Rationality

In concluding this basic discussion of agency, it is useful to introduce the concept of rationality. The very idea of an agent is associated with some standards of performance or functioning, which we call 'standards of rationality'. These must be satisfied at some minimal level if a system is to count as an agent at all. They apply to the way an agent's attitudes connect with its environment; to the way they connect with one another, both within a category like that of representation and motivation, and across such categories; and to the way they connect with the actions by which the agent intervenes in its environment. We call these three kinds of standards 'attitude-to-fact', 'attitude-to-attitude', and 'attitude-to-action' standards of rationality.

Attitude-to-fact standards rule in favor of representations that fit with how things are and rule against those that don't. They include standards of how to look out for evidence, how to respond to perceptual evidence in forming perceptual representations, and, moving beyond the world of our robots, how to respond to accumulating evidence in forming general representations or how to respond to the testimony of others. Attitude-to-action standards rule in favor of actions that are required – or at least permitted – by the agent's representations and motivations and rule against those that aren't. Where attitude-to-fact failures are often associated with inattention, *idées fixes*, or paranoia, attitude-to-action failures are linked with ailments like weakness of will, compulsion, and obsession.

Attitude-to-attitude standards of rationality are a particularly important category for our present purposes. They rule out representations that take propositions to be true that are not co-realizable, or motivations that require such propositions to be true, at least when these serve as bases for action. That is, they rule out failures of consistency; more on this below. They also rule out deriving a motivation or intention to perform a specific action from a more general motivation without respecting the agent's representations; thus they rule out means–end failures. They rule in deductive closure, as far as feasible; this consists in representationally or motivationally endorsing any proposition entailed by other propositions so endorsed. Finally, if some of the agent's representations have evaluative propositions as their objects – that is, propositions about goodness, desirability, or rationality itself – they rule out combining such representations with attitudes that breach such presumed values; we discuss evaluative representations in the next section.

Achieving consistency is of special importance. It matters, first, when the agent's actions respond to the attitudes involved and, second, when the actions of others respond to those attitudes: for example, because others form expectations based on the attitudes they ascribe to the agent. Let an agent try to act on inconsistent representations or motivations, or let others try to orientate by the ascription of such attitudes, and there will be a straightforward breakdown: actions will be supported that cannot be realized. If an agent forms inconsistent attitudes on matters far removed from action, this may matter less, at least if the inconsistency can be blocked from migrating into the agent's attitudes as a whole. But with representations and motivations near the coal-face of action, inconsistency is a serious problem.

1.2 Complications in agency

We have seen that every representation or motivation held by an agent consists in a pair of things: an attitude, which may be either representational or motivational, and a proposition that is the object of that attitude. But there are two ways in which an attitude-proposition pair may vary. One involves the attitude, the other the proposition. Representational and motivational attitudes can come in one of two forms: they can either have an on-off, binary form or come in degrees.[13] And the propositions that are the objects of such attitudes can be simple or sophisticated. We now look at these complications.

Binary and non-binary attitudes

Consider representational attitudes. A binary representational attitude towards some proposition 'p' is what we call a 'judgment' on 'p', where we assume that an agent either judges that p or doesn't judge that p, with no halfway houses. With any given cylinder, for example, our little robot either judges that the cylinder is upright, or doesn't judge that this is so. Under this assumption, there is no such thing as judging with one or another degree of strength that p. A jury either judges a defendant to be guilty, or does not do so; there is (typically) no possibility in between. However, it is compatible with this on-off assumption that judgments are formed on propositions that themselves have a probabilistic content, such as the proposition 'there is a probability of 0.5 that p', as we discuss later.

By contrast, a typical non-binary representational attitude towards 'p' is what decision theorists call a 'credence' or 'degree of belief' the agent assigns to 'p', which may take any value between zero and one. A weather forecaster, for example, may assign a credence of 0.2, 0.5, or 0.8 to the proposition that it will rain tomorrow. A financial trader may assign a credence of 0.1 to the proposition that a particular company will go bankrupt in the next couple of months.

Similarly, the motivational attitudes that prompt action can be binary or non-binary. An illustrative binary motivational attitude towards proposition 'p' is what we may call a 'preference' concerning 'p', where we assume that the agent either prefers that p or doesn't prefer that p, with nothing in between. Our robot, for example, prefers that the cylinders be in an upright position and doesn't prefer that they be on their sides, period. By contrast, a paradigmatic non-binary motivational attitude towards proposition 'p' is, again in the language of decision theory, a 'utility' or 'degree of satisfaction' the agent assigns to 'p'. A bird searching for a nest site may get a utility of 0.1 from a site being

Table 1.1: Representational and motivational attitudes

	Binary	Non-binary
Beliefs	Judgments	Credences or degrees of belief
Desires	Preferences	Utilities or degrees of satisfaction

bad, a utility of 0.5 from the site being mediocre, and a utility of 0.9 from the site being good.

Let us use the word 'beliefs' for representational attitudes in general, and 'desires' for motivational attitudes in general. As we have seen, beliefs can take the form of judgments or credences, and desires that of preferences or utilities. We set aside further, more complicated possibilities (see, for example, Dietrich and List 2010a). Table 1.1 shows the possibilities we have considered.

Simple and sophisticated propositions

So much for variations in the attitudinal element of an attitude-proposition pair. The propositions towards which agents hold their attitudes also come in one of at least two forms. They may be expressible in a relatively sparse, single language; or their expression may require a richer language or a combination of two languages: an 'object language' and a 'metalanguage'. We describe the first sort of proposition as 'simple', the second as 'sophisticated'.

Simple propositions can be formulated with just the resources of propositional logic. They include 'atomic' propositions, the basic building blocks of the language, and 'compound' propositions formed out of atomic propositions together with logical connectives such as 'not', 'and', 'or', 'if then', 'if and only if'.

To express sophisticated propositions we require the use of a richer language, for example with the quantifiers 'some' and 'all' or with modal operators 'it is necessary that' and 'it is possible that' or with deontic operators 'it is obligatory that' and 'it is permissible that'. Alternatively, we may require a metalanguage, which can express propositions that assign properties to other, 'object-language' propositions. Let 'p' and 'q' be propositions expressed in the object language. Sufficiently complex agents can form intentional attitudes not only towards 'p' and 'q' but also towards metalanguage propositions that assign certain properties or relations to 'p' and 'q'. Thus they may believe – or also desire – that 'p' is true; that 'p' and 'q' are consistent; that 'p' and 'q' jointly entail 'r'; that 'p' is probable, or evidentially warranted, or believed by one or another agent; or that 'p' is an attractive or desirable scenario, or one that someone desires; and so on.

Human beings are able to draw on much richer linguistic resources in forming their attitudes than non-human animals or simple robots. Precisely because they are able to hold attitudes over sophisticated, and not just simple, propositions, they can come to believe entire theories about how different events in the world are causally related, what would have happened under this or that counterfactual circumstance, and why these beliefs are warranted. Similarly, the reference to sophisticated propositions allows them to desire the most complex scenarios, conditional on various contingencies and pertaining to times far in the future. Such contents are outside the scope of our robot's or a simpler animal's attitude formation.

Functional similarities between different attitude-proposition pairs

As attitude-proposition pairs can vary both attitudinally and propositionally, it is worth noting that two or more structurally different such pairs may sometimes play a similar functional role in an agent. It is then not clear from that functional role alone which pair correctly captures the agent's intentional state. Consider, for example, the following two scenarios:

> **First scenario.** The agent assigns a degree of belief of one in a million to the proposition that the lottery ticket on offer will be a winning one.

> **Second scenario.** The agent judges that there is a probability of one in a million that the lottery ticket on offer will be a winning one.

In the first scenario, the agent's attitude is non-binary – a degree of belief of one in a million – but the proposition towards which it is held – 'the ticket will win' – expresses an on-off matter, formulated in a relatively simple language. In the second, the attitude – a judgment – is binary, but the proposition – 'there is a probability of one in a million that the ticket will win' – has a probabilistic content; it is a reformulation of the earlier proposition in a richer language containing an operator of probability. When it comes to guiding action, at least in a narrow sense, the non-binary belief in the first scenario may play the same role as the binary judgment in the second one, so that the agent can, on the face of it, be interpreted as holding either of these attitude-proposition pairs. For example, the agent's decision on whether to buy the lottery ticket may be exactly the same in the two scenarios. Each scenario may in this sense be re-expressed as the other. Put more abstractly, a credence of x assigned to 'p', i.e. a non-binary attitude towards a simple proposition, may play a similar role as a judgment whose content is the proposition 'there is a probability of x that p', i.e. a binary attitude towards a more sophisticated proposition.[14]

A second kind of functional similarity between different proposition-attitude pairs crosses the desire–belief divide. To illustrate, consider the following two scenarios:

> **First scenario.** The agent prefers that the cylinders be in an upright position.

> **Second scenario.** The agent judges that it is preferable that the cylinders be in an upright position.

Here the agent's attitude is motivational – a preference – in the first scenario and representational – a judgment – in the second. The proposition towards which it is held, however, is a simple (and factual) one in the first scenario and a more sophisticated (and normative) one in the second, involving a predicate of preferability. In terms of guiding action, once again, the two attitude-proposition pairs may play similar roles, at least if the agent is motivated to achieve what he or she deems preferable. As in the earlier example, the agent's intentional state is open to more than one interpretation. More generally, a preference in favor of proposition 'p' may play a similar role as a judgment whose content is the proposition 'it is preferable that p' or ' "p" is preferable', where the language contains an appropriate operator or predicate of preferability.[15] With modifications, similar points apply to the non-binary case as well.[16]

In the cases considered, we require interpretive criteria over and above the observed functional role to settle the question of which attitude-proposition pairs to ascribe to the agent. Intentional explanation may thus become quite interpretive, especially when we move from simple to more complex agents.

Interpreting an agent

What interpretation should we give when the agent's behavior is consistent with more than one hypothesis as to what its representations and motivations are? When an agent acts so as to make it the case that p, and the agent does not seem to act in error, should we ascribe to the agent a preference in favor of 'p', a belief whose content is the proposition 'it is preferable that p', or a belief with content ' "p" is preferable', for example? And should we interpret these attitudes as binary or non-binary? Should we ascribe to our robot a preference for the cylinders to be in an upright position, or a belief that it is preferable for them to be so?

The first thing to stress is that the choice of which attitude-proposition pair to ascribe must be driven, under our functionally oriented approach, only by how the agent behaves, not by its physical make-up. That make-up – be it neural, electronic, or perhaps of another kind – may provide indirect evidence about what performance to expect in different situations, but the performance itself should dictate the representations and motivations we ascribe to the agent. There are many different ways our little robot may be constructed, consistently with its performance in putting the cylinders into an upright position. What determines the intentional ascriptions it deserves is how it interacts with its environment.

But under such a performance-driven interpretation, as we have seen, we can be faced with a choice between several functionally similar proposition-attitude pairs. Only if we were to stipulate that there is no significant difference between beliefs in preferability and attitudes of preference, for example, could we be completely relaxed about which formulation to choose, say whether to ascribe to the robot a preference for the cylinders to be upright or a judgment that it is preferable for them to be so. But without such a stipulation, the choice often carries a message, and it is then important to get the message right. Ascribing to the agent a preference concerning a simple proposition, for example, may carry a very different message from ascribing to it a judgment on a more sophisticated one. The ascription of intentional attitudes to an agent usually leads us to form certain expectations about its performance. The counsel against sending the wrong message, then, supports the following ceiling and floor constraints:

The ceiling constraint. The ascription chosen should not give rise to expectations the agent is unable to meet.

The floor constraint. The ascription chosen should not fail to give rise to expectations the agent is able to meet.

The ceiling constraint is the central principle employed in the intentional interpretation of animal minds (Hauser 2000). Here the danger, recognized on all sides, is one of anthropomorphism or over-interpretation: the danger of formulating the intentional attitudes ascribed to a non-human animal in a way that suggests cognitive capacities it does not have. To say that an animal believes that all plants of such and such a kind are poisonous, for example, might be misleading if it were taken to suggest that the animal understood the logic of 'all' and 'some' and could reason about what 'all'-sentences and 'some'-sentences imply. It may be better to say that the animal believes of each plant it recognizes as being of the kind in question that it is poisonous (Bennett 1976).

The floor constraint is equally important, though less often invoked. The danger addressed in this case is one of under-interpretation rather than over-interpretation: the danger of ascribing intentional attitudes to the agent that fail to register its capacities. Consider, for example, the traditional emotivist or expressivist view that the correct way to ascribe an evaluational attitude – say, a moral one – to human agents is not to say that they believe that something is desirable, or obligatory, but rather to say that they have a non-representational, pro-attitude towards it (Ayer 1982). On this view, human agents do not strictly speaking believe that harming people is wrong, for example, but they have a con-attitude (or 'boo'-attitude) towards harming people. Similarly, they do not strictly speaking believe that helping people is right, but they have a pro-attitude (or 'hurrah'-attitude) towards it. From the perspective of those, like us, who think that there are genuine evaluative beliefs – or from the perspective of expressivists of a recent, more sophisticated cast (Blackburn 1984; Gibbard 2003) – this is a case of under-interpretation. The interpretation fails to signal that human beings reason with evaluative propositions just as they reason with descriptive ones, that they form beliefs in such propositions, draw inferences from them, and so on. On the traditional expressivist interpretation, the implicature is that any appearance of such evaluative reasoning is misleading.

From rationality to reasoning

Fully rational agents, we have argued, satisfy three sorts of standards of good functioning: attitude-to-fact, attitude-to-action, and attitude-to-attitude standards. We are now able to see, however, that rationality in this sense is not the same as reasoning. An agent may be rational without being aware of it or without any capacity to aim to be rational. Our little robot only has beliefs about the cylinders in its environment and desires in respect of those objects. It has no beliefs or desires about its rationality as it updates its beliefs in light of evidence, as they connect with other beliefs and desires, and as they lead to actions. The same is likely to be true of almost any device or any non-human animal – certainly outside the realm of primates – that we can imagine.

But things are different with any creature capable of having beliefs about the properties of propositions, such as truth and consistency, entailment and support, and the like. Simple animals that are able to have beliefs about objects in the environment can seek out information about those objects and ask themselves questions about them; a dog does this, for example, when it attends to the sound it hears or the light that catches its attention. But since we human beings can form beliefs about propositions, not just about objects in the environment, we can ask questions about these more abstract entities, for example questions about their truth, their logical relations, or their evidential support. And we can do so out of a desire to maximize the prospect of having true beliefs, or consistent beliefs, or beliefs that are deductively closed or well supported. Not only can we rejoice in whatever rationality comes spontaneously to us from the impersonal processing we share with any agent. We can take intentional steps to reinforce our rationality (Pettit 1993).[17]

To see this point, we must recognize that just as rationality requires us to be disposed like any animal to believe that q when we believe that p and that if p then q, so it requires us to adjust appropriately when we believe metalanguage propositions. Our rationality will, ideally, stop us, not only from believing that not p if we believe that p but also from believing that not p if we believe that 'p' is true; and not only from believing that not q if we believe that p and that if p then q but also from believing that not q if we believe that 'p' is true and that the truth of 'p' entails the truth of 'q'; and so on.

Thus we human beings have more resources than simpler agents in the pursuit of rationality. Take the rational process whereby we spontaneously move from the belief that p and that if p then q to the belief that q. We may reinforce the expectation of rationality in such a process by intentionally putting an extra check in place to govern it. We may intentionally ask ourselves whether it is the case that 'p' and 'if p then q' are true and whether their truth entails the truth of 'q'. And we may expect that while the rational processing at either the lower or higher level is vulnerable to failure, the chance of failure is lowered when both levels are in place. If either fails on its own, the divergence from the other puts on a red light and leads to further, more careful processing.

The intentional pursuit of beliefs in metalanguage propositions, so as to impose extra checks on rational processing, is what we call 'reasoning'. The 'so as' may hold on a stronger or weaker basis: stronger, if the agent has an explicit goal of imposing extra checks; weaker, if it is likely that the agent would give up the activity did it not impose such checks. We rationally and non-intentionally process beliefs when the belief that p and the belief that if p then q lead us to the belief that q. And we rationally and non-intentionally process beliefs when the belief that 'p' and 'if p then q' are true and the belief that they entail the truth of 'q' lead us to the belief that 'q' is true. But taking active steps to form beliefs in metalanguage propositions, so as to check lower-level processing, is an intentional exercise and constitutes reasoning. Reasoning does not always require the explicit use of words like 'true' and 'entails'. Often our reasoning may go: p; if p then q; so, q. The fact that we are forming beliefs about the relation between those propositions – as the word 'entails' would make explicit – shows up only in the little word 'so'. Reasoning may reinforce not just the rational, deductive processing illustrated here but also inductive or probabilistic processing, and the more practical processing that leads an agent to form intentions or perform actions; we set the details aside here.

We should note, in concluding this discussion, that a reasoning agent can give evidence of agency even in the absence of much rationality. If a non-reasoning system like our robot agent fails to be rational – say, it persistently fails to put the cylinders upright or to sustain any other systematic pattern – then, unless circumstances are discernibly inappropriate, it won't be clear that it is an agent. But if a reasoning agent fails to be rational, then the fact that it self-corrects, recognizing its failure in a manner open only to a reasoning agent, will provide a ground for continuing to view it as an agent. Suppose, for example, a human being behaves erratically, but is able to recognize that he or she fell short of our expectations and even demonstrates a willingness to rectify the problem; then we have every reason to continue to view him or her as an agent.

We noticed earlier that the more extended the scope of an agent's attitudes and actions, the more likely are breakdowns and failures of rationality. Our present observations explain why those breakdowns can mount significantly without leading us to deny agency. If a system displays increased sophistication and extended scope, there may still be a ground for thinking that no matter how egregious a failure, this is truly an agent. The sensitivity to the demands of rationality displayed in the acknowledgment that criticism is appropriate may be evidence of agency, albeit of an underperforming sort.

1.3 The idea of group agency

Groups as agents

We have now built up the conceptual resources to approach the topic of groups as agents. Collections of individuals come in many forms. Some change identity with any change of membership. An example is the collection of people in a given room or subway carriage. Other collections have an identity that can survive changes of membership. Examples are the collections of people constituting a nation, a university, or a purposive organization. We call the former 'mere collections', the latter 'groups'. Our focus here is on groups.

There are enormous differences among groups. They may be unified by properties that members or outsiders do not register and that do not affect anyone's behavior; an example may be the group of those third-born in their families. They may be unified by a property that isn't salient but that affects their behavior or that of outsiders, such as (perhaps) being the eldest in the family, or by one that is salient but that doesn't affect anyone's behavior, such as (perhaps) being red-haired. Alternatively, a group may be unified by a property that is both epistemically salient and behaviorally influential: being of a certain ethnicity, religion, or gender is often like this. In addition, the members may not just be unified by such a property but their sharing it may be a matter of common awareness. The property may be a pre-existing marker or one created by the members, for example by signing up to some commitment; the members may construe themselves around the identity provided by that property, though not necessarily in exclusion of other identities.

What, then, is a 'group agent'? It is a group that exhibits the three features of agency, as introduced above. However this is achieved, the group has representational states, motivational states, and a capacity to process them and to act on that basis in the manner of an agent. Thus the group is organized so as to seek the realization of certain motivations in the world and to do so on the basis of certain representations about what that world is like. When action is taken in the group's name – say, by its members or deputies – this is done for the satisfaction of the group's desires, and according to the group's beliefs.

When a group of individuals form an agent, they may relate to one another in a more or less coordinate manner, with each playing a similar role. Alternatively, they may be divided up into different subgroups, each with its distinctive tasks. In either case their relations with one another may involve a hierarchy or a more or less egalitarian arrangement. We abstract for the moment from such differences, postponing them until the third chapter.

Could mere collections, and not just groups, count as agents? We do not think so. Any multi-member agent must be identifiable over time by the way its beliefs and desires evolve. So there must be a basis for thinking of it as the same entity, even as its membership changes due to someone's departure or the addition of new members. Thus it is a candidate for being taken as a group, not just a mere collection.[18]

Group agents without joint intention

Individuals may combine into group agents in two very different ways, depending on whether or not any joint intention is involved. We discuss group agents without joint intention in this section, and turn to ones with joint intention in the next.

How might a group agent materialize if members do not jointly intend to form such an agent? There are at least two ways in which this could happen. The first would involve a process of natural or cultural evolution in which members are selected for possessing traits that lead them to act as required for group agency. They would each adjust to one another and to their circumstances such that the resulting group acts in the service of common desires according to common beliefs. And they might do this without being aware of the group agency achieved.

But while cultural evolution may plausibly shape existing group agents, just as competition shapes commercial corporations (Nelson and Winter 1982), we are not aware of any examples of new group agents coming into existence among human beings in this way. It is hard to see how individuals, each with his or her own beliefs and desires, could be organized without any joint intention, or continuing intervention, so as to sustain and enact group-level beliefs and desires distinct from their individual ones. We know that bees can combine, on the basis of simple signals, so as to perform as a simple group agent (Seeley 2001); they coalesce into a group agent through the interaction and coordination for which nature has selected them (for a formal model, see List, Elsholtz, and Seeley 2009). It is harder to imagine, though not conceptually impossible, that nature or culture could work to similar effect on human beings, eliciting coalescent agents (Pettit 1993).

A second way in which a group agent may form without joint intention is perhaps more plausible. This would involve one or several organizational designers co-opting others into a structure underpinning group agency, without making them aware of their agency at the group level and without seeking their intentional acquiescence in the arrangement. Think of the cellular organization by which, so we are told, many terrorist organizations have operated. We can imagine that a cellular network may be established for the promotion of some goals, without those recruited to the different cellular tasks being aware of the overall purpose; they may be kept in the dark or even deceived about it. The organization would be composed of a group of people, in perhaps a thin sense of group, and would function as an agent. But it would do so without a joint intention among its members, with the possible exception of a few coordinators.

Group agents with joint intention

To discuss group agents with joint intention, we must define the notion of a joint intention more precisely. This notion has been analyzed in several ways in an important literature (e.g. Gilbert 1989; Searle 1990; 1995; Tuomela 1995; Bratman 1999; Gilbert 2001; Bacharach 2006; Gold and Sugden 2007; Tuomela 2007), but we shall abstract from some differences between these approaches and adopt the following stipulative approach, broadly inspired by Bratman (1999). We say that a collection of individuals 'jointly intend' to promote a particular goal if four conditions are met:

Shared goal. They each intend that they, the members of a more or less salient collection, together promote the given goal.

Individual contribution. They each intend to do their allotted part in a more or less salient plan for achieving that goal.

Interdependence. They each form these intentions at least partly because of believing that the others form such intentions too.

Common awareness. This is all a matter of common awareness, with each believing that the first three conditions are met, each believing that others believe this, and so on.[19]

Examples of collections forming joint intentions are abundant. Suppose we are on the beach, everyone's attention is called to the plight of a swimmer in difficulty, and we form a chain that enables someone to throw a lifebelt. Our coordination involves a joint intention. The collection of helpers is salient. We each intend that we, the members of that collection, provide the required help, and, expecting others to do so too, we each do our part in the more or less salient plan to form a chain. That we each satisfy these conditions is something we each recognize, each recognize that we each recognize, and so on.[20] What is true of the rescue party on the beach is equally true of the coordination displayed when several people carry a piano downstairs together, or combine in a brilliant play on the football field, or sing together in a choir. They do not combine in the blind way, for example, in which bargain hunters drive market prices to the competitive level. They combine with awareness of acting together and adjust as required for a successful performance of that action.

The bargain hunters in a market have a common effect but do not perform a common action. Those who act on the basis of a joint intention do perform a common action: they do something together intentionally. But their doing so does not imply that they constitute a group agent (for an earlier discussion of the relationship between group agency and joint intention, see Pettit and Schweikard 2006); it does not imply that they form and enact a single system of belief and desire, or give life to a single vision (Rovane 1997). They may perform only one action together, such as saving the swimmer. And even if they perform several actions, they may do so without forming and enacting a single system of belief and desire.[21] Thus there may be no basis for predicting what they will do together in future or for speculating about what they would do under various counterfactual possibilities. In short, there may be no basis for thinking of them as a unified agent.

With the notion of joint intention in place, however, we can see that a group of individuals may go beyond performing a joint action and form a joint intention to become a group agent. They each intend that they together act so as to form and enact a single system of belief and desire, at least within a clearly defined scope; they each intend to do their own part in a salient plan for ensuring group agency within that scope, believing that others will do their part too. And all of this is a matter of common awareness.

The natural image of how people may form a jointly intentional group agent suggests that they will be equal and willing partners in a coordinate organization. But this is not required. Think of a group agent in which individuals are segmented into different, specialized subunits and some are subordinated to others. The members of such an organization may jointly intend that they together form a group agent, even when many of them are reluctant or unwilling; they may prefer a different organization, or no organization at all, and go along with the existing arrangement only under pressure or for lack of an accessible alternative.

The intentions of those who form a jointly intentional group agent may be not only reluctantly endorsed but also rather shallow. The fact that a group of individuals jointly intend that they form a group agent does not mean that with everything the group does they jointly intend that it be done. It only means that they jointly intend that the group form for the satisfaction of certain desires according to certain beliefs, whether these beliefs and desires are already established or only to be determined later. The group may form and enact certain attitudes without all its members jointly intending that these particular attitudes be formed and enacted.

Indeed, some, or even many, group members may not participate in any joint intention at all. Generally, all we require for a group agent to count as 'jointly intentional' is that the group's performance involve joint intentions on the part of some of its members. This definition is deliberately broad and flexible in order not to restrict our theory unnecessarily. However, we should now say more about the question of who the members of a group agent are.

The roles of group members

The members of a jointly intentional group agent may play one or both of two roles. The first is that of 'authorizing' the group agent, in the sense of accepting its claim to speak and act for the group. If the group agent is a trade union, this means accepting its right to negotiate in one's name as a member. If it is a church, it means accepting its right to speak for one's religious beliefs. If it is a corporation, it means accepting its right to use the resources in which one owns shares for corporate purposes, as defined in the corporation's charter and the law.

The second role members may play is an 'active' one, that is, acting in full awareness for the pursuit of the group's ends. It may mean performing some part within the group or acting in its name in dealing with outside parties or fellow members. The members of a trade union may play this part in standing on a picket line or in paying their dues; the members of a church in participating in religious ceremonies or in proselytizing among non-believers; the members of a corporation in attending the annual general meeting or in assuming responsibility on the board.

The members' authorization or activity in relation to a group agent is always licensed authorization or activity. We do not authorize a group agent, having it speak and act for us, just by our say-so. We must be licensed by the group as being fit to do this, for example by belonging to a suitable category or meeting a criterion such as having paid a fee or being accepted by other members. The license may be given explicitly by the group's charter or a contract of affiliation, or implicitly through the informal acceptance by others. The same goes for activity. We do not act for a group agent just by virtue of trying to help; we must be licensed by the group, formally or informally, as being fit to act on its behalf.

We assume that playing at least one of these two roles is necessary and sufficient for membership in a jointly intentional group agent. Every member is thus an authorizing or active member, and anyone who is suitably authorizing or active is a member. The variation in the basis for membership means that different group agents can be distinguished by how far the members play an authorizing or an active role.[22]

At one extreme, we can imagine group agents most of whose members authorize the group but few of whom act within or for it. Members may, for instance, authorize a 'dictator' to form the group agent's attitudes, without doing anything more active on the group's behalf; we discuss the technical meaning of 'dictatorship' in the second chapter. The dictator may then be the sole member acting for the group, with other group members being merely complicit in the group agent's existence, under the dictator's direction.

Can we imagine the opposite extreme, where few if any members authorize the group, but many act for it? This could be illustrated by a jointly intentional group agent in which only a few members participate in the joint intention. The active members might be hired by the (few) authorizing members, for example, to implement group projects. Alternatively, it could be illustrated by a group agent that is not jointly intentional at all. As mentioned above, individuals may form a group agent in virtue of evolutionary selection or cleverly designed incentives to act as required for group agency, perhaps within independent cells. Here the individuals contribute to the group agent's performance, but do not explicitly authorize the group agent; they need not even be aware of its existence.

In a jointly intentional group agent, the two types of members are typically present and often overlap. In a participatory group like a voluntary association, members have the same status within the group agent; they equally authorize the group agent and take roughly equal parts in acting on its behalf. In a hierarchical organization, such as a commercial corporation or a church, there may be differences in the members' roles, for example through holding different offices or through belonging to subgroups with different tasks. Ordinary believers are usually not as active in a church as priests and bishops but they still authorize the church equally, taking it to speak for the group in religious matters. Ordinary workers do not authorize a commercial company in the manner of shareholders and directors – it is these agents who provide the money and the votes that keep the firm on track – but they play a similar if not greater part in acting on behalf of the group.

Intentional agent-formation and rational performance

To count as an agent, a group must exhibit at least a modicum of rationality. And so its members must find a form of organization that ensures, as far as possible, that the group satisfies attitude-to-fact, attitude-to-action, and attitude-to-attitude standards of rationality.

On the attitude-to-fact front, the group must ensure, as far as possible, that its beliefs are true about the world it inhabits – and, ideally, that its desires are at least in principle realizable. We assume that this requires the group to form its attitudes based on inputs from its members, since the members are typically the eyes and ears of the group, providing it with information about the world. We return to this point at various places. In the next chapter, we discuss how the members' attitudes can be aggregated into group attitudes; in the third chapter, we discuss the resulting supervenience relationship between individual-level inputs and group-level outputs. The attitude-to-fact theme is also relevant to the second part of the book, where we ask, among other things, how a group agent can be constituted so as to enable it to track the facts better than any of the individual members; and whether members have an incentive to reveal their attitudes truthfully to the group.

On the attitude-to-action front, the group must ensure, as far as possible, that whenever its attitudes require an action, suitable members or employees – for simplicity, we call them 'enactors' – are selected and authorized to take the required action. To ensure a robust performance, the group's organizational structure must further include some back-up arrangements for finding substitutes in case the original candidates fail to do their part. It is not difficult to see how an organization may provide, formally or informally, for the recruitment of suitable enactors. But such an arrangement raises serious questions about the responsibility of group agents and their members. We address these questions in the seventh chapter. In particular, we ask whether a group agent can be held responsible in its own right for the actions its chosen enactors perform in its name.

The third front on which a group must organize itself relates to the satisfaction of attitude-to-attitude standards of rationality. The group must ensure that whatever beliefs and desires it comes to hold, say on the basis of its members' beliefs and desires, form a coherent whole. This is certainly the case with attitudes close to action: those desires on which it acts and those beliefs on which it relies for directing its action. Otherwise the group won't be able to enact its intentional attitudes in the manner of a well-functioning agent. It turns out that a group can fulfill the requirement of attitude-to-attitude rationality only if it breaches certain initially plausible conditions on how its attitudes relate to those of its members. This issue is of pressing importance, because it puts in question the very possibility of group agency. We address it in the next chapter in our discussion of attitude aggregation.

Our focus on binary attitudes

One assumption underlying our account of group agency – specifically, jointly intentional group agency – must be made explicit at this stage. We assume that, whatever the group's organizational structure is, it must lead the group to form binary attitudes, not attitudes that come in degrees of strength. The group agents we are concerned with form and enact their attitudes on the basis of communication among the members, and this requires a method for communicating the proposed or accepted group attitudes. We think that, in practice, this will lead the group to form binary attitudes: on-off judgments that something is or is not the case, and on-off preferences that something should or should not be the case. Although there are conceivable ways in which a group agent might arrive at non-binary credences or utilities in respect of certain propositions – for example, via bets or prediction markets among members – we do not consider this possibility in this book.[23]

Group agents that generate their attitudes by communication may do so in a variety of ways. One is deliberation among group members or among those in a relevant subgroup. Another is voting among some or all of the members, whether majoritarian or otherwise. A third is 'dictatorship', in a sense defined in the next chapter, as when a particular individual is authorized to determine the group's judgments or preferences. But in each case, the typical result is the formation of binary attitudes.

When group members deliberate together, they offer each other the kinds of considerations that come up in reasoning: for example, that the evidence supports 'p', or that 'not p' is inconsistent with something already judged or preferred to be the case. Similarly, when members vote on the group's attitudes, they usually cast their votes in an on–off manner rather than on a continuous scale. And when they accept the pronouncements of a chair or director, these pronouncements are likely to take the form of a judgment that something is or is not the case, or a preference that something should or should not be the case. Similar considerations could be given to support the claim that, just as the communication involved in the formation of group attitudes tends to require those attitudes to be binary, so the communication involved in the group's enactment of its attitudes shares that requirement.

Even attitudes explicitly involving degrees of belief are usually communicated in this binary manner. Language leads us to report a degree of belief in a proposition 'p' not by placing 'p' itself on some continuous scale but by expressing a binary judgment on a suitably adjusted proposition with the degree in its content, such as the proposition 'the probability of "p" is x'. Since it is always possible, as we have seen, to re-express a non-binary attitude towards a simple proposition as a binary attitude towards a more sophisticated one, our assumption about the group agent's restriction to binary attitudes is no major loss of generality.

We should also emphasize that this restriction does not entail any deep departure from the way we think about individual human beings. While decision theory ascribes credences and utilities to individual agents, less formal accounts develop the kinds of explanations people give of themselves: the explanations in which they report their core beliefs and desires in any area and the attitudes to which reasoning leads them from that base. And those explanations tend to be given in terms of binary attitudes. We human beings are usually unable by introspection to tell our precise degrees of belief or desire in a given proposition; by almost all accounts, we lack that self-scanning capacity. And even if we do have fine-grained credences and utilities, we are no better than others at identifying them and cannot reveal them directly (Harman 1986). When we ask ourselves about our attitude to a proposition we usually consider whether the evidence supports it or, in the case of desire, whether it describes an attractive scenario or one that is more attractive than something else. We then announce that we do in fact judge that p or prefer that p, or that we don't. To express a degree, as we have seen, we normally refer to it in the content of the proposition rather than in the attitude towards it, using the re-expression indicated above. In particular, we tend to express degrees only to the extent that they are supported by considerations of evidence and attractiveness. The identification and communication of attitudes thus seems to require those attitudes to be binary, in the ordinary human case as well as in the case of a group agent, though there is theoretical scope for generalization.

The variety of group agents

We have distinguished between mere collections and groups, between mere groups and group agents, and between those group agents that are formed without joint intention and those that are formed with joint intention. Figure 1.1 shows the possibilities. In this book we are almost entirely concerned with jointly intentional group agents.

It is methodologically defensible to regard a group as an agent only if it makes sense to ascribe intentional attitudes to it. But we often also ascribe intentional attitudes to groups that are not agents. For example, we ascribe beliefs and desires, on the basis of majority polling, to various random samples and the populations they exemplify. So how do we draw the line between non-agential and agential groups? Our discussion suggests that we regard a group as an agent just when we think something is amiss if those attitudes are inconsistent, or otherwise irrational. We assume that only group agents as opposed to mere groups should acknowledge that this is a fault that should be rectified. Although a pioneer of opinion polling reportedly claimed that 'the collective judgment of the people is amazingly sound' (George Gallup quoted in Chaffee 2000), none of us takes an opinion poll sample as a group agent: we are not disturbed at all by discovering that it holds inconsistent beliefs.

Which groups prompt us not only to ascribe attitudes to them but also to fault them if these attitudes fail to respect the appropriate standards of rationality? There are many different groups that meet this test and therefore pass as group agents. They come in at least three categories, depending on whether they have a political, commercial, or civic character.

Political group agents include the town meeting that regularly assembles and forms and enforces a consistent system of attitudes as to how things should be done in the locality. They also include political parties, and the executives or governments established by them. In each case the members intend that they together espouse and

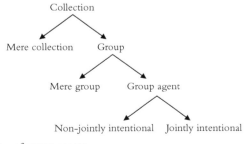

Figure 1.1 The variety of group agents

promote consistent policies, as set out in their party programs, campaign or mission statements, or coalition agreements. They could not do their job properly, or avoid electoral failure or ridicule, if they failed to achieve consistency.

Political entities such as the people, the legislature, and the judiciary are more problematic than town meetings, political parties, and governments. Philosophers and political scientists disagree about whether or not they are group agents; the disagreement is precisely on whether inconsistency or irrationality on the part of such entities is a problem or not (see, for example, Kornhauser and Sager 2004; and our response in List and Pettit 2005). By many accounts, however, the state is an agent. It is an entity that deals across changes of government with its own members and with other states; and, as befits an agent, it is routinely held to expectations of consistency in legal and other forums (McLean 2004). Indeed, an entire research tradition within international relations theory, the so-called 'realist' tradition, is based on modeling states as unitary rational agents (Waltz 1979; for a related discussion, see Wendt 2004). While not uncontroversial, this approach to thinking about international relations was hugely influential, for example, in devising political and military strategies during the Cold War.

Although states act through their executives or other organs of government, they can count as distinct group agents, as they have their own goals and commitments, which their subsidiary organs need not share. This suggests that group agents may nest within one another: the members of a larger entity like the state may also form smaller group agents like the executive.

Commercial entities are almost as various as political ones. They include partnerships of relatively few members in which each plays an active role. They include trade unions, professional associations, and industry groupings. Most conspicuously of all, they include firms and corporations. Such entities pursue the financial welfare of their shareholders as their ultimate purpose, at least on common lore, and exhibit the characteristics of agency in full dress. Shareholders, directors, managers, and workers combine, often in subsidiary units, to ensure that they pursue the overall goals of their corporations according to a single body of representations; these may bear on which sub-goals to adopt, their relative importance, the best means of attaining them, and so on. Shaped in an environment of commercial competition, corporations are paradigm examples of instrumentally rational group agents.

The civic or cultural world also provides a great variety of entities that count as group agents by our criteria. They include voluntary associations that support popular causes, whether environmental, philanthropic, or more directly political; recreational bodies that run particular activities, such as local athletics organizations, chess clubs, and cycling societies; and more formal bodies like schools, churches, and universities.

Even a coherently edited newspaper can count as a group agent if it forms collective judgments and preferences, promotes certain goals, holds itself accountable across time and announces revisions of its views explicitly. An amusing example is *The Economist*

Newspaper. On its webpage, *The Economist* explains why its articles are published anonymously, rather than in individual authors' names:

Many hands write *The Economist*, but it speaks with a collective voice. Leaders are discussed, often disputed, each week in meetings that are open to all members of the editorial staff. Journalists often co-operate on articles. And some articles are heavily edited. ('About us', www.economist. com, accessed on 11 July 2007)

The Economist articulates some of its judgments and preferences as follows:

What, besides free trade and free markets, does *The Economist* believe in?. . .It is to the Radicals that *The Economist* still likes to think of itself as belonging. . .[It] considers itself the enemy of privilege, pomposity and predictability. It has backed conservatives. . .[but also] espoused a variety of liberal causes, opposing capital punishment from its earliest days, while favouring penal reform and decolonization, as well as – more recently – gun control and gay marriage. Lastly, *The Economist* believes in plain language. (Ibid.)

Such self-ascriptions of intentional attitudes are clear markers of a joint intention to form a group agent, and it is group agents of this kind that this book is about.

2

The Aggregation of Intentional Attitudes

An agent, we have seen, is a system that forms representations and motivations about the world and acts so as to realize its motivations according to its representations. The agent's representations and motivations can be modeled as attitudes held towards certain propositions. An agent's representational attitude towards a proposition (or scenario) captures its belief in that proposition, its motivational attitude towards it its desire for it.

We are familiar with the idea of individual human agents holding such attitudes towards propositions, and even in the case of a robot we have little difficulty in making sense of it. Human beings as well as robots may believe that a particular cylinder is on its side, for example, and desire that the cylinder be in an upright position, and they may then act to satisfy the desire according to the belief, by putting the cylinder upright. It is less obvious, however, how a jointly intentional group agent could hold such attitudes. How could a multi-member group move from the distinct and possibly conflicting intentional attitudes of its members to a single system of such attitudes endorsed by the group as a whole?

In this chapter we want to answer this question. To do so, we introduce the theory of attitude aggregation, which investigates possible ways of merging, or 'aggregating', the intentional attitudes of several individuals into attitudes held by the group as a whole.[24] As explained in the first chapter, we assume that the attitudes are binary so as to meet the requirements of interpersonal communication in a jointly intentional group agent. Representational attitudes thus take the form of judgments, and motivational attitudes that of preferences: to judge that p is to believe that 'p' is the case, and to prefer that p is to desire that 'p' be the case. But our account of attitude aggregation can in principle be generalized beyond the binary case (e.g. Dietrich and List 2010a).[25]

The chapter is divided into three sections. The first explains a paradox of majoritarian attitude aggregation, which shows that an initially plausible approach to the formation of group attitudes does not generally work; the second presents an impossibility theorem generalizing the paradox; and the third discusses possible routes out of the impossibility, pointing towards ways in which a multi-member group can successfully come to hold rational intentional attitudes.

2.1 A paradox of majoritarian attitude aggregation

The problem

The problem of attitude aggregation has recently received most attention in the case of judgments: how can a group of individuals make collective judgments on some propositions based on the group members' individual judgments on them? This problem arises, for example, in legislatures or committees deciding what factual and normative propositions to accept in legislation, in multi-member courts adjudicating cases, and in expert panels giving advice on complex issues. And it also arises outside the human realm, in information processing systems consisting of multiple data-generating devices whose outputs need to be reconciled, such as 'meta search engines' on the internet that combine the results of several other search engines.[26]

Because of the wide variety of applications, judgment aggregation has generated interest in several disciplines, including law, economics, philosophy, political science, and computer science. Sparked by the discovery of a paradox in jurisprudence – the 'doctrinal paradox' (Kornhauser and Sager 1986; 1993), later generalized as a 'discursive dilemma' (Pettit 2001b; 2001c, Ch. 5) – there is now a growing body of technical work on the problem, beginning with a formal model and an impossibility result in List and Pettit (2002; 2004a).[27] We explain the paradox and some of the more general results in a moment.[28] This recent literature has some important precursors, most notably a 1920s discovery by the Italian lawyer Roberto Vacca (1921) of something essentially equivalent to the 'doctrinal paradox',[29] the 1950s work on 'Theories of the General Interest, and the Logical Problem of Aggregation' by the French mathematician George Théodule Guilbaud (partially translated in Guilbaud 1966), and some mathematical work from the 1970s and 1980s on aggregation problems that are more abstract than, but formally related to, the now-familiar judgment-aggregation problems (Wilson 1975; Rubinstein and Fishburn 1986).[30]

Judgments are just one of the two kinds of binary intentional attitudes we have identified, namely representational ones. But an agent must also hold motivational attitudes, that is, preferences. In what follows we therefore consider not just the aggregation of judgments but that of binary intentional attitudes more generally.

So, how can a group of individuals form binary intentional attitudes – judgments or preferences – towards some propositions based on the group members' individual attitudes towards them? A seemingly natural solution to this problem is to generate group-level attitudes by majority voting. This was prominently advocated by Thomas Hobbes, John Locke, and Jean Jacques Rousseau:

[I]f the representative consist of many men, the voice of the greater number must be considered as the voice of them all. For if the lesser number pronounce, for example, in the affirmative, and the greater in the negative, there will be negatives more than enough to destroy the affirmatives, and thereby the excess of negatives, standing uncontradicted, are the only voice the representative hath. (Hobbes 1994, Ch. 16)

[I]n assemblies empowered to act by positive laws where no number is set by that positive law which empowers them, the act of the majority passes for the act of the whole, and of course determines as having, by the law of Nature and reason, the power of the whole. (Locke 1960, bk. 2, Ch. 8.96)

[T]he vote of the majority always obligates all the rest ... [W]hen a law is proposed in the People's assembly, what they are being asked is not exactly whether they approve the proposal or reject it, but whether it does or does not conform to the general will, which is theirs; everyone states his opinion about this by casting his ballot, and the tally of the votes yields the declaration of the general will. Therefore when the opinion contrary to my own prevails, it proves nothing more than that I made a mistake and that what I took to be the general will was not ... This presupposes, it is true, that all the characteristics of the general will are still in the majority. (Rousseau 1997, Bk. 4, Ch. 2)

But as we now show, this solution does not generally work: it does not generally lead to group-level attitudes that meet the requirements of rationality. Let us first consider the case of judgments, then that of preferences.

Majoritarian judgment aggregation

Our first example is the 'doctrinal paradox', as presented by Kornhauser and Sager (1986; 1993) (see also Vacca 1921; Chapman 1998). Suppose a three-member court has to make a decision in a breach-of-contract case. The court seeks to make judgments on the following propositions:

- The defendant was contractually obliged not to do a certain action (the first premise).
- The defendant did that action (the second premise).
- The defendant is liable for breach of contract (the conclusion).

According to legal doctrine, obligation and action are jointly necessary and sufficient for liability; that is, the conclusion is true if and only if both premises are true. Suppose, as shown in Table 2.1, judge 1 believes both premises to be true; judge 2 believes the first but not the second premise to be true; and judge 3 believes the second but not the first to be true. Then each premise is accepted by a majority of judges, yet only a minority, that is, judge 1, individually considers the defendant liable.

The 'doctrinal paradox' consists in the fact that the court's verdict depends on whether it votes on the conclusion or on the two premises: a majority vote on the

Table 2.1: The doctrinal paradox

	Obligation?	Action?	Liable?
Judge 1	True	True	True
Judge 2	True	False	False
Judge 3	False	True	False
Majority	True	True	False

issue of the defendant's liability alone would support a 'not liable' verdict, whereas majority votes on the two premises would support a 'liable' verdict. This shows that, even for a single given combination of individual judgments, the court's verdict is highly sensitive to its method of decision making. If the court wishes to respect the judges' majority opinions on the premises of a case, this can lead to a different verdict than if it wishes to respect the majority opinion on the case's overall conclusion. We come back to the difference between 'premise-based' and 'conclusion-based' procedures of decision making at various points below.

We can make a further observation from the example. Relative to the given legal doctrine – that obligation and action are jointly necessary and sufficient for liability – the set of propositions accepted by a majority, namely that the defendant had an obligation, did the action, and yet is not liable, is inconsistent. If adherence to legal doctrine is considered a requirement of rationality in a court, then majority voting will prevent the court from meeting this requirement in the present case. The problem can also arise in the absence of any legal doctrine or any other exogenous constraint. This more general problem has become known as the 'discursive dilemma' (Pettit 2001c, Ch. 5; List and Pettit 2002). As an illustration, imagine an expert panel that has to give advice on global warming, such as a stylized version of the Intergovernmental Panel on Climate Change. The panel seeks to form judgments on the following propositions (and their negations):

- Global carbon dioxide emissions from fossil fuels are above 6500 million metric tons of carbon per annum (proposition 'p').
- If global carbon dioxide emissions are above this threshold, then the global temperature will increase by at least 1.5 degrees Celsius over the next three decades (proposition 'if p then q').
- The global temperature will increase by at least 1.5 degrees Celsius over the next three decades (proposition 'q').

The three propositions are complex factual propositions on which the experts may reasonably disagree. Suppose the experts' judgments are as shown in Table 2.2, all individually consistent. Could the expert panel form its collective judgments by taking majority votes on all the propositions?

Table 2.2: A discursive dilemma

	Emissions above threshold?	If emissions above threshold, then temperature increase?	Temperature increase?
Individual 1	True	True	True
Individual 2	True	False	False
Individual 3	False	True	False
Majority	True	True	False

Given the judgments in Table 2.2, a majority of experts judges that emissions are above the relevant threshold ('p'), a majority judges that, if they are above this threshold, then the temperature will increase by 1.5 degrees Celsius ('if p then q'), and yet a majority judges that there will be no such temperature increase ('not q'). Thus the set of propositions accepted by a majority is inconsistent. The 'discursive dilemma' consists in the fact that majority voting on interconnected propositions may lead to inconsistent group judgments even when individual judgments are fully consistent (for a related discussion of this problem of 'collective incoherence', see also Brennan 2001).

Majoritarian preference aggregation

Let us now look at the aggregation of preferences, that is, binary motivational attitudes. Consider a legislature deciding on a new budget. The legislature seeks to form preferences on the following propositions (and their negations):

- Taxes are increased (proposition 'p').
- Spending is reduced (proposition 'q').
- Taxes are increased or spending is reduced (so that there is no budget deficit) (proposition 'p or q').

Suppose the preferences of the individual legislators are as shown in Table 2.3, each individually consistent. Could the legislature form its collective preferences by majority voting?

Given the individual preferences in Table 2.3, a majority of legislators prefers that taxes be increased or spending reduced so as to avoid a budget deficit ('p or q'), yet a majority prefers that there be no tax increase ('not p'), and a majority prefers that there be no spending reduction ('not q'): the set of propositions preferred by a majority is inconsistent. If consistency is deemed a rationality requirement on preferences, then majority voting does not generally secure rational group preferences.

The upshot

We have seen that the initially plausible approach of aggregating judgments or preferences by majority voting fails to guarantee rational group attitudes, assuming

Table 2.3: A paradox of majoritarian preference aggregation

	Increase taxes?	Reduce spending?	Increase taxes or reduce spending (to avoid a budget deficit)?
Individual 1	Preferred	Dispreferred	Preferred
Individual 2	Dispreferred	Preferred	Preferred
Individual 3	Dispreferred	Dispreferred	Dispreferred
Majority	Dispreferred	Dispreferred	Preferred

we impose consistency as a rationality condition on such attitudes. This problem is very general. As soon as the propositions on which group-level attitudes are to be formed are interconnected in a non-trivial way and there are three or more group members, majoritarian inconsistencies like the ones in the examples can occur.[31] We must therefore look for alternatives to majoritarian attitude aggregation.

Before we do so, it is worth noting that the problem just reviewed resembles a much older paradox of majority voting: 'Condorcet's paradox'. The Marquis de Condorcet (1785) noticed that, in a multi-member group choosing between three options, say electoral candidates x, y, and z, majorities may prefer x to y, y to z, and yet z to x, a 'cycle', even when the group members' preference rankings over x, y, and z are individually rational. An example is the case in which a third of the group prefers x to y to z, a second third prefers y to z to x, and the last third prefers z to x to y.[32]

Condorcet's paradox found a dramatic generalization in Kenneth Arrow's celebrated impossibility theorem (1951/1963), showing that majority voting is not alone in failing to guarantee rational collective preference rankings, but that any decision rule satisfying some plausible axioms will fail to do so. Arrow's theorem and his axiomatic approach to the study of aggregation inspired an enormous body of work. Some scholars went so far as to interpret Arrow's theorem as a proof of the meaninglessness of populist democracy (e.g., Riker 1982), while others regarded it primarily as an insightful mathematical result throwing light on what axioms can and cannot be met by a decision rule.

Given Arrow's work, the resemblance of the present problem to Condorcet's paradox raises a particularly pressing question. Does the present problem also illustrate a more general impossibility theorem – here on attitude aggregation – just as Condorcet's paradox turned out to illustrate a more general impossibility theorem on the aggregation of preference rankings? If the answer to this question is positive, this could undermine the very possibility of group agency. We now turn to this question.

2.2 An impossibility result

Intentional attitudes formalized

Our first step is to define the problem of attitude aggregation more formally. A group of two or more individuals seeks to form intentional attitudes towards a set of propositions. The attitudes are binary and can be either judgments or preferences, but only one kind of attitude at a time. Thus our model can be interpreted either as one of judgment aggregation or as one of preference aggregation, but not as both at once.[33]

To use a language compatible with both interpretations, we speak of 'positive' and 'negative' attitudes towards propositions. In the case of judgments, saying that an individual's attitude on a proposition 'p' is positive means that the individual judges that p; saying that it is negative means that he or she does not judge that p (which is not the same as judging that not p).[34] In the case of preferences, saying that the individual's attitude on 'p' is positive means that he or she prefers that p; saying that it is negative means that he or she does not prefer that p (which, again, is not the same as preferring that not p).

The propositions are formulated in propositional logic, which can express 'atomic' propositions without logical connectives, such as 'p', 'q', 'r', and so on, and 'compound' propositions with the logical connectives 'not', 'and', 'or', 'if-then', 'if and only if', such as 'p and q', 'p or q', 'if p then q', and so on. The model can be extended to richer logical languages, which can express what we have called sophisticated as well as simple propositions (Dietrich 2007), but for expositional simplicity we set these technicalities aside.

The set of propositions towards which attitudes are held is called the 'agenda'. To exclude trivial cases, we assume that the agenda contains at least two distinct atomic propositions ('p', 'q'), one of their conjunction, disjunction, or material implication (that is, any one of 'p and q', 'p or q', 'if p then q'), and the negations of all propositions contained in it.[35] This assumption can be weakened, but the technical details are not central to our overall argument.[36]

Formally, an individual's 'attitudes' towards the propositions on the agenda are modeled as an assignment of Yes's and No's to these propositions, where 'Yes' stands for a positive attitude and 'No' for a negative one.[37] A combination of attitudes across all individuals in the group is called a 'profile'.

The concept of an aggregation function

To move from a profile of individual attitudes to group-level attitudes, the group requires an 'aggregation function'. As illustrated by the input-output scheme in Figure 2.1, an aggregation function is a mapping that assigns to each profile of individual attitudes towards the propositions on the agenda (assuming the profile is admissible, more on this later) the collective attitudes towards these propositions, which are also modeled as an assignment of Yes's and No's to them.[38]

In our earlier examples, the aggregation function was majority voting, according to which the group forms a positive attitude towards any proposition if and only if a majority of group members does so. But majority voting is just one of many possible aggregation functions. Other examples are supermajority or unanimity rules, where the group forms a positive attitude towards any proposition if and only if a certain qualified majority of group members – for example, two thirds, three quarters, or all of them – does so; dictatorships, where the group's attitudes are always those of an

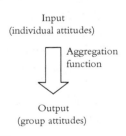

Input
(individual attitudes)

Aggregation
function

Output
(group attitudes)

Figure 2.1 An aggregation function

antecedently fixed individual; inverse dictatorships, where the group's attitudes are always the reverse of those of an antecedently fixed individual; and constant rules, where the group's attitudes are always the same, regardless of its members' attitudes.

The total number of logically possible aggregation functions, even for a small group and a small agenda of propositions, is truly breathtaking. For example, if an attitude is to be formed just on a single proposition, a 10-member group already has a choice between $2^{2^{10}}=2^{1024}$ logically possible aggregation functions (List 2006a), a number that on some estimates exceeds the total number of elementary particles in the universe. Most of these aggregation functions are completely useless for the purpose of group-attitude formation. We have already seen that majority voting does not generally secure rational group attitudes, and even some of the formally well-defined alternatives to majority voting, such as constant rules or inverse dictatorships, are of little practical use. We must therefore restrict our attention to aggregation functions that satisfy certain minimal conditions of plausible group-attitude formation.

Four conditions on an aggregation function

We now introduce four conditions that we may, at least initially, expect an aggregation function to satisfy. The first two specify what inputs the aggregation function should accept as admissible and what outputs it should produce, the next two how these inputs and outputs should hang together. To state the first two conditions, call an agent's attitudes 'consistent' if the propositions on which the agent has a positive attitude constitute a consistent set, that is, they are co-realizable; call them 'complete' relative to the given agenda of propositions if, for every proposition-negation pair on the agenda, the agent has a positive attitude on either the proposition or its negation, that is, the agent is 'opinionated' on every such pair.

Universal domain. The aggregation function admits as input any possible profile of individual attitudes towards the propositions on the agenda, assuming that individual attitudes are consistent and complete.

Collective rationality. The aggregation function produces as output consistent and complete group attitudes towards the propositions on the agenda.

Anonymity. All individuals' attitudes are given equal weight in determining the group attitudes. Formally, the aggregation function is invariant under permutations of any given profile of individual attitudes.

Systematicity. The group attitude on each proposition depends only on the individuals' attitudes towards it, not on their attitudes towards other propositions, and the pattern of dependence between individual and collective attitudes is the same for all propositions.

Although these four conditions may seem initially plausible, we argue below that they can, and should, be relaxed in various contexts. Nonetheless, it is useful to begin by asking what aggregation functions, if any, can satisfy them all. Majority voting, for example, satisfies universal domain, anonymity, and systematicity but violates collective rationality, as illustrated by the paradox we have discussed.

An impossibility theorem

In analogy to Arrow's impossibility theorem on the aggregation of preference relations, it turns out that our four conditions on attitude aggregation are mutually inconsistent.

Theorem. There exists no aggregation function satisfying universal domain, collective rationality, anonymity, and systematicity (List and Pettit 2002).

It is important to emphasize that this result is not the same as Arrow's impossibility theorem. The present result applies to the aggregation of intentional attitudes towards logically connected propositions, while Arrow's theorem applies to the aggregation of preference relations (which, if rational, take the form of 'rankings' of options).[39] In the more technical literature, however, many generalizations and extensions of the present result have been obtained, including one that is sufficiently general to imply Arrow's original theorem as a formal (though interpretationally distinct) corollary.[40] Although we refer to a few of these results in the next section, we are unable to do justice to this rich body of technical work in this primarily philosophical book. We restrict our discussion to the simplest results illustrative of the ideas we are concerned with.

How should we interpret this impossibility theorem? If we regarded all four conditions as indispensable requirements on group-attitude formation, we would have to interpret it as demonstrating the impossibility of forming such attitudes and thus as undermining the possibility of group agency: as soon as the propositions on the agenda are non-trivially interconnected, it is impossible for a group to form intentional attitudes in accordance with universal domain, collective rationality, anonymity, and systematicity.

But we think this would be the wrong interpretation of the result. More constructively, our result can be taken to show that, if a group seeks to form intentional attitudes, it must relax at least one of the four conditions. As we now demonstrate, any three of them can be satisfied together. The question therefore is which one, or which ones, to relax. In the next section, we go through the conditions one by one and ask what possibilities open up if we relax each.[41] Sometimes it turns out that the impossibility is quite persistent, in that a rather counterintuitive relaxation of the given condition is necessary in order to obtain convincing possibilities. In the context of group agency, we argue, the most promising route is to relax systematicity. The possible modes of group agency considered in the next chapter all involve a relaxation of this condition.

2.3 Escape routes from the impossibility

Relaxing universal domain

Universal domain requires the aggregation function to admit as input any possible profile of individual attitudes towards the propositions on the agenda. An aggregation function satisfying universal domain exhibits a certain kind of 'robustness': it works not only for certain special inputs but for all possible inputs that may be brought to it. But suppose we require successful group-attitude formation only when there is sufficient agreement among group members, not regardless of the level of diversity in the group. Then it becomes possible for majority voting to generate rational group attitudes.

Suppose, in particular, that the group members can be aligned from left to right – we may interpret this as capturing their cognitive or ideological positions – such that the following pattern holds: for every proposition on the agenda, the individuals with a positive attitude towards the proposition are either all to the left, or all to the right, of those with a negative one. Call a profile of attitudes with this pattern 'unidimensionally aligned'. It is then guaranteed that majority voting generates consistent group attitudes, assuming that the group members' attitudes are individually consistent (List 2003b).[42]

To see why this is the case, consider the following example. Suppose a five-member group seeks to form attitudes towards propositions 'p', 'if p then q', 'q', and their negations, as in the global warming example above, and suppose the individual attitudes – here judgments – are as shown in Table 2.4.

We then have the pattern of unidimensional alignment: the individuals with a positive attitude towards any proposition are either all to the left, or all to the right, of those with a negative one. What are the group's attitudes under majority voting? It is easy to see that they coincide with the attitudes of the median individual on the left–right alignment of the individuals, that is, with the attitudes of the individual who has an equal number of others on both sides, here individual 3. Under the pattern of unidimensional alignment, no proposition can be accepted by a majority without being accepted by the median individual. As long as individual attitudes are consistent, then, so are the resulting majority attitudes. The median individual may differ from profile to profile, of course; but for any profile exhibiting unidimensional alignment, the consistency of the median individual's attitudes guarantees that of the majority attitudes.

In short, if universal domain is relaxed to the requirement that the aggregation function admit as input only those profiles of individual attitudes exhibiting

Table 2.4: Unidimensionally aligned judgments

	Individual 1	Individual 2	Individual 3	Individual 4	Individual 5
'p'	False	False	False	False	True
'if p then q'	True	True	True	True	False
'q'	True	True	False	False	False

unidimensional alignment, then majority voting satisfies collective rationality, anonymity, and systematicity. It can further be shown that, instead of unidimensional
alignment, some less restrictive patterns, which are easier to achieve, are already
sufficient to secure the same result (Dietrich and List 2010b). So Hobbes's, Locke's,
and Rousseau's proposals on how to arrive at group-level intentional attitudes can be
made to work, after all, so long as group members exhibit the required level of
agreement (see also List 2002, where a distinction between 'substantive' and 'meta-
agreement' is developed).

How plausible is this escape route from our impossibility theorem? It is perhaps most
compelling if the aggregation of attitudes is preceded by a period of group deliberation.
Such deliberation may transform individual attitudes so as to make them more cohesive
and bring about a pattern like unidimensional alignment. In response to Condorcet's
paradox on the aggregation of preference relations, theorists of deliberative democracy
have hypothesized the existence of a mechanism along these lines (Miller 1992; Knight
and Johnson 1994; Dryzek and List 2003). This hypothesis is supported, with certain
qualifications, by empirical data from deliberative opinion polls (List, Luskin, et al.
2000/2006). Each of these polls focused on one particular controversial public issue,
such as the future of the monarchy in Australia or in Britain, energy policies in Texas,
or whether to close down, maintain, or expand the local airport in New Haven,
Connecticut. In each case, a random sample of people from the relevant community
was first interviewed on the issue in question, then gathered for a weekend of
deliberation about this issue, and finally interviewed again. A before–after comparison
of the participants' answers to the interview questions suggested that deliberation
transformed individual attitudes in such a way as to make them more structured in
terms of a shared cognitive or ideological dimension.

Nonetheless, this solution cannot be expected to work in general, especially with
judgments as opposed to preferences. Even in an idealized expert panel making judgments on factual matters without any conflicts of interest, disagreement may still be
pervasive, and there is no guarantee that the intentional attitudes of several individuals,
each with his or her own exposure to the world, will neatly fall into a pattern like
unidimensional alignment. The empirical fact of pluralism must be expected to hold not
only in the world at large but also among the members of a group agent.

Relaxing collective rationality

Collective rationality is a two-part condition requiring the aggregation function to
produce as output group attitudes that are both consistent and complete. Thus there
are two ways of relaxing it: we may drop either consistency or completeness (or both).
Allowing inconsistent group attitudes seems unattractive, especially if the group seeks
to achieve agency and the attitudes are near the coal-face of action, as we put it earlier.
Outside the context of agency, liberals sometimes argue that inconsistency of a
democratic decision-making body need not be a bad thing (Brennan 2003), but we
remain unconvinced.

Let us therefore turn to the second way of relaxing collective rationality, that of allowing incomplete group attitudes while upholding the requirement of consistency. Suppose a group is willing not to be opinionated on some proposition-negation pairs; it is willing to refrain from forming a positive attitude on both the proposition and its negation. The group may then be able to generate consistent group attitudes in accordance with the other conditions introduced above. For example, it may use a supermajority or unanimity rule, under which it forms a positive attitude on a proposition if and only if a certain supermajority of group members – all of them in the case of unanimity rule – do so. If the required supermajority threshold is sufficiently high – in our examples above, any threshold above two thirds would work – this aggregation function produces consistent group attitudes, while satisfying universal domain, anonymity, and systematicity (List 2001; Dietrich and List 2007b).

Groups operating in a strongly consensual manner, such as the UN Security Council or the EU Council of Ministers, often take this approach, with the result that they frequently have to suspend attitude. But if a group is to perform robustly as an agent, it must generally avoid attitudinal incompleteness; it must be able to make up its mind on the main issues it confronts. Recall, for example, the multi-member court deciding a breach-of-contract case or the expert panel giving advice on global warming. Incompleteness may not be an option in such groups, as they may be expected to take a clear stance on every proposition-negation pair brought to them for adjudication.[43]

Relaxing anonymity

Anonymity requires the aggregation function to treat all group members equally in determining the group attitudes. This is obviously a fundamental democratic requirement. But suppose a group gives it up and appoints one member as a 'dictator' whose attitudes always determine those of the group. The resulting aggregation function – a 'dictatorship' – clearly satisfies universal domain, collective rationality, and systematicity. In fact, it does so uniquely: there is no other way of meeting these three conditions (Pauly and van Hees 2006; Dietrich and List 2007a). This implies that the impossibility theorem above continues to hold if anonymity is replaced by the weaker condition of 'non-dictatorship'.[44]

Is the relaxation of anonymity a plausible escape route, then, from the impossibility result? The answer depends on the group in question. A dictatorship is unappealing in a democratically oriented group, while we can imagine a hierarchical group in which an individual plays a dictatorial role – the director of a company or the head of an organization, for example. But even if we set democratic concerns aside, there is a distinct problem to be confronted. A dictatorship fails to use information dispersed among the group members in forming the group's judgments. As we show in Chapter 4, a dictatorially organized group loses out on the epistemic advantages of a democratic structure (for a case study, see Ober 2008).[45]

However, there are also some more benign ways of relaxing anonymity, specifically in the context of relaxing systematicity. It turns out that there exist some plausible non-anonymous and non-systematic aggregation functions that capture a division of labor in the group's attitude formation. We discuss such aggregation rules – under the name 'distributed premise-based procedures' – in the next section and the following two chapters.

Relaxing systematicity

Like collective rationality, systematicity has two parts. First, the group attitude on each proposition should depend only on the individuals' attitudes towards it, not on their attitudes towards other propositions, and second, the same pattern of dependence should hold for all propositions. Call these the 'independence' and 'neutrality' parts, respectively. Unlike in the case of collective rationality, however, the two parts are nested; that is, the second part strengthens the first. We may thus consider either relaxing just neutrality while preserving independence, or relaxing both neutrality and independence. These two routes correspond to different ways of implementing a differential treatment of propositions.

First possibility: Giving up neutrality

It turns out that relaxing neutrality alone while keeping independence does not get us very far. The relevant results are somewhat technical, and we mention them primarily to illustrate the robustness of the original impossibility. We turn to more positive results in a moment, when we consider the more radical move of giving up independence as well.

Here we want to make two points. The first is that, although, for our simple examples, we can actually find aggregation functions satisfying the rest of our conditions without neutrality, these aggregation functions are not very appealing. Secondly, and more strongly, even those unappealing aggregation functions cease to be possible once we go beyond simple examples.

In the example of the expert panel above, an aggregation function satisfying all of our conditions except neutrality is given by the following stipulation: proposition 'p' is accepted by the group if and only if all individuals accept it; and each of propositions 'q' and 'if p then q' is accepted if and only if at least one individual accepts it. In other words, every group member can veto a positive group attitude on 'p' and a negative one on the other two propositions. Obviously, no real-world expert panel would use such an aggregation function. Why should unanimous agreement be needed for the group to judge that carbon dioxide emissions are above the critical threshold, while a single individual's vote is enough for the group to conclude that there is a causal mechanism by which emissions lead to a temperature increase and that there will be such an increase? Why should individuals each have a veto in the one case, and an 'anti-veto' in the other?

Technical work has revealed that only aggregation functions that give everyone either a veto or an anti-veto on each proposition in this manner can satisfy our conditions (in slightly strengthened form) with systematicity weakened to independence (Nehring and Puppe 2008; 2010a).[46] This establishes our first point: the aggregation functions that become possible if we drop just neutrality are not very appealing.

What about our second point, that these aggregation functions, besides being unappealing, are not available more generally? In each of our examples, the agenda of propositions towards which attitudes are formed is very simple: it contains only a small number of propositions and among them only one compound proposition (and its negation). Real-world group agents typically have to form attitudes on more complex agendas of propositions; and for many such agendas, an impossibility theorem holds even with systematicity weakened to the independence part alone. To state this theorem, let us impose one further condition on the aggregation function.

Unanimity preservation. If all individuals hold the same attitudes towards all propositions, then these unanimously held attitudes are the group attitudes.

Suppose now the agenda is more complex than assumed above, exhibiting richer logical interconnections between propositions, in a sense that can be made technically precise but whose details do not matter for the informal discussion.[47] An example of such an agenda is the one containing two atomic propositions and both their conjunction and their disjunction (rather than just one of them), as well as the negations of these propositions.

Theorem. An aggregation function satisfies universal domain, collective rationality, unanimity preservation, and independence if and only if it is a dictatorship (Dietrich and List 2007a; Dokow and Holzman 2010).[48]

These considerations show that relaxing only the neutrality part of systematicity does not open up a satisfactory escape route from the original impossibility theorem. Even for relatively simple agendas, only unappealing aggregation functions, such as those with a veto/anti-veto structure, satisfy the remaining conditions, and as soon as the agenda is richer in logical interconnections, even these aggregation functions become unavailable, as the new theorem shows (see also Nehring and Puppe 2010a). To find a compelling escape route from the impossibility theorem, we must therefore drop systematicity altogether, that is, give up both its neutrality part and its independence part.

Second possibility: Giving up independence and neutrality

The different relaxation possibilities reviewed so far do not offer much hope of evading the impossibility result and identifying a reliable, generally available recipe for constructing a robustly rational group agent. But we have left the best prospect until last. It turns out that by relaxing independence as well as relaxing neutrality, thereby taking a radical line on systematicity, we can begin to see how individuals can routinely incorporate as group agents.

The most obvious possibility for forming a group-agent that is opened up by relaxing independence involves prioritizing some propositions over others and letting the group attitudes on the first set of propositions determine its attitudes on the second.

Suppose, for example, that the group designates some propositions as 'premises' and others as 'conclusions' and assigns priority either to the premises or to the conclusions. We already encountered the choice on whether to prioritize premises or conclusions in the example of the three-member court, where the propositions about action and obligation were the premises of the case and the proposition about liability the conclusion.

If a group prioritizes the premises, it may use a 'premise-based procedure', whereby it generates a group attitude towards each premise by taking a majority vote on that premise and then derives its attitudes on the conclusions from its majority attitudes on the premises. Independence is clearly breached here, since the group attitudes on the conclusions depend no longer on individual attitudes on those conclusions alone but also on individual attitudes on other propositions, namely the premises. In the court example, with the individual judgments shown in Table 2.1, the premise-based procedure leads to the acceptance of all the displayed propositions, resulting in a 'liable' verdict.

Alternatively, if the group prioritizes the propositions designated as conclusions, it may use a 'conclusion-based procedure', whereby it takes a majority vote on each conclusion and forms no opinion on any of the premises, accepting neither it nor its negation. Apart from violating systematicity, this aggregation function thus produces incomplete group attitudes. In the court example, the conclusion-based procedure leads to the acceptance of the negation of the conclusion: a 'not liable' verdict.

The premise- and conclusion-based procedures are not the only possible aggregation functions when systematicity is dropped altogether. Both are special cases of a 'sequential priority procedure' (List 2004b), although this is more obvious in the case of the premise-based procedure than in the case of the conclusion-based one.[49] To define a sequential priority procedure, let some order among the propositions on the agenda be given, where earlier propositions in the order are interpreted as 'prior to' later ones, capable of serving as reasons for or against these later ones. For example, 'premises' could come before 'conclusions'. Now the group considers the propositions in the given order. For each proposition considered, if the group's attitude towards the proposition is unconstrained by its attitudes on earlier propositions, then it forms its attitude on the new proposition by majority voting; but if the attitude on the new proposition is constrained by attitudes on earlier propositions, then the group lets those earlier attitudes determine the new one. In our expert-panel example, the propositions could be considered in the order 'p', 'if p then q', 'q', resulting in positive attitudes towards all three propositions (and thus negative attitudes towards their negations).

Further possibilities open up when the group relaxes anonymity as well as systematicity. It can then use an aggregation function that not only assigns priority to certain premises but also implements a division of labor among its members: a 'distributed premise-based procedure' (List 2005). Here different group members are assigned to different premises and form attitudes only on these premises; they each 'specialize' on their assigned premises. The group then determines its attitude on each premise by taking a majority vote on that premise among the assigned individuals – the 'specialists' – and derives its attitudes on other propositions from these attitudes on the premises. We discuss the properties of this aggregation function in Chapter 4.

Another important class of aggregation functions that become possible when we give up independence and therefore systematicity is that of 'distance-based aggregation functions' (Konieczny and Pino-Perez 2002; Pigozzi 2006). Unlike premise-based or sequential priority procedures, these aggregation functions are not based on prioritizing some propositions over others. Rather, they are based on a 'distance metric' between different combinations of attitudes on the propositions in the agenda. For example, we can calculate the 'distance' between two particular combinations of attitudes by counting the number of propositions on the agenda on which they disagree. A distance-based aggregation function now assigns to each profile of individual attitudes that consistent and complete combination of attitudes that minimizes the total distance from the given individual attitudes (with some further rule for breaking any ties).[50] In this way, the collective attitude to any particular proposition depends not just on individual attitudes to that proposition but on whether it occurs in a combination of attitudes that has this distance-minimizing property. Such distance-based aggregation functions have some interesting properties. In particular, they capture the idea of reaching a compromise between different individuals' attitudes. Moreover, they can be generalized in a number of ways, for instance by giving different 'weights' to different propositions in the distance calculation, depending on their particular status (for further generalizations, see also Miller and Osherson 2009).

Giving up systematicity comes, of course, at a cost. If a group uses an aggregation function that treats different propositions differently – either by designating some as premises and others as conclusions, or by specifying a more general order of priority among them, or alternatively by giving different weights to different propositions in a distance calculation – then the question arises of how to justify this differential treatment. Although there may sometimes be a natural order of priority, or a ranking of status, among a given set of propositions, propositions do not generally carry an independent mark of priority or status, and people often differ in their background assumptions as to which propositions matter most. One person's conclusion may be another person's premise. If a premise-based procedure is applied to the legislators' preferences in Table 2.3, for instance, the choice of premises can make a big difference. If 'p' and 'q' are chosen as premises, then all three propositions, 'p', 'q', and 'p or q', are dispreferred by the group; if 'p' and 'p or q' are chosen as premises, then 'p' is dispreferred and both 'q' and 'p or q' are preferred; and if 'q' and 'p or q' are chosen as premises, then 'q' is dispreferred and both 'p' and 'p or q' are preferred.

Obviously, the fact that the group's attitudes depend on the way propositions are prioritized may be strategically exploited by group members with agenda-setting power. In Chapter 5, we further show that aggregation functions violating the independence part of systematicity are vulnerable to another, equally important form of strategic manipulation: the members of a group using such an aggregation function do not generally have an incentive to reveal their individual attitudes truthfully (Dietrich and List 2007c).[51]

Despite these problems, giving up systematicity may be our best way to avoid the impossibility of rational attitude aggregation (see also Chapman 2002). If we do not require systematicity, we can find several aggregation functions that guarantee rational intentional attitudes at the group level, albeit at some cost. The premise-based or sequential priority procedures, for example, make the pursuit of agency explicit: they lead a group to perform in the manner of a reason-driven agent by deriving its attitudes on conclusions (or 'posterior' propositions) from its attitudes on relevant premises (or 'prior' ones). Thus they lead the group to 'collectivize reason', in the sense of guaranteeing that the attitudes of the group are consistent as well as derived in a rational process.[52]

Impossibility avoided?

Let us recapitulate our opening question: How can a multi-member group move from the distinct and possibly conflicting intentional attitudes of its members to a single system of such attitudes endorsed by the group as a whole? In answering this question, we have encountered a paradox and a more general impossibility theorem.

The paradox shows that an initially plausible approach to the formation of group attitudes – majority voting on all propositions – does not generally work. The impossibility theorem, similar in spirit to Arrow's theorem on the aggregation of preference relations, demonstrates that majority voting is not alone in its failure to solve the problem: no aggregation function will generate rational group attitudes in accordance with some minimal conditions. At first sight, this result seems to put the very possibility of group agency in question. We have argued, however, that some of the theorem's conditions can and should be relaxed.

The most promising escape route from the theorem, we have suggested, is given by relaxing systematicity. An aggregation function such as a premise-based or sequential priority procedure enables a group not only to form rational intentional attitudes but also to do so in a way that collectivizes reason. By using such an aggregation function, a group explicitly acknowledges that propositions stand in certain relationships of priority to each other and takes these relationships seriously in deriving its attitudes on some propositions from its attitudes on others. We should emphasize that the possible aggregation functions reviewed in this chapter are only illustrative of the large space of possibilities that open up once the restriction of systematicity and particularly independence is lifted.

We show in the next chapter that the pursuit of this escape route has some surprising implications for the relationship between what goes on at the level of the group and what goes on at the level of its members, establishing a certain kind of autonomy for group agents.

3

The Structure of Group Agents

We have argued that it is possible, at least in principle, for a group to aggregate the intentional attitudes of its members into a single system of such attitudes held by the group as a whole. But in doing so, a group cannot satisfy all of universal domain, collective rationality, anonymity, and systematicity: it must either disallow certain profiles of individual attitudes, or permit less than fully rational group attitudes, or make one member a dictator, or treat different propositions differently in determining the group's attitudes. While the first two of these routes are of limited use for achieving group agency, the last two seem more promising. But only the last is genuinely attractive. By contrast, a group agent that is constructed around a dictator is intuitively a rather degenerate case: it can be seen as just an extension of that individual's agency rather than as a group agent proper.

What picture of the structure of a jointly intentional group agent emerges from this? How should we expect such a group agent to form, and what relationship should we expect between its group-level performance and that of its members? We discuss these questions in this chapter. Our discussion is divided into three sections. In the first, largely descriptive section, we review some possible ways in which a group may organize itself for the pursuit of agency. Aggregation functions, as discussed in the last chapter, are explicit or implicit parts of these. In the second, more philosophical section, we investigate the relationship between what goes on at the level of the group and what goes on at the level of its members. We describe this relationship as one of 'supervenience' and argue that the group's attitudes cannot generally be determined by the attitudes of its members in a 'proposition-wise' way, only in a 'holistic' one. This, in turn, suggests a surprising degree of autonomy for group agents. In the third, concluding section, we contrast our account of group agency with two traditional accounts that have dominated the literature. Our account differs, on the one hand, from the emergentist one in which group agency is recognized but its supervenience denied and, on the other, from the eliminativist one in which group agency is denied and thus the issue of supervenience not considered. Instead, our account recognizes the reality of group agents but does so in a non-mysterious way.

3.1 The organizational structure of a group agent

It is one thing to map out the logical space of possible aggregation functions a group may use to generate its intentional attitudes, as we have done in the last chapter. It is another to identify actual organizational structures by which a group can implement a given aggregation function and perform as an agent. We now turn to this issue.

Organizational structures versus aggregation functions

It is important to distinguish between an aggregation function in the thin, formal sense of a functional relation between individual and group-level attitudes on certain propositions and an 'organizational structure' in the thicker, more practical sense of the rules and procedures the group uses to implement, and subsequently to enact, such a function.[53] There are several ways, for example, in which a group could implement majority voting as its aggregation function. It could do so through explicit voting, which can itself be conducted in various ways: through different forms of balloting, such as open or anonymous ballots, paper ballots, or electronic ones, and so on. Alternatively, majority voting could be implemented in a more implicit manner, for example through some process of deliberation that leads group members to converge on the attitudes of the majority. Thus different organizational structures can be compatible with the same aggregation function. Occasionally, it can also happen that there is no feasible organizational structure for implementing a particular aggregation function, perhaps because group members would never reveal their preferences or judgments truthfully. We discuss these issues in Chapter 5.

In what follows, we characterize different organizational structures in terms of two distinctions: first, between 'functionally explicit' and 'functionally inexplicit' ones, and second, between 'non-reasoning' and 'reasoning' ones.[54] Within the category of functionally inexplicit organizational structures, we also comment on the role of 'feedback'. Our aim is to give a sense of the variety of ways in which group agents can form and function. We do not make much of the difference between participatory and hierarchical group agents here, as our main distinctions apply in each category. This difference becomes crucial, however, in subsequent chapters: for example, when we discuss the epistemic advantages of a democratic organizational structure as compared with a dictatorial one (in Chapter 4) and when we turn to the question of how group members can be protected against excesses of the group agent's power (in Chapter 6).

Functionally explicit versus functionally inexplicit structures

We call a group's organizational structure 'functionally explicit' if the group explicitly uses a given aggregation function, such as majority voting, applies it mechanically to the attitudes of its members, and then enacts the resulting group attitudes in an equally mechanical way. The group may do this by setting up a suitable balloting and vote-counting system for arriving at its preferences and judgments and by assigning to some of its members or deputies the task of acting as required by these group attitudes. A legislature that uses a rigid voting protocol for its decisions may fall into this category.[55] While majority voting can easily be implemented in this way, however, a majoritarian organizational structure does not generally ensure group agency, as we have seen, since it may generate inconsistent group attitudes on logically interconnected propositions. But there are other functionally explicit organizational structures that avoid this problem. Examples are implementations of premise-based or sequential priority procedures, as introduced in the last chapter. These require the group to prioritize some propositions over others, either by designating some as premises and others as conclusions or by specifying some other, more general order of priority over the propositions. The group's attitudes on conclusions or propositions lower in that order are then derived from its attitudes on premises or propositions higher in it.[56] In the real world, precedent-based decision procedures under which prior decisions constrain posterior ones, such as in judicial contexts, may be examples of such organizational structures.

An important problem with this kind of organizational structure, however, is its lack of flexibility. There need not always be a satisfactory way of prioritizing propositions, as we have already noted, and the same proposition may figure as fundamental in one person's reasoning and as derivative in that of another. To be sure, some propositions may stand out because of their logical form, status, generality, or the point in time at which they come up for consideration. Examples may be propositions falling under constitutional law in a judicial or legislative context, or propositions constituting basic theoretical principles in scientific contexts. But more generally, one person's premise may be another person's conclusion, as it is often said. Moreover, an agent may change the relative weighting of propositions as attitudes develop and then reconsider his or her attitudes on initially adjudicated propositions when confronting their implications for other propositions. An organizational structure that mechanically implements a premise-based or sequential priority procedure, for instance by rigidly enforcing the rule of precedents, denies this flexibility to a group agent. It denies the group the sort of to-and-fro adjustment that John Rawls (1971) calls the 'reflective equilibrium' method. This method involves going back and forth between different mutually inconsistent judgments – the idea might be extended to preferences too – so as to decide where to adjust in order to achieve consistency and other requirements of rationality; no judgment is forever privileged.

In view of the rigidity of a functionally explicit structure, a group may well resort to a 'functionally inexplicit' one. This involves a heuristic for determining, from proposition to proposition, the way for the group to go on, perhaps through deliberation, giving the group the flexibility to adjust its attitudes whenever appropriate. The group attitudes generated in this process, assuming it is non-random, are still a function of individual attitudes and perhaps other contributions by the individuals.[57] Thus a functionally inexplicit structure may turn out to *mimic* some aggregation function, though in all likelihood a rather complex one. The aggregation function implemented is not one the members of the group set out to implement *ex ante*; rather, its implementation is a consequence of the functionally inexplicit organizational structure adopted. We give an illustration in a moment.

A functionally inexplicit structure can have practical advantages over the explicit implementation of any underlying aggregation function. As an illustration, consider what we may describe as a 'straw-vote procedure'. This functionally inexplicit organizational structure requires a group to follow roughly these steps in determining its attitudes.

- Consider the propositions on the agenda one by one in a sequence, which may reflect either a temporal order or some other order of priority.
- Take a majority vote on each proposition considered.
  o If the attitude formed is consistent with attitudes already formed, let it stand as the group attitude.
  o If the attitude formed is not consistent with these attitudes, consider all the different possible ways in which previously formed attitudes or the new attitude could be revised so as to restore consistency. Take a vote under a suitable procedure, or deliberate, on which of the possible revisions to make.
- Assign suitable members or deputies to enact the resulting group attitudes.

Although we have suggested that some real-world precedent-based decision procedures implement a premise-based or sequential priority procedure and thus count as functionally explicit, they are perhaps better described as instances of a straw-vote procedure, especially if past decisions are not always rigidly prioritized.

As we have argued, despite its functionally inexplicit character, the straw-vote procedure may still implement some aggregation function. Which one it is depends on several factors, especially the group members' dispositions in choosing between different possible attitude revisions. If they are conservatively disposed, always favoring the revision of new attitudes over that of earlier ones, the straw-vote procedure mimics a sequential priority procedure. But if they have another, less conservative disposition, it may mimic a very different aggregation function, for instance a 'reverse' sequential priority procedure in which the revision of old attitudes is favored.

The role of feedback

The straw-vote procedure requires group members not just to vote as required under any aggregation function but to form a view about whether the resulting attitudes are consistent and, if not, about how consistency can be restored. It thus requires 'feedback' from the group-level attitudes that are being formed to the individual members involved in forming them. It seems clear that feedback, of one form or other, is a key ingredient in any functionally inexplicit organizational structure.

Two points about feedback are worth noting. First, up to now, we have implicitly assumed that when the members of a group cast their votes on proposition 'p', they vote solely on the basis of whether they individually judge or prefer that p. But this cannot generally be the case under the straw-vote procedure, when members are deciding about whether to revise the group attitude on some proposition. When they vote for 'p' here, they do so, not necessarily because they individually accept 'p' but rather because they prefer, or judge that it is better, for the group to accept 'p'. Feedback thus brings to the fore the possibility of more complex voting motives: the attitudes expressed by members may be driven not – or not only – by their individual judgments or preferences on the propositions in question but by their judgments that it is better for the group to form certain judgments or preferences or by their preferences over what the group should judge or prefer.[58]

The second point to note is that feedback introduces a causal relationship between what is happening at the group level and what is happening at the level of individuals. Under the straw-vote procedure, the members of the group become aware of the group attitudes formed up to a certain point and respond to those attitudes. Does the presence of sophisticated voting motives and of causal inter-actions between group-level attitudes and individual votes contradict our claim that the group still implements some aggregation function? We do not think so. Even under an organizational structure with feedback like the straw-vote procedure, member attitudes are ultimately mapped to group attitudes. The fact that this mapping is more complicated, perhaps involving an initial transformation of the members' attitudes or their mediation through complex voting motives, is consist-ent with the existence of a functional relation between member attitudes and group attitudes (for a formal model of the transformation of opinions through group communication, see List forthcoming-a).

Non-reasoning versus reasoning structures

By the account offered in Chapter 1, an agent counts as reasoning, not just rational, only if it is able to form not only beliefs *in* propositions – that is, object-language beliefs – but also beliefs *about* propositions – that is, metalanguage beliefs. Examples of the latter are the belief that a given proposition is true, well supported, or desirable and the belief that one proposition entails or is consistent with another. As we have seen, an agent forming metalanguage beliefs can use them to put rational checks on its object-language beliefs and desires. Coming to believe that 'p' and 'q' are inconsistent, for example, the agent is rationally led to suspend a belief that p and q. Coming to believe that 'r' is desirable, the agent is rationally led to reconsider a desire that not r. The agent can thus take intentional steps, by asking itself suitable metalanguage questions, to enhance its own rational performance.

In practice, it seems difficult to achieve group-level reasoning through a functionally explicit organizational structure, given its rather mechanical nature.[59] But what about functionally inexplicit organizational structures, which incorporate feedback? Does such an organizational structure automatically give a group agent the ability to reason? Not necessarily. Imagine a group agent that tries to conduct its business by majority voting and avoids inconsistencies through covert adjustments by some canny individuals. In a small, open group, some individuals may keep track of the votes of others and predict how those others will vote on logically connected issues. Suppose that whenever they predict an inconsistent pattern of votes, they change their own votes so as to sustain the overall rationality of the group agent, perhaps at a cost of individual-level consistency; there is some evidence that this occasionally happens in collegial courts (Stearns 2000). In such cases feedback from the group level to the individual level plays a crucial role, and the individuals who stand ready to change their votes reason on the basis of meta-language beliefs about the consistency or inconsistency of propositions the group is likely to endorse. But the group itself does not reason. It cannot do so since it does not itself form any metalanguage beliefs.

Although feedback alone is insufficient for group reasoning, we can imagine cases where group reasoning does occur due to feedback. A group using a straw-vote procedure, for instance, may form group-level beliefs about the consistency or inconsistency of the propositions towards which attitudes have already been formed, and it may rely on its own rationality — sustained by its members — to ensure that it does not violate the constraints of rationality. The reasoning group is like the reasoning individual. It forms metalanguage beliefs intentionally, asking itself suitable questions and adjusting in light of them to advance its own rationality. The adjustment is ensured by the group's members, just as the rational adjustment of an individual is ensured by the subpersonal mechanisms in his or her cognitive make-up.

We think that organizational structures with feedback often give rise to group-level reasoning (though nothing much in our argument depends on this claim). This is because individuals who notice an actual or potential inconsistency in the group's attitudes are likely to draw this to the other members' attention rather than adjusting covertly so as to compensate. But if group members address such metalanguage issues together — and in common awareness of doing so — then in effect the group addresses them. And when the group adjusts in order to avoid the inconsistency, this is naturally explained as a case of the group reasoning its way out of the difficulty. Figure 3.1 summarizes the different types of organizational structures we have reviewed in this section.

3.2 The supervenience of a group agent

Given this understanding of organizational structures, how should we expect the performance of a group agent to relate to its members' contributions, that is, their attitudes, actions, or dispositions to act?[60] The things a group agent does are clearly determined by the things its members do; they cannot emerge independently. In particular, no group agent can form intentional attitudes without these being deter-mined, in one way or other, by certain contributions of its members, and no group agent can act without one or more of its members acting. But what is the precise sense of determination involved?

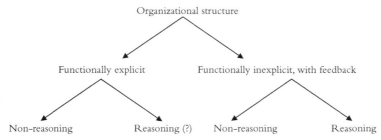

Figure 3.1 Organizational structures

The notion of supervenience

Think of the relation between the shapes made by dots on a grid and the positions or coordinates of the dots. The positions of the dots do not cause the shapes to be such and such, as there is no lag between the dots assuming those positions and the shapes materializing. Nothing causal needs to happen in order for the positions to give rise to the shapes; suitably positioned, the dots simply constitute the shapes and are not distinct enough to be causes. But although the positions of the dots do not causally determine the shapes, they still determine those shapes.

One way of expressing the nature of that determination is to say that, assuming the stock of dots is fixed, no variation is possible in the shapes – none is even logically possible – without a variation in the positions of the dots. Thus, if we produce a duplicate of the grid by duplicating the original stock of dots and their positions, then we will also have duplicated the shapes. Fix the number and positions of the dots and, as a matter of logical necessity, the shapes will be fixed as well. This mode of determination is called 'supervenience'. Formally, we say that one set of facts, say B, 'supervenes' on another, say A, if and only if, necessarily, fixing the A-facts also fixes the B-facts.[61] In the grid example, the facts about the number and positions of the dots are the A-facts, and the facts about the shapes the B-facts.

The notion of supervenience is useful for formulating theories about the relationship between facts, intuitively, of different levels. Many people have argued, for example, that the evaluative characteristics of things supervene on their non-evaluative characteristics; that the mental properties of a person supervene on his or her physical properties, at least in the context of the physical laws; and that the features of a culture supervene on the dispositions of members of that culture.

A supervenience relation leaves open the possibility that while the 'lower-level' pattern determines the 'higher-level' pattern, the higher-level pattern may be realized in a number of lower-level ways. Although the shapes produced by the dots may be fixed by the actual number and positions of these dots, the same shapes may still be maintained with a slight shift or reconfiguration in the dots or with an increase in their number. Supervenience may thus be a many–one relation with multiple lower-level patterns being capable of sustaining the same higher-level pattern. This property is called the 'multiple realizability' of B-facts in configurations of A-facts.

The notion of supervenience enables us to express formally our thesis about the relationship between what goes on at the level of the group and what goes on at the level of its members:

> **The supervenience thesis.** The attitudes and actions of a group agent supervene on the contributions of its members.

In other words, any individual-level duplicate of the group agent will be a group-level duplicate as well; let the individual contributions be fixed and the attitudes and actions of the group agent will be fixed as well.[62] The supervenience thesis does not sideline the role of the group agent's organizational structure. It is perfectly possible that the members of two different group agents individually have exactly the same intentional attitudes on some propositions, while the two group agents, due to their different organizational structures, hold different attitudes and act differently. But the difference in the two organizational structures will show up in some individual-level differences between the two groups; their different forms of organization mean that their members will act and be disposed to act in different ways. If one group is democratically organized while the other is dictatorial, for example, this difference will show up in different dispositions among members with regard to counting votes.

The supervenience of group attitudes on individual ones

Let us focus on the intentional attitudes of a group agent, since they are at the heart of the group's agency. The claim that these attitudes supervene on contributions of members is logically consistent with the possibility that they are fixed entirely by the members' actions and dispositions to act and do not depend on their individual attitudes on the relevant propositions. Take Ned Block's China-body system (Block 1980). In this scenario each of the billion members of the Chinese population takes charge of some task in the Turing-machine replication of someone's mental life. We can think of this system as a giant computer in which the mechanical role of transistors is played by individual human beings. Although individuals themselves do not form intentional attitudes on the propositions that are the objects of the system's representations and motivations, their mechanical interconnections ensure that the system as a whole manifests agency.[63] The attitudes of the group agent clearly supervene on the contributions of individuals, but only on their non-attitudinal contributions.

Nonetheless, this possibility is not a very realistic one. In most real-world examples of jointly intentional group agents, the members' actions and dispositions sustain the group's organizational structure, but under that structure the group's intentional attitudes are formed on the basis of the intentional attitudes that members manifest.[64] In what follows we therefore restrict ourselves to cases where the members' attitudes play this role and look at the nature of the supervenience relation between individual and group attitudes.[65]

If our account of group agency is to be vindicated, that supervenience relation must secure rational attitudes at the group level.[66] First, the supervenience relation must determine the group attitudes on the relevant propositions for any possible profile of members' attitudes. Unless this condition is met, the relation is not one of supervenience – that is, of necessary determination – but only one of contingent determination. Second, the group attitudes determined by the supervenience relation must robustly meet the appropriate attitude-to-attitude standards of rationality, such as consistency and completeness. Unless this second condition is met, the supervenience relation does not secure the robust presence of group-level agency. We can express these two requirements in terms of the following condition.

Robust group rationality. The supervenience relation determines consistent and complete group attitudes on the relevant propositions for any possible profile of consistent and complete member attitudes on these propositions.

It is easy to see that a supervenience relation satisfies robust group rationality if and only if it can be modeled as an aggregation function satisfying universal domain and collective rationality, as defined in the last chapter. But what are the other properties that the supervenience relation must satisfy? We now go through a number of possible theses about the nature of that relation; each of these can be seen as a possible 'precisification' of our main supervenience thesis. We argue for two general claims, one negative, the other positive. The negative claim is that the supervenience relation cannot be proposition-wise, as we put it. The positive is that it may be of a holistic rather than proposition-wise form.

The negative claim: proposition-wise supervenience conflicts with robust group rationality

The first and simplest thesis about the supervenience relation between individual and group attitudes is that of majoritarian supervenience. Recall that Hobbes (1994, Ch. 16) argued that 'the voice of the greater number must be considered as the voice of them all'; Locke (1960, Bk. 2, Ch. 8.96) held that 'the act of the majority passes for the act of the whole . . . and determines as having . . . the power of the whole'; and Rousseau (1997, Bk. 4, Ch. 2) maintained that 'the tally of the votes yields the declaration of the general will [in a majoritarian way]'.

Majoritarian supervenience. The group attitude on each proposition is the majority attitude on that proposition.

It is clear from our discussion of the paradox of majoritarian attitude aggregation in the last chapter, however, that majoritarian supervenience conflicts with robust group rationality. To recapitulate the argument, suppose a group agent forms intentional attitudes on some logically connected propositions. Could these attitudes supervene on the members' attitudes in a majoritarian way? If they did, it would be possible for the group simultaneously to accept propositions such as 'p', 'if p then q', and 'not q', for instance when individual attitudes are as shown in Table 2.2 in Chapter 2. But this would violate robust group rationality. Similar violations arise for any group size and any agenda of propositions with certain logical connections. We can summarize this observation as follows.

First fact. If the propositions on the agenda have non-trivial logical connections, majoritarian supervenience is inconsistent with robust group rationality.

For a group to be an agent, then, the relation between the group attitudes and those of its members cannot be that of majoritarian supervenience. Could the relation still resemble a majoritarian one in certain respects? Consider the following weaker thesis.

Uniform proposition-wise supervenience. The group attitude on each proposition is determined by the individual attitudes on that proposition, where the mode of determination is the same for all propositions.

While majoritarian supervenience permits only a single mode of determination between individual and group attitudes – a majoritarian one – uniform proposition-wise supervenience permits a large variety of such modes. Nonetheless, uniform proposition-wise supervenience requires the implementation of an aggregation function satisfying systematicity and thus comes into conflict with robust group rationality, as shown in the last chapter.[67]

Second fact. If the propositions on the agenda have non-trivial logical connections, uniform proposition-wise supervenience is inconsistent with robust group rationality, unless the supervenience relation is degenerate (in the sense that the group attitudes are determined by a dictator).

Therefore the relation between a group agent's attitudes and those of its members cannot be that of uniform proposition-wise supervenience either, unless the group is willing to install a dictator, such as a Hobbesian sovereign. Let us weaken the supervenience thesis further. Perhaps the problem lies in the 'uniformity' of the supervenience relation, that is, the fact that the mode of determination between individual and group attitudes is the same for all propositions. Let us drop this restriction and consider a weakened version of the thesis.

Proposition-wise supervenience. The group attitude on each proposition is determined by the individual attitudes on that proposition, where the mode of determination may differ from proposition to proposition.

Proposition-wise supervenience permits, for example, that on some propositions the group attitude is the majority attitude, while on others it is a different function of individual attitudes; it could be the attitude of some sub- or super-majority, the attitude of a particular subgroup, or the attitude held by an odd number of individuals, for example. But as soon as the agenda of propositions is sufficiently rich in logical connections, even proposition-wise supervenience, which requires the implementation of an aggregation function satisfying the independence part of systematicity, conflicts with robust group rationality, as we have noted in the last chapter as well.[68]

Third fact. If the propositions on the agenda have rich logical connections, proposition-wise supervenience is inconsistent with robust group rationality, unless the supervenience relation is degenerate (in the sense that the group attitudes are determined by a dictator or fail to preserve unanimous attitudes).

In summary, for a group to form rational attitudes on an agenda of propositions with certain logical connections, the relation between individual and group attitudes cannot generally be that of proposition-wise supervenience in any of its various forms, assuming a non-degenerate supervenience relation.[69] Although this finding does not refute our main thesis that a group agent's attitudes supervene on the contributions of members, it does show that the supervenience relation cannot be as simple as one may have thought. The group's attitude on a particular proposition cannot generally be a function of the members' attitudes on that proposition. The supervenience relation must be more complex. Can we find such a supervenience relation?

The positive claim: holistic supervenience is consistent with robust group rationality

The following thesis preserves the core idea that group attitudes supervene on members' attitudes, while dropping the restriction to proposition-wise supervenience.

Holistic supervenience. The set of group attitudes across propositions is determined by the individual sets of attitudes across these propositions.

As we will now see, the results reviewed in the last chapter, specifically those on relaxing systematicity, imply that several aggregation functions are available whose implementation ensures robust group rationality and a holistic supervenience relation between individual and group attitudes. This finding supports the logical possibility of group agency on our account.

Fourth fact. Holistic supervenience is consistent with robust group rationality.

Important examples of organizational structures giving rise to a holistic supervenience relation between individual and group attitudes while ensuring robust group rationality are those that implement a premise-based or sequential priority procedure, as discussed above. Under such a structure, the set of group attitudes across the propositions on the agenda is determined by, and thus holistically supervenient on, the individual sets of attitudes on these propositions; and by the given organizational design, consistent and complete group attitudes are guaranteed.

It is instructive to see how the premise-based and sequential priority procedures, while giving rise to a holistic supervenience relation between individual and group attitudes, breach proposition-wise supervenience. This breach shows that individual and group attitudes can come apart in surprising ways, thereby establishing a certain autonomy for the group agent. Suppose, for example, a group employs a premise-

based procedure to form collective judgments on three propositions (and their negations), 'p', 'q', and 'p and q', taking 'p' and 'q' as premises. Initially, consider the
individual judgments shown in Table 3.1.

Here both premises are accepted by a majority, and hence the premise-based
procedure leads the group to accept the conclusion as well. But now consider a second
combination of individual judgments, shown in Table 3.2.

In this second case, neither premise is accepted by a majority, and so the premise-based
procedure leads the group to reject the conclusion as well. But all individuals hold exactly
the same judgments on 'p and q' in the profiles in Tables 3.1 and 3.2; the rightmost
columns of Tables 3.1 and 3.2, showing the individuals' judgments on 'p and q',
coincide. Yet, under the premise-based procedure, the group forms opposite judgments
on 'p and q' in the two cases: 'p and q' is accepted in Table 3.1 and rejected in Table 3.2.
Therefore the group's judgment on 'p and q' is not determined by the individual
judgments on 'p and q' alone, a clear breach of proposition-wise supervenience.

It is worth noting a further point. Under the premise-based procedure, the supervenience relation between individual and group attitudes has not only a holistic as
opposed to proposition-wise character but also an additional property. The individual
attitudes on the premises alone are sufficient to determine the group attitudes on all the
propositions. Thus the group attitudes on the conclusion are 'autonomous' in relation
to the members' attitudes in two senses. The individual attitudes on the conclusion are
both insufficient for determining the group attitudes on it and unnecessary. We call the
lack of sufficiency a 'weak autonomy' and the lack of necessity a 'strong autonomy'.
Similar points apply to the sequential priority procedure and *a fortiori* to any function-

Table 3.1: A profile of individual judgments

	'p'	'q'	'p and q'
Individual 1	True	True	True
Individual 2	True	False	False
Individual 3	False	True	False
Premise-based procedure	True	True	⇒ True

Table 3.2: A modified profile of individual judgments

	'p'	'q'	'p and q'
Individual 1	True	True	True
Individual 2	False	False	False
Individual 3	False	False	False
Premise-based procedure	False	False	⇒ False

ally inexplicit organizational structure such as the straw-vote procedure. We return to the autonomy theme in the last section of this chapter.

While the organizational structures we have identified give rise to a holistic supervenience relation between individual and group attitudes, they are still 'homogeneous' in the sense that all group members play exactly the same role in determining the group's attitudes. Permute the attitudes across group members, and the resulting group attitudes will remain the same; this follows from the fact that the premise-based and sequential priority procedures satisfy anonymity, as defined in the last chapter. This raises the question of whether there are also organizational structures that give rise to a holistic and 'heterogeneous' supervenience relation, where different members play different roles in determining the group's attitudes. Recall the distributed premise-based procedure, under which the group is subdivided into several subgroups, each 'specializing' on a particular premise and independently determining the group attitude on that premise, before the resulting premise-attitudes are combined into the group attitudes on other propositions. It is easy to see that the distributed premise-based rule generates a holistic and heterogeneous supervenience relation between individual and group attitudes, while securing robust group rationality. Although the group's set of attitudes across the propositions on the agenda is determined by the members' attitudes on various subsets among these propositions, different members play different roles in this determination, by specializing on different premises.

We have already seen that, under a regular premise-based or sequential priority procedure, group attitudes can enjoy a certain kind of autonomy in relation to individual attitudes. The distributed premise-based procedure yields further forms of autonomy between these two levels. First, for each premise, the attitudes of some subgroup – the relevant 'specialists' – suffice to determine the group attitude on that premise, whereas other individuals' attitudes are not necessary; and the subgroups in question differ across premises. Second, to determine the group attitudes on the entire agenda of propositions, each individual needs to contribute only a single attitude on a single proposition, namely on the premise he or she 'specializes' on; no contribution on other propositions is needed. And third, no individual attitudes on the conclusion are at all required for determining the group attitude on that conclusion. Under a distributed premise-based procedure, then, the supervenience relation between individual and group attitudes displays both holism and heterogeneity.

A map of possible supervenience relations and their implications for group agency

We conclude our discussion of supervenience relations by sketching a map of possible such relations and their implications for group agency. The most basic distinction is that between proposition-wise and holistic supervenience relations. Among proposition-wise supervenience relations, we have further distinguished between uniform ones and others, and among uniform proposition-wise supervenience relations between majoritarian ones and others. In the proposition-wise category, we have considered some degenerate special cases, and in the holistic category we have distinguished

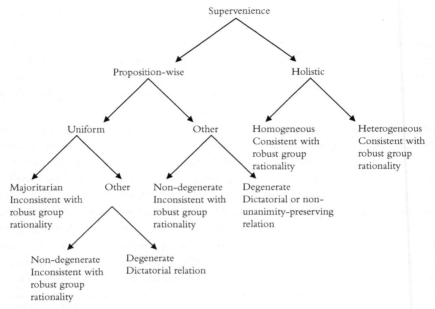

Figure 3.2 A map of supervenience relations

between homogeneous and heterogeneous relations. Figure 3.2 summarizes the range of possible supervenience relations and their status vis-à-vis robust group rationality, assuming in each case an agenda of propositions with sufficiently rich logical connections.

Our starting point was the observation that majoritarian supervenience is inconsistent with robust group rationality. A majoritarian supervenience relation, however, is a very special case. It is only one among many possible proposition-wise supervenience relations and still only one among many possible uniform ones. But we have seen that, even if the majoritarian and uniform restrictions are dropped, proposition-wise supervenience remains inconsistent with robust group rationality, except in degenerate cases. Holistic supervenience, by contrast, is consistent with robust group rationality. The regular and distributed premise-based procedures as well as sequential priority procedures are examples of aggregation functions whose implementation allows a group to meet both conditions (that is, holistic supervenience and robust group rationality). Here the supervenience relation is homogeneous in the case of regular premise-based and sequential priority procedures and heterogeneous in the case of a distributed premise-based one. Needless to say, the organizational structures sustaining holistic supervenience relations in real-world group agents will typically be much more complex than the ones in our simple, stylized examples.

3.3 The unmysterious autonomy of the group agent

Two traditions

There are two extreme and starkly opposed traditions of thinking about group agents in the literature, as we saw in the Introduction. One is the 'emergentist' tradition in law and history, sociology, and political theory that prospered in the late nineteenth and early twentieth centuries. The other is a debunking, 'eliminativist' tradition, associated with analytical philosophy and economics, which arose in the nineteenth century and became mainstream from about the middle of the twentieth. The one tradition held that group agents emerge as new phenomena over and above the individuals constituting them. The other held that group agents can be eliminated from any serious inventory of the world; they are nothing but individual agents acting in concert.

The emergentist tradition was influenced by the German legal historian Otto von Gierke and emphasized the institutional personality of group agents and its significance for legal, political, and social theory (Hager 1989; Runciman 1997; McLean 1999). Those who embraced the approach generally wanted to assert the reality of groups, particularly group agents, arguing that these collective entities had a life and mind of their own, and that they were creatures neither of individuals nor of states (Nicholls 1975; Vincent 1987, Ch. 6). Often described as group pluralists, proponents of this approach included historians like J. N. Figgis, legal theorists like F. W. Maitland, political thinkers like H. J. Laski, and guild socialists like G. D. H. Cole. All of them saw the emphasis on the reality of group agents as a way of rejecting the claims of an individualistic atomism on the one hand and a monistic statism on the other. While they would have seen Hegel as excessively statist, they were nevertheless inspired by the broadly Hegelian thought that the abstract individual is a creature of the imagination – an abstraction from the embedding groups in which individuals live. The flavor of this Hegelian approach is caught well in the work of the nineteenth-century philosopher F. H. Bradley: 'To know what a man is', he wrote, 'you must not take him in isolation . . . The mere individual is a delusion of theory' (Bradley 1876, pp. 173–174).

For the emergentist tradition, it went without saying that group agents were agents in their own right, over and above their members. The idea seems to have been that, as members join together in a group, a new force animates them and gives rise to a single center of agency. Certainly this is the idea communicated by the organicist metaphors on which pluralists, as we mentioned in the Introduction, routinely drew. The group agent that members constitute emerges at the moment they come together but it appears as an extra reality over and above anything they themselves contribute – or anything contributed by the state that gives the group legal recognition. The spirit of the approach appears in a question posed by Figgis (1914, p. 40) about the standing of a group like a church: 'Does the church exist by some inward living force, with powers of self-development like a person; or is she a mere aggregate, a fortuitous concourse of ecclesiastical atoms?' His own view is clear, if strikingly worded: 'to deny this real life is to be false to the facts of social existence, and is of the same nature as that denial of human personality which we call slavery' (p. 42).

The emergentist idea is vague and typically expressed in elusive metaphors. Those metaphors are drawn from a now discredited theory of what gives life to organic entities, according to which living entities do not live just by virtue of their chemical structure but rather by the presence of some *vis vitalis*, or 'life force'. The idea was that the chemical elements in an organic entity assume a living form only when this force appears. The parallel idea with groups is that the individual members give rise to a single agent only when a counterpart force comes on stream with its transforming effect.

If the emergentist tradition reified and mystified group agents, hailing them like transcendent realities, the eliminativist tradition went to the other extreme. It was fostered in the nineteenth-century English school of economic, utilitarian thinking and prided itself on its no-nonsense approach. One of its founders, Jeremy Bentham, held that '[t]he community is a fictitious body' (Bentham 1970), and this view was main-tained among Bentham's followers. Thus John Austin, a mid-century utilitarian theorist of law, wrote that groups are considered as subjects or agents 'only by figment, and for the sake of brevity of discussion' (Austin 1869, p. 364). To speak of group agents is a *façon de parler*, not a serious form of speech.

The opposition to any reification of groups was supported in Anglophone twentieth-century philosophy and related disciplines by the association between the emergentist, organicist tradition and the appearance of fascism. One of the lessons drawn from Karl Popper's arguments in *The Poverty of Historicism* (1960), for example, was that it was philosophically confused, and politically dangerous, to ascribe autonomous agency to groups. For perfectly understandable reasons, the established view came to be that there were no agents but individuals and that any talk of group agents should be taken as metaphorical or misconceived. We might describe this view in positive terms as 'singu-larism', borrowing a term from Margaret Gilbert (1989). Singularism asserts that there are no pluralistic agents, in any literal sense of the term, only the singular agents constituted by individual human beings and perhaps some other creatures.

Beyond the traditions

The difference between these two traditions can be illuminated with the help of the notion of supervenience. Taken at its word, emergentism holds that group agents are real entities whose properties as agents do not supervene on the contributions of their individual members. Those who believed in the *vis vitalis*, the life force, held that the properties in virtue of which an entity is living do not supervene on the properties of its chemical components but derive from a life force that comes on stream in certain chemical organizations of matter. Emergentists about group agents held, in similar vein, that the force by which a collection of individuals constitutes a group agent is an add-on to the individual contributions of the members; it is something that accompanies those contributions but does not logically derive from them.

Put in this way, the emergentist view assumes a more precise form than the organicist metaphors give it. But it also assumes a form under which it becomes very difficult to take it seriously. If a collection of individuals needs some add-on factor to become a group agent, then it must be logically possible that a duplicate collection of agents, indiscernible in attitudes, actions, and relations, might not have that add-on factor and might thus fail to constitute a group agent. This possibility is hard to countenance. As we imagine a collection of agents assuming all the attitudes and undertaking all the roles associated with group agency, we cannot hold open the possibility that group agency might not materialize. We might as well try to imagine that the dots constituting a certain shape on a grid are exactly duplicated on a similar grid without the same shape materializing.

If emergentism makes group agents into non-supervenient realities, eliminativism denies the reality of group agents altogether and so denies that the issue of super-venience even arises in any interesting way. Where emergentism makes group agents into hyper-realities, eliminativism makes them into non-realities. On this view, group agents are not entities of any kind and thus not even candidates for an emergent or non-supervenient status.

The approach taken in the foregoing chapters shows us a way beyond these two extremes. The argument of the first chapter draws on a broadly functionalist theory of agency in order to establish that groups of individuals can in principle count as agents. Let a collection of individuals form and act on a single, robustly rational body of attitudes, whether by dint of a joint intention or on some other basis, and it will be an agent; let it function or perform in the role of an agent, and it will indeed be an agent. The argument of the second and third chapters shows that despite the difficulties of aggregation, it is possible for collections of individuals to coordinate their individual contributions so as to achieve this level of functioning. Hence group agents exist.

Autonomy with moderation

Stated like this, the view we defend is a moderate one, not big news. Take the case of consciousness within an individual, rather than group agency. Emergentists about consciousness hold that conscious experience is something over and above what the neurons contribute and eliminativists say it is nothing at all; consciousness, in the ordinary conception, is an illusion. The moderate position in relation to these extremes is that consciousness exists but that it is supervenient on the contributions of the neurons. In almost exact parallel, our view about group agency avoids emergentist and eliminativist extremes and asserts that group agency exists but that it materializes superveniently on the contributions of group members. Moderation rules and moderation makes no big news.

But in one way this understates what our position implies. We put aside the mystery associated with the emergentist tradition in building our account of group agency on the thesis that this phenomenon supervenes on the contributions of individuals. But to put aside mystery is not to put aside surprise. And our account has some surprising implications. It is in virtue of these implications that we distinguish our approach from the one we associated in the Introduction with Hobbes – that is, with the Hobbesian view, shorn of the mistake about majoritarian aggregation – according to which it is the authorization of a spokesperson that turns a collection of people into a group agent. Where Hobbes would only offer us a thin, rather redundant realism that allows easy translation from talk of group agents into talk of individual agents, our approach supports a non-redundant realism under which groups have an important sort of autonomy.

While the agency achieved by a group supervenes on the contributions of its members – while it is not ontologically autonomous – it is autonomous in another, related sense. The agency of the group relates in such a complex way to the agency of individuals that we have little chance of tracking the dispositions of the group agent, and of interacting with it as an agent to contest or interrogate, persuade or coerce, if we conceptualize its doings at the individual level. We might be able to deal quite satisfactorily with a Hobbesian, individually 'personated' group – a degenerate group agent, as we described it – by focusing just on the spokesperson and taking the other members as functionaries at his or her disposal. But we will be unable to recognize the kind of group agent we have in mind as an agent, and to predict how it is likely to perform and what we can do to affect it, if we keep our gaze fixed at the level of individuals. We will fail to see the wood for the trees.

The autonomy we ascribe to group agents under our approach is epistemological rather than ontological in character and has two aspects, negative and positive. We have seen that to gain knowledge of group agents is to make an important advance in learning about the social world and how to intervene in it (our positive claim). And we have argued that this knowledge is unavailable in practice – even the most idealized practice – on the basis of observing individual agents alone (our negative claim). We commented already on the positive claim in the Introduction. In particular, we saw that by recognizing group agents in their own right, abstracting away from individual-level detail, we can interact with them, criticize them, and make demands on them, in a manner not possible with non-agential systems; we gain a perspective that opens up new possibilities of interacting within the social world. But in the Introduction we were not able to comment in any detail on the negative claim, that an understanding of group agents is unavailable if we focus on individual agents alone. The formal arguments we have presented in this chapter show that there is no easy translation between some of the things we can know about group agents and the things we know about their members. This is because the beliefs and desires of a group agent generally supervene on the beliefs and desires of its members only in a holistic manner that allows the group's attitudes on some propositions to come apart from its members' attitudes on them.

A group agent is autonomous in the relevant sense to the extent that the features that make it an agent – particularly its attitudes – are not readily reducible to features of the individual members: again, crucially, their attitudes. Under our account, there are a number of reasons why the required reduction or translation is difficult. Although the supervenience of the group's attitudes on individual contributions means that the former can in principle be derived from the latter, there are at least three practical difficulties that stand in the way of an easy reduction. We present them in ascending order of seriousness.

First, even in the special case in which the group attitude on a given proposition is determined by the individuals' attitudes on that proposition, it may still be hard to ascertain what the precise individual attitudes are. Moreover, many different possible combinations of individual attitudes on the proposition can give rise to the same group attitude. Just think of the many different ways in which a majority can materialize. The multiple realizability of any given group attitude in terms of individual attitudes makes the reductive analysis of group attitudes in terms of individual-level realizers quite unparsimonious.

Second, the multiple realizability of group attitudes in terms of individual ones and the resulting lack of an easy reduction are amplified in the case where the group attitude on a given proposition is determined, not by individual attitudes on it, but by sets of individual attitudes across multiple connected propositions. This scenario is bound to obtain in many cases, according to the argument defended here. It materializes whenever group attitudes supervene on individual attitudes in a merely holistic way, as they would, for example, under a premise-based or sequential priority procedure. We have seen that the individual attitudes on some conclusion, or posterior proposition, may be not only insufficient but even unnecessary for determining the group attitude on it. Thus a relatively simple set of group attitudes can result from a vast and complex variety of individual sets of attitudes.

This second difficulty is amplified if the group's attitudes are formed on a heterogeneous basis, involving individual specialization. To know what the group's attitude on some proposition is, we will not only have to know which propositions are relevant: which propositions are such that the members' attitudes to them determine the group's attitude to the proposition we seek knowledge about. We will also have to know which members are relevant: which members are in a position, with each of those propositions, to determine the group's attitude towards it.

Third, an additional difficulty occurs when the group's organizational structure is functionally inexplicit, as for example under the straw-vote procedure. Here there is feedback between individual and group-level attitudes, leading individuals to revise their attitudes in light of the resulting group attitudes or to adjust their votes over what the group attitudes should be. In this scenario it is even more difficult than in the previous one to reduce the group agent's attitudes to those of the members. The individualistic supervenience base for the group attitudes may not only be extensive, as holistic supervenience implies; it may also have an evolving character.

In view of these considerations, we must think of group agents as relatively autonomous entities – agents in their own right, as it is often said, groups with minds of their own (Pettit 2003b). We may even have grounds for giving credence to some of the emergentists' claims, though – and this is crucial – reinterpreting them in our terms. Thus there is a sense, albeit not his own sense, in which Sir Ernest Barker (1915, p. 74) was correct to say:

There is a college mind, just as there is a trade union mind, or even a 'public mind' of the whole community; and we are all conscious of such a mind as something that exists in and along with the separate minds of their members, and over and above any sum of these minds.

The arguments for our claim about the autonomy of group agency are epistemological, bearing on the difficulty of deriving a group agent's attitudes from the attitudes of its members. But this should not be surprising, since it is similarly epistemological arguments that support the stance of many psychologists, as well as the commonsense view, that individual agents cannot be understood merely as complexes of neuronal organization. Under standard approaches to the individual subject, mind and agency supervene on what happens at the neuronal level. But the difficulty of predicting from a neuronal base what an agent does provides a justification for making sense of the agent in terms that abstract from the way its neuronal parts operate. Analogously, the difficulty of predicting from an individualistic base what a group agent does provides a justification for making sense of the group agent in terms that abstract from the way its members perform. It is true that in the case of a group agent we make sense of parts and whole in the same intentional vocabulary, whereas we do not use that vocabulary with reference to neurons. But this disanalogy does not undermine the fundamental similarity between the two cases.

Donald Davidson (1984) once wrote that the secret in philosophy is to maintain the excitement of an idea while increasing its intelligibility. We think that the approach developed in these first three chapters maintains the excitement of the idea that groups can be agents over and above their individual members. But we also hope that it increases its intelligibility by banishing the aura of mystery that has made the emergentist theory unpalatable and given plausibility to the eliminativist alternative.

PART II

The Organizational Design of Group Agents

4

The Epistemic Desideratum

In the first part of the book, we have defended the logical possibility of group agency. We have identified basic conditions of agency and argued that a group can, at least in principle, meet them. We have also seen that a group's performance as an agent depends on how it is organized: on its rules and procedures for forming its propositional attitudes – its preferences and judgments – and for putting them into action. Although we have reviewed different types of organizational structures, we have said relatively little about their concrete design, apart from identifying basic constraints they must fulfill to ensure rational group attitudes.

In this second part of the book, we examine some more demanding desiderata of good organizational design. We discuss an 'epistemic' desideratum in this chapter, an 'incentive-compatibility' desideratum in Chapter 5, and a 'control' desideratum in Chapter 6. In each case, we ask what constraints the given desideratum imposes on the group's methods of attitude formation, particularly its aggregation function, and its procedures for translating attitudes into action.

This chapter is concerned with the 'epistemic' desideratum.[70] To function well, a group agent must form true rather than false beliefs about the world. Think of a multi-member court or a jury adjudicating a case, an expert committee advising the government on its actions, or a central bank's monetary policy committee setting the interest rate. We expect the decisions of such bodies to be based on true rather than false beliefs. Moreover, these beliefs should be true not just accidentally but reliably. What is reliability, however? And how can it be achieved? We address these questions in three sections. In the first section, we formulate the epistemic desideratum by introducing the notion of truth-tracking and discussing its relation with the notion of truth-indication; both are aspects of reliability. In the second section, we investigate how a group agent can meet the epistemic desideratum and show that, in setting up its organizational structure, a group agent can benefit from what we call 'democratization', 'decomposition', and 'decentralization'. In the third section, we raise some complications and make some concluding remarks. Although we include some mathematical formulas, their details are not essential for following our main argument.

4.1 Formulating the epistemic desideratum

The notion of truth-tracking

Consider some proposition 'p', which is factually true or false. For example, 'p' could be the proposition that a defendant is guilty of some crime, or that a patient has a particular disease, or that, given no change in the *status quo*, the average global temperature will increase by 1.5 degrees Celsius over the next three decades. Following Robert Nozick's classic definition (1981), we say that an agent 'tracks the truth' on 'p' if the following two conditionals hold. First, if 'p' were true, the agent would judge that p. Second, if 'p' were false, the agent would not judge that p.

Most agents are fallible and meet Nozick's two conditionals only approximately. As a rough quantitative measure of how well an agent meets them, it is useful to consider two conditional probabilities, corresponding to Nozick's two conditionals (List 2006b): first, the conditional probability that the agent judges that p, given that 'p' is true; and, second, the conditional probability that the agent does not judge that p, given that 'p' is false.[71] Let us call these two conditional probabilities the agent's 'positive' and 'negative tracking reliability' on 'p', respectively. In some cases these two probabilities coincide, in others they differ. An agent may be better at identifying the truth of 'p' than its falsehood, or the other way round. For example, a doctor performing a diagnostic test on a patient may be better at detecting the presence of some disease if the patient has the disease than its absence if the patient does not. Or an expert advisory committee may be better at detecting the presence of some risk if there is such a risk than its absence if there is not.

An agent is a good truth-tracker on 'p' only if it has a high positive tracking reliability on 'p' and also a high negative one. One of the two alone is not enough. We offer a more formal argument for this claim below, but, to illustrate the point informally, imagine a medical advisory panel that always – invariably – judges that a particular chemical is safe – call this proposition 'p' – regardless of how carcinogenic the chemical is. This committee would have a positive tracking reliability of one – certainty – on 'p': if the chemical were truly safe, the committee would certainly say so: it never says anything else. But it would have a negative tracking reliability of zero: even if the chemical were strongly carcinogenic, the committee would still deem it safe. As a truth-tracker the committee would be useless: its judgments would not co-vary at all with the truth.

The notion of truth-indication

Although we assess a group agent's epistemic performance mainly in terms of its ability to track the truth, it is useful to contrast the notion of truth-tracking with that of truth-indication. Our discussion of truth-indication should also clarify why achieving both a high positive and a high negative tracking reliability is so important.[72]

As just noted, when we ask how well an agent tracks the truth on 'p', we are interested in how well the agent's judgment on 'p' co-varies with the actual truth-value of 'p', as captured roughly by Nozick's two conditionals. An agent who is a good truth-tracker on 'p' has a process in place under which it is highly likely that, if 'p' is true, the agent judges that p, and if 'p' is false, the agent does not do so. But now put yourself in the position of an outside observer who learns about some agent's judgment on 'p'. For example, you learn that a medical advisory panel has judged that a particular chemical is safe, or you learn that a court has judged that a defendant is guilty. What do you make of that judgment? Do you take it to indicate the truth of the proposition in question?

To answer this question, we must reverse the two conditionals in Nozick's definition of truth-tracking introduced above. We say that an agent 'indicates the truth' on proposition 'p' if the following two conditionals hold. First, if the agent were to judge that p, 'p' would be true. Second, if the agent were not to judge that p, 'p' would be false. Notice the reversed order of conditionalization, compared with the two conditionals introduced above. Just as a good truth-tracker on 'p' has the property that its judgment on 'p' co-varies with the truth-value of 'p', so a good truth-indicator has the property that the truth-value of 'p' co-varies with the agent's judgment on 'p'.

As in the case of truth-tracking, we need to quantify how well a given agent meets the two conditionals of truth-indication. To do this, it is once again useful to consider two conditional probabilities: first, the conditional probability that 'p' is true, given that the agent judges that p; and, second, the conditional probability that 'p' is false, given that the agent does not judge that p. We call these two conditional probabilities the agent's 'positive' and 'negative indicating reliability' on 'p', respectively.

An agent's indicating reliability has a natural interpretation in terms of rational belief updating by an outside observer. An agent's positive indicating reliability on 'p' is the credence that you, the outside observer, are entitled to assign to 'p' on learning that the agent has judged that p. Likewise, the agent's negative indicating reliability on 'p' is the credence that you, the observer, are entitled to assign to 'not p' on learning that the agent has *not* judged that p. For example, if a medical diagnostic test has a positive indicating reliability of 0.7 on the proposition that a patient has a particular disease and a negative one of 0.9, this means that upon observing a positive test result you are entitled to assign a credence of 0.7 to the patient's being ill, and upon observing a negative one you are entitled to assign a credence of 0.9 to the patient's being healthy.

How is an agent's indicating reliability related to his or her tracking reliability? Does a high tracking reliability guarantee a high indicating reliability? To answer these questions, we must introduce Bayes's theorem.

Bayes's theorem

One of the most famous insights into the properties of conditional probabilities is due to the Reverend Thomas Bayes, a British clergyman and mathematician in the eighteenth century. Having studied both theology and logic, Bayes worked on a number of topics ranging from 'Divine Benevolence, or an Attempt to Prove that the Principal End of the Divine Providence and Government is the Happiness of His Creatures' to 'An Introduction to the Doctrine of Fluxions, and a Defence of the Mathematicians against the Objections of the Author of the Analyst', on which he published books in 1731 and 1736, respectively. But his best-known work, an 'Essay towards Solving a Problem in the Doctrine of Chances' (Bayes 1763), which contains the theorem now named after him, was published only posthumously in 1763.

Bayes's insight can be described as follows, using the language of hypothesis testing. Suppose we want to test some hypothesis H based on some evidence E. As before, H could be the proposition that a patient, who has come to see a doctor, has a particular disease, and E could be a positive diagnostic test obtained by the doctor. Suppose further that, although we do not know whether H is true, we do know its prior, unconditional probability – for example, the base rate of the disease in the population, say one in a thousand – and we know the conditional probabilities of observing evidence E given that H is true and of observing evidence E given that H is false. How can we use this information to calculate the conditional probability of H being true given that we observe evidence E?

Let $\Pr(H)$ denote the prior, unconditional probability of H, and let $\Pr(E|H)$, $\Pr(E|\text{not-}H)$, and $\Pr(H|E)$ denote the conditional probabilities of E given H, of E given not-H, and of H given E, respectively. Bayes's theorem states that these probabilities are related as follows:

$$\Pr(H|E) = \frac{\Pr(H)\ \Pr(E|H)}{\Pr(H)\ \Pr(E|H) + \Pr(\text{not-}H)\ \Pr(E|\text{not-}H)}.$$

Although this formula may take a moment to parse, it can easily be derived from the principles of the probability calculus. To see this, note that the probability of the conjunction of any two events is always given by the product of two probabilities: the probability of one of the two events multiplied by the conditional probability of the other event given the first. For example, in order to calculate how probable it is that your neighbor will win the lottery next week, you must consider the probability that he or she will buy a lottery ticket and multiply it by the probability that a given lottery ticket will win, that is, the conditional probability of winning given that one has bought a ticket. Accordingly, we can express the probability of the hypothesis H being true – one event – *and* observing the evidence E – another event – as follows:

$$\Pr(H \text{ and } E) = \Pr(H)\,\Pr(E|H).$$

By the same reasoning, we can also derive an alternative expression of the same probability:

$$\Pr(H \text{ and } E) = \Pr(E)\,\Pr(H|E).$$

Combining the two different expressions for $\Pr(H \text{ and } E)$ yields the identity

$$\Pr(E)\,\Pr(H|E) = \Pr(H)\,\Pr(E|H),$$

and dividing both sides of this identity by $\Pr(E)$ leads to the basic version of Bayes's theorem, namely

$$\Pr(H|E) = \frac{\Pr(H)\,\Pr(E|H)}{\Pr(E)}.$$

To obtain the theorem's canonical version stated earlier, it suffices to substitute $\Pr(E) = \Pr(H)\,\Pr(E|H) + \Pr(\text{not-}H)\,\Pr(E|\text{not-}H)$ in the denominator. This completes the derivation.

An analogous formula, derived in exactly the same way, holds for the negations of H and E, obtained by negating every proposition in the first formula:

$$\Pr(\text{not-}H|\text{not-}E) = \frac{\Pr(\text{not-}H)\,\Pr(\text{not-}E|\text{not-}H)}{\Pr(\text{not-}H)\,\Pr(\text{not-}E|\text{not-}H) + \Pr(H)\,\Pr(\text{not-}E|H)}.$$

Relating truth-tracking and truth-indication

With these remarks about Bayes's theorem in place, we can turn to the relationship between an agent's tracking and indicating reliabilities. Let our hypothesis H be proposition 'p' and our evidence E the fact that the agent judges that p. Then the agent's positive and negative tracking reliability on 'p' are, respectively, $\Pr(E|H)$ and $\Pr(\text{not-}E|\text{not-}H)$, and the agent's positive and negative indicating reliability on 'p', $\Pr(H|E)$ and $\Pr(\text{not-}H|\text{not-}E)$. The prior, unconditional probability of 'p' is $\Pr(H)$. Thus the two Bayesian formulas describe precisely how the agent's tracking and indicating reliabilities are related. Two observations can be made immediately.

First, the positive indicating reliability depends not only on the positive tracking reliability but also on the negative one; and the negative indicating reliability depends not only on the negative tracking reliability but also on the positive one. Even if the positive tracking reliability is fixed, the positive indicating reliability still increases with increases in the negative tracking reliability, and decreases with decreases in it. And even if the negative tracking reliability is fixed, the negative indicating reliability still increases with increases in the positive tracking reliability, and also decreases with decreases in it.

Second, the positive and the negative indicating reliability each depend also on the prior, unconditional probability of 'p'. Even if the positive and the negative tracking reliability are fixed, the positive indicating reliability increases, and the negative indicating reliability decreases, with increases in the unconditional probability of 'p'.

In the example of the medical advisory panel that always certifies the safety of the chemical under consideration, regardless of its actual danger, the positive indicating reliability would be rather low, namely equal to the base rate of safe chemicals, and the negative indicating reliability would be undefined, because the panel would never reach a negative verdict on the chemical's safety. Similar points hold even in less extreme cases where the agent's judgment exhibits at least some correlation with the truth.

More surprisingly, even the possession of a high positive *and* negative tracking reliability is no guarantee of a high positive *and* negative indicating reliability. The indicating reliability could still be distorted by a particularly low or high base rate. To illustrate this point (e.g. Gigerenzer 2003), consider a mammogram, a diagnostic test for breast cancer. Suppose that, if a woman has breast cancer, the probability of a positive mammogram is 0.8, and if she does not, the probability of a negative mammogram is 0.904. Thus the mammogram has a relatively high positive and negative tracking reliability, at 0.8 and 0.904, respectively. Suppose further that the base rate of women with breast cancer in the relevant population is 0.01. By substituting these numbers into the formulas above, we can calculate the mammogram's positive and negative indicating reliability. While the negative indicating reliability is 0.998, the positive one is only 0.078. Therefore a positive mammogram is still a poor indicator of breast cancer. In other words, while a positive mammogram should certainly give a patient a reason for undergoing further diagnostic tests, it is not yet a cause for alarm. In all likelihood – namely with a probability of 1–0.078 = 0.922 – the patient does not have breast cancer. This fact is due to the fortunately low base rate of the disease in the population.

But although a high positive and negative tracking reliability is not sufficient for a high positive and negative indicating reliability – the latter could still be affected by the base rate – it is clearly necessary. Having a high positive and negative tracking reliability is therefore an important desideratum that a well-functioning agent should satisfy.

4.2 Satisfying the epistemic desideratum

The power of information pooling

Can a group agent ensure that its judgments track the truth?[73] At first sight, one may think that the best a group agent can do is to match the truth-tracking reliability of its most reliable members. But it is now well known that, by pooling the diverse information of multiple individuals, a group can outperform all of its members at truth-tracking. This is an implication of a statistical phenomenon called the 'law of large numbers'.

Consider two examples. First, in a frequently cited experiment (Surowiecki 2004; Sunstein 2006), the scientist Francis Galton investigated a contest at an agricultural fair in rural England, in which about 800 participants were asked to estimate the weight of an ox on display. While few participants were individually accurate, the average estimate across the group of participants turned out to be 1197 pounds, almost identical to the true weight of 1198 pounds.

Second, the political scientist Nicholas Miller (1996) investigated multiple-choice tests taken by several classes of undergraduate students and computed not only each student's individual score but also that of one hypothetical 'collective student' per class, whose answer to each question was deemed to be the plurality answer given by the students in the class, that is, the answer given by the most students. Thus he treated each student's answer to each question as a vote on that question, with each class forming one electorate. The answers of the 'collective student' for that class were the winning answers in this election. While the mean fraction of correct answers among students across 127 different classes was about 0.617, the mean fraction of correct answers of the 'collective student' across these 127 classes was 0.866 and thus significantly higher than the individual-level mean. Although the hypothetical 'collective student' did not always outperform the best students in each class, it was among the top 5% of students overall.

Just as information pooling was responsible for the impressive collective performance in these two examples, so a group agent that seeks to track the truth in its judgments must organize itself so as to facilitate information pooling. In what follows we consider a group making judgments on one or several propositions and investigate its tracking reliability on these propositions under various aggregation functions and various scenarios. Our discussion shows that it is possible for a group agent to meet the epistemic desideratum, but that the group's aggregation function – more broadly, its organizational structure – plays a crucial role in determining its success. We argue that three principles of organizational design may be beneficial to the group: 'democratization', 'decomposition', and 'decentralization'.

Epistemic gains from democratization

Suppose that a group seeks to make a judgment on one factual proposition, such as the proposition that a defendant is guilty or that the global temperature will increase by a certain amount, as in the examples above. Suppose, as an initial scenario, that the group members' individual judgments on proposition 'p' satisfy two favorable conditions, as originally suggested by the Marquis de Condorcet (1785):

> **The competence condition.** Each group member has a positive and negative tracking reliability above a half, but below one, on proposition 'p', so that individuals are fallible in their judgments but biased towards the truth. For simplicity, all individuals have the same tracking reliability, denoted r.

As an illustration, let us assume that r equals 0.6.

> **The independence condition.** The judgments of different group members are mutually independent.

These conditions should be understood as describing a best-case scenario, and they have been challenged from various directions.[74] Later we consider cases in which they are violated, but it is helpful to begin with the idealized scenario in which they both hold.

The group now requires an aggregation function to make its collective judgment on 'p' based on the group members' individual judgments on 'p'. What is the group's positive and negative tracking reliability on 'p' under various aggregation functions? Consider three aggregation functions: first, a dictatorship of one individual, where the group's judgment on 'p' is always determined by the same fixed individual group member; second, the unanimity rule, where agreement among all group members is necessary and sufficient for reaching a collective judgment on 'p'; and third, majority voting on 'p'.

Figures 4.1, 4.2, and 4.3 show the group's tracking reliability on 'p' under these three aggregation functions. Recall that the group's positive tracking reliability on 'p' is its probability of judging that p when 'p' is true, and its negative one the probability of not judging that p when 'p' is false.[75] The group size is plotted on the horizontal axis, the group's positive and negative tracking reliability on 'p' on the vertical one.

Under a dictatorship, the group's positive and negative tracking reliability on 'p' equals that of the dictator, which is 0.6 in our examples. Here the group performs no

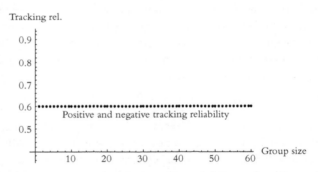

Figure 4.1 The group's positive and negative tracking reliability under a dictatorship

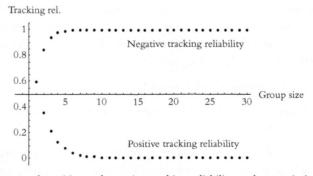

Figure 4.2 The group's positive and negative tracking reliability under unanimity rule

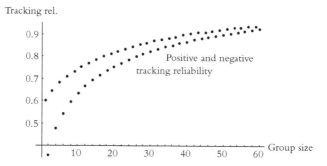

Figure 4.3 The group's positive and negative tracking reliability under majority voting

Note: The difference between the tracking reliability for an odd group size (top curve) and an even one (bottom curve) is due to the fact that majority ties are impossible under an odd group size but possible under an even one.

better and no worse at truth-tracking than any of its members. Under the unanimity rule, the group's positive tracking reliability on 'p' approaches zero as the group size increases: it equals r^n. For example, in a ten-member group with an individual tracking reliability of 0.6, this is 0.006. But the group's negative tracking reliability on 'p' approaches one as the group size increases: it equals $1-(1-r)^n$. In the same example of a ten-member group, this is 0.999. Moreover, a determinate group judgment on 'p' — that is, a judgment that p or that not p — is reached only if all individuals agree on the truth-value of 'p'. If they do not, no group judgment on 'p' is made. In a large group, the unanimity rule is almost certain to produce no group judgment on 'p' at all, which makes it useless as a truth-tracker. Finally, let us turn to majority voting. Here, the group's positive and negative tracking reliability on 'p' exceeds that of any individual group member[76] and approaches one as the group size increases. This is the famous 'Condorcet jury theorem' (e.g. Grofman, Owen, et al. 1983; Boland 1989; List and Goodin 2001).

Why does the jury theorem hold? By the competence condition, each individual has a probability r above a half of making a correct judgment on 'p', and by the independence condition different individuals' judgments are independent from each other. So each individual's judgment is akin to an independent coin toss, where one side of the coin, for example heads, corresponds to a correct judgment, which comes up with a probability of r, say 0.6, and the other side, tails, corresponds to an incorrect judgment, which comes up with a probability of 1-r, say 0.4. Think about how often you expect the coin to come up heads when it is tossed many times. Statistically, you expect heads in 6 out of 10 cases and tails in 4 out of 10 cases. However, in the case of ten tosses, the actual heads–tails pattern may still deviate from the expected pattern of 6–4: it may be 7–3, or 5–5, or sometimes even 4–6. But now consider the case of a hundred tosses. Here the expected heads–tails pattern is 60–40. Again, the actual pattern may deviate from this; it may be 58–42, or 63–37, or 55–45. But it is less likely than in the case of ten tosses that we get heads less often than tails. Finally, consider the case of a thousand, ten thousand, or a million tosses. Given the expected frequency of 0.6, it is less and less likely that the coin comes up heads less often than tails. The law of large numbers implies that the actual frequency of heads will increasingly approximate the expected one as the number of coin tosses increases. This implies that the probability of getting a majority of heads rather than tails exceeds the probability of the coin coming up heads in any single toss and approaches one as the number of tosses increases. Translated back into the language of judgments, the probability of a majority of individuals making a correct judgment exceeds the probability of any individual making a correct judgment and approaches one as the group size increases. And this is, of course, Condorcet's jury theorem.

What lesson can we draw from this? If group members are independent, fallible, but biased towards the truth in their judgments, majority voting outperforms both dictatorial and unanimity rules in terms of maximizing the group's positive and negative tracking reliability on a given proposition 'p'. Hence, when a group agent seeks to track the truth in its judgments, there may be epistemic gains from 'democratization', that is, from adopting a majoritarian democratic structure.

False positives versus false negatives

In some judgmental tasks, there is an asymmetry between false positive judgments and false negative ones. These two types of error occur, respectively, when the agent judges that p although 'p' is false and when the agent does not judge that p although 'p' is true. In jury decisions, false positives – that is, convicting the innocent – are usually considered worse than false negatives – that is, acquitting the guilty. As nicely summarized by the much-quoted words of the eighteenth-century English legal scholar William Blackstone, it is 'better that ten guilty persons escape than that one innocent suffer' (Blackstone 1978). In medical decisions, by contrast, we usually prefer diagnostic tests that minimize the occurrence of false negatives at the expense of more false positives. If a woman has a negative mammogram, for example, we want to be confident that she is free from breast cancer, whereas if she has a positive one, we are prepared to accept that a conclusive judgment requires further tests, and indeed hope that the positive mammogram has been a false alarm.

While a dictatorship and majority voting each avoid false positives and false negatives essentially at the same rate – they have the same positive and negative tracking reliability – the unanimity rule implements a strong asymmetry between the two types of error. By requiring all individuals' agreement for a positive judgment, unanimity rule is very good at avoiding false positives, but very bad at reaching true positive ones.[77] On the other hand, if we seek to implement the opposite asymmetry, then the anti-unanimity rule is a suitable aggregation function: its default judgment is a positive one, with a negative judgment being made only if all individuals agree on it. Finally, supermajority rules, under which a proposition is collectively accepted if and only if a particular supermajority of group members – say, two thirds or three quarters – accept it, lie in between unanimity rule and majority voting in terms of implementing an asymmetry between false positives and false negatives.

Generally, we can use the profile of individual judgments on 'p' to make some inferences about the probability that 'p' is true (List 2004c). The reasoning is an application of Bayes's theorem. Under the competence and independence conditions introduced above, the conditional probability that 'p' is true given that x individuals accept 'p' and y individuals reject 'p', is given by the formula

$$\frac{t\ r^{x-y}}{t\ r^{x-y} + (1-t)(1-r)^{x-y}},$$

where, as before, r is each individual's positive and negative tracking reliability on 'p' and t is the prior, unconditional probability of 'p' being true. In the terminology of truth-indication, the formula expresses the positive indicating reliability on 'p' associated with a profile in which x individuals accept 'p' and y individuals reject 'p'. Surprisingly, this indicating reliability depends only on the margin between the number of individuals accepting 'p' and the number rejecting 'p' (and of course the individuals' tracking reliability and the prior, unconditional probability of 'p'), but not on the total number of individuals in the group or the proportion accepting 'p'. Thus the positive indicating reliability of a 'guilty' verdict in a 12-member jury supported by 12 versus 0 votes is the same as that of a 'guilty' verdict in a 1000-member jury supported by 506 versus 494 votes. This result is counterintuitive, since a majority of 12 out of 12 corresponds to 100% of the jurors, whereas a majority of 506 out of 1000 corresponds to only 50.6% of the jurors (albeit in a much larger jury). But in both cases, there is a margin of 12 between the number of individuals accepting the proposition that the defendant is guilty and the number rejecting it.

Suppose we want to avoid false positives and make a positive group judgment on 'p' only when the group's positive indicating reliability on 'p' exceeds a given threshold. We can then use the formula just stated to calculate how large the margin between the number of individuals accepting 'p' and the number rejecting 'p' must be in order to push the indicating reliability above the required threshold. For example, if each individual's tracking reliability is 0.6 and the prior, unconditional probability of 'p' is 0.5, then 12 more individuals must accept 'p' than reject 'p' for the group's positive indicating reliability on 'p' to exceed 0.99, which could be interpreted as a threshold of 'reasonable doubt'. Under the given assumptions, our two 'guilty' verdicts – 12 versus 0 in a 12-member jury and 506 versus 494 in a 1000-member jury – would therefore be sufficient to meet the specified threshold of 'reasonable doubt'. In a 50-member group, to give another example, at least 31 individuals would have to accept 'p' and at most 19 could reject 'p' for 'p' to be acceptable beyond 'reasonable doubt'.[78]

This completes our discussion of the epistemic gains from 'democratization', and we turn now to the gains that 'decomposition' makes possible.

Epistemic gains from decomposition

Suppose a group seeks to make a judgment not just on a single factual proposition but on multiple interconnected ones (for detailed analyses on which the present discussion draws, see Bovens and Rabinowicz 2006; List 2006b). For example, the group could be a university committee deciding on whether a junior academic should be given tenure, with three relevant propositions involved: first, the candidate is excellent at teaching; second, the candidate is excellent at research; and third, the candidate should be given tenure, where excellence at both teaching and research is necessary and sufficient for tenure. More generally, there are k (say two, three, four, . . .) different premises and a conclusion, which is true if and only if all the premises, and thereby their conjunction, are true. Alternatively, the conclusion could be true if and only if at least one premise, and thereby their disjunction, is true; the analysis would be very similar to the one given here for the conjunctive case.

In this case of multiple propositions, an individual does not generally have the same tracking reliability on all propositions. A member of a tenure committee, for example, may be better at making a correct judgment on each of the separate premises about teaching and research than on the overall conclusion about tenure. More formally, if each individual has the same positive and negative tracking reliability r on each premise and makes independent judgments on different premises, then his or her positive tracking reliability on the conclusion will be r^k, which is below r and can be below a half,[79] while his or her negative tracking reliability on the conclusion will be above r. Here each individual is worse at detecting the truth of the conclusion than the truth of each premise, but better at detecting the falsehood of the conclusion than the falsehood of each premise. Other scenarios can be constructed, such as ones in which each individual is overall more reliable on the conclusion than on the premises, but it remains the case that an individual typically has different levels of reliability on different propositions (List 2006b).

What is the group's positive and negative tracking reliability on the various propositions under different aggregation functions? As before, let us assume that the group members' judgments are mutually independent. Majority voting performs well only on those propositions on which the individuals each have a positive and negative reliability above a half. In other words, majority voting performs well on a proposition if the individuals satisfy Condorcet's competence condition on that proposition, assuming they also satisfy the independence condition. But as just argued, individuals may not meet this condition on every proposition; they may meet it only on premises, for example, but not on conclusions. In addition, majority voting may fail to ensure rational group judgments on interconnected propositions, as we have already seen. We therefore set majority voting aside and compare dictatorial, conclusion-based, and premise-based procedures, as introduced in Chapters 2 and 3. The latter two procedures restrict majority voting to a subset of the agenda: the premise-based procedure applies majority voting only to premises, the conclusion-based procedure only to conclusions.

Suppose, as an illustration, there are two premises as in the university committee example and individuals each have a positive and negative tracking reliability of 0.6 on every premise and are independent in their judgments across different premises. Figures 4.4 and 4.5 show the group's probability of judging all propositions correctly under a dictatorship and the premise-based procedure, respectively. Figure 4.6 shows the group's positive and negative tracking reliability on the conclusion under the conclusion-based procedure. As in the earlier figures, the group size is plotted on the horizontal axis and the probabilities in question on the vertical one.

Generally, under a dictatorship of one individual, the group's positive and negative tracking reliability on each proposition equals that of the dictator. In particular, the probability that all propositions are judged correctly is r^k, which may be very low,

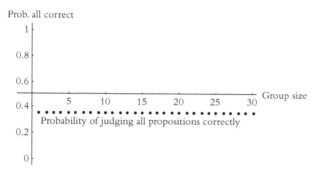

Figure 4.4 The group's probability of judging all propositions correctly under a dictatorship

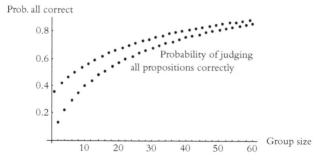

Figure 4.5 The group's probability of judging all propositions correctly under the premise-based procedure

Note: The difference between the tracking reliability for an odd group size (top curve) and an even one (bottom curve) is due to the fact that majority ties are impossible under an odd group size but possible under an even one.

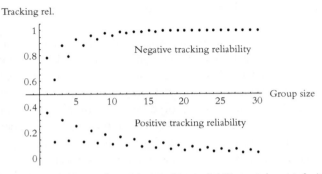

Figure 4.6 The group's positive and negative tracking reliability on the conclusion under the conclusion-based procedure

Note: The difference between the tracking reliability for an odd group size (top curves) and an even one (bottom curves) is due to the fact that majority ties are impossible under an odd group size but possible under an even one.

especially when the number of premises k is large. Under the conclusion-based procedure, unless individuals have a very high reliability on each premise,[80] the group's positive tracking reliability on the conclusion approaches zero as the group size increases. Its negative tracking reliability on the conclusion approaches one, since, under the present assumptions, the conclusion-based procedure almost always leads to the rejection of the conclusion – and thereby also in cases in which the conclusion is genuinely false. Under the premise-based procedure, finally, the group's positive and negative tracking reliability on every proposition approaches one as the group size increases. This result holds because, by the Condorcet jury theorem, the group's positive and negative tracking reliability on each premise approaches one with increasing group size, and therefore the probability that the group derives a correct judgment on the conclusion also approaches one with increasing group size.

What lesson can we draw from this second scenario? Under the assumptions made, the premise-based procedure outperforms both dictatorial and conclusion-based procedures in terms of simultaneously maximizing the group's positive and negative tracking reliability on every proposition. Again, a dictatorship is bad at pooling the information contained in the judgments of multiple individuals. And the conclusion-based procedure, like the unanimity rule in the single-proposition case, is good at avoiding false positive judgments on the conclusion, but usually bad at reaching true positive ones (Bovens and Rabinowicz 2006; List 2006b). If the conclusion is logically equivalent to the disjunction of the premises, the asymmetry is reversed.

In summary, if a larger judgmental task such as making a judgment on some conclusion can be decomposed into several smaller ones such as making judgments on certain relevant premises, there may be epistemic gains from 'decomposition', that is, from making collective judgments on the conclusion based on separate collective judgments on those premises. This involves the application of what we have called a holistic aggregation function: it is no longer the case that the group judgment on every proposition is a function of individual judgments on that proposition.

Epistemic gains from decentralization

When a group is faced with a complex judgmental task involving several propositions, different group members may have different levels of expertise on different propositions. Not everyone can be a specialist on everything. This is an important characteristic of many group agents, such as expert committees, groups of scientific collaborators, large organizations, and so on. Even in a tenure committee, the representatives of the university's teaching and learning center may be better placed to assess the candidate's teaching than some of the other committee members, whereas the latter may be better placed to assess the candidate's research. Furthermore, individuals may lack the temporal, computational, and informational resources to become sufficiently good truth-trackers on every proposition. If we take this problem seriously, can we improve on the premise-based procedure?

Suppose, as before, a group seeks to make collective judgments on k different premises and a conclusion, which is true if and only if all the premises are true. Instead of requiring every group member to make a judgment on every premise, we may partition the group into several subgroups, for simplicity of roughly equal size: one subgroup for each premise, whose members specialize on that premise and make a judgment on it alone. In the tenure committee example, one subgroup may consist of the teaching assessors and the other of the research assessors. Instead of using a regular premise-based procedure as in the previous scenario, the group may now use a distributed premise-based procedure, as introduced in Chapters 2 and 3. Here the collective judgment on each premise is made by taking a majority vote within the subgroup specializing on the given premise, and the collective judgment on the conclusion is then derived from these collective judgments on the premises.

Will it ever happen that the distributed premise-based procedure outperforms the regular one at maximizing the group agent's truth-tracking reliability? Two effects pull in opposite directions here. On the one hand, individuals may become more reliable on the proposition on which they specialize. We may describe this first effect as 'epistemic gains from specialization'. But on the other hand, each subgroup voting on a particular proposition is smaller than the original group: it is only roughly 1/k the size of the original group when there are k premises, and this may reduce the information-pooling benefits of majority voting on that proposition. Let us describe this second effect as 'epistemic losses from lower numbers'.

Whether or not the distributed premise-based procedure outperforms the regular one depends on which of these two opposite effects is stronger. Obviously, if there were no epistemic gains from specialization, then the distributed premise-based procedure would suffer only from losses from lower numbers on each premise and would thus perform worse than the regular premise-based procedure. On the other hand, if the epistemic losses from lower numbers were relatively small compared to the epistemic gains from specialization, then the distributed premise-based procedure would outperform the regular one.

Suppose, to give a very simple example, there are ten individuals making judgments on two premises, where each individual's tracking reliability on each premise is 0.6 without specialization. And suppose further that if we subdivide the group into two halves specializing on one premise each, then each individual's tracking reliability on the assigned premise goes up to 0.9. Clearly, the group is better off by opting for the decentralized arrangement and using the distributed premise-based procedure. Each five-member subgroup with an individual tracking reliability of 0.9 will make a more reliable judgment on its assigned premise than the ten-member group as a whole with each individual's tracking reliability at 0.6. The following theorem generalizes this point:

Theorem. For any group size n (divisible by k), there exists an individual tracking-reliability level $r^* > r$ such that the following holds. If, by specializing on proposition 'p', individuals achieve a positive and negative tracking reliability above r^* on 'p', then the majority judgment on 'p' in a subgroup of n/k specialists, each with tracking reliability above r^* on 'p', is more reliable than the majority judgment on 'p' in the original group of n non-specialists, each with tracking reliability r on 'p' (List 2005).

Hence, if by specializing on one premise individuals achieve a tracking reliability above r^* on that premise, then the distributed premise-based procedure outperforms the regular one. How great must the reliability increase from r to r^* be in order to have this effect? Does it have to be as great as that from 0.6 to 0.9 in our simple example? Surprisingly, a much smaller increase is already sufficient. Table 4.1 shows some illustrative calculations. For example, when there are two premises, if the original individual reliability was 0.52, then a reliability above 0.5281 after specialization is sufficient; if it was 0.6, then a reliability above 0.6393 after specialization is enough.

Figure 4.7 shows the group's probability of judging all propositions correctly under regular and distributed premise-based procedures, where there are two premises and individuals have positive and negative tracking reliabilities of 0.6 and 0.7 before and after specialization, respectively. Again, the group size is plotted on the horizontal axis, and the relevant probability on the vertical one.

Table 4.1: Tracking reliability increase from r to r* required to outweigh the loss from lower numbers

	k = 2, n = 50			k = 3, n = 51			k = 4, n = 52		
r	0.52	0.6	0.75	0.52	0.6	0.75	0.52	0.6	0.75
r*	0.5281	0.6393	0.8315	0.5343	0.6682	0.8776	0.5394	0.6915	0.9098

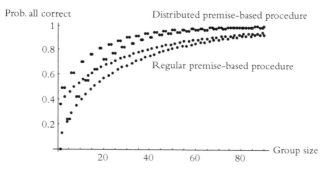

Figure 4.7 The group's probability of judging all propositions correctly under the distributed and regular premise-based procedures

Note: The difference between the tracking reliability for an odd group size (top curves) and an even one (bottom curves) is due to the fact that majority ties are impossible under an odd group size but possible under an even one.

The lesson from this third scenario is that, even when there are only relatively modest gains from specialization, the distributed premise-based procedure may outperform the regular one in terms of maximizing the group's positive and negative tracking reliability on every proposition. Hence there may be epistemic gains from 'decentralization'. If a group agent has to perform a complex judgmental task, it may benefit from subdividing the task into several smaller ones and distributing them among multiple subgroups. Plausibly, such division of cognitive labor is the mechanism underlying the successes of collectively distributed cognition in science (Knorr Cetina 1999; Giere 2002) or the division of cognitive labor in large corporations and organizations.

4.3 Complications

Throughout this chapter we have assumed that Condorcet's competence and independence conditions hold, at least on some relevant propositions. That is, we have assumed that all group members have the same positive and negative tracking reliability above a half on at least those propositions on which majority votes are taken, and that their judgments are mutually independent. The satisfaction of these two conditions ensures the benefits of information pooling under a suitable aggregation function, through the statistical phenomenon of the law of large numbers. What happens, however, if these favorable conditions are violated? To what extent can a group agent still meet the epistemic desideratum in this case? A lot can be said about this question, but for brevity we here concentrate on four salient challenges to a group agent's epistemic performance: three challenges to the competence condition and one to the independence condition.

Insufficiently high or decreasing individual reliability

If individuals are independent and competent in the sense of having the same positive and negative tracking reliability above a half on a given proposition, then the group's positive and negative tracking reliability on it under majority voting exceeds that of any group member and approaches one with increasing group size. But what happens if individuals have a positive and negative tracking reliability below a half? Just as the law of large numbers implies that when a coin's probability of coming up heads is above a half the majority outcome is overwhelmingly likely to be heads, so it implies that when its probability of coming up heads is below a half then the majority outcome is overwhelmingly likely not to be heads. In other words, when individuals have a positive and negative tracking reliability below a half on some proposition then the group's positive and negative tracking reliability on it under majority voting falls below that of any group member and approaches zero with increasing group size. The latter effect can be described as the 'reverse Condorcet jury theorem'.

While it may not be surprising that Condorcet's jury theorem is undermined if individuals are worse than random at making correct judgments, it is perhaps more surprising that the theorem may be undermined even in some less extreme cases (Berend and Paroush 1998). Suppose, for example, that while individuals are each better than random at making a correct judgment on a given proposition, their positive and negative tracking reliability on it is an exponentially decreasing function of the group size, as illustrated in Figure 4.8 (List 2003a). It is then no longer true that the group's positive and negative tracking reliability on the proposition under majority voting approaches one as the group size increases.[81]

Reasons for the decrease of individual reliability with group size could be one of the following. There may be only a limited pool of competent individuals, and as the group enrolls more members, it ends up enrolling less competent ones. Or an individual's tracking reliability may be a function of his or her effort, and that effort decreases as the group size increases, perhaps because individuals realize that in a large group their marginal influence on the group's judgment is low or because there are

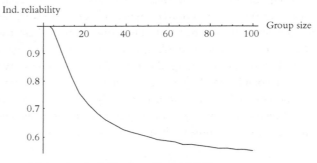

Figure 4.8 A case of decreasing individual tracking reliability

weaker reputational incentives for individuals to make an effort, given their lower visibility in a larger group.[82] Condorcet himself acknowledged the challenge that an insufficient or decreasing individual reliability poses to truth-tracking by the group:

A very numerous assembly cannot be composed of very enlightened men. It is even probable that those comprising this assembly will on many matters combine great ignorance with many prejudices. Thus there will be a great number of questions on which the probability of the truth of each voter will be below a half. It follows that the more numerous the assembly, the more it will be exposed to the risk of making false decisions. (Condorcet, quoted in Waldron 1999, pp. 51–52)

Heterogeneous individual reliability

A simplifying assumption built into the competence condition as stated above is that individual tracking reliability (positive as well as negative) is the same across all individuals. This simplification is not just a matter of convenience; it has substantive implications. Without it, it is no longer true in general[83] that majority voting outperforms a dictatorship of the most reliable group member in terms of maximizing the group's positive and negative tracking reliability (see also Grofman, Owen, et al. 1983; Boland 1989; Goldman 1999). Consider, for example, a group of five individuals three of whom have a positive and negative tracking reliability of 0.6 on proposition 'p' and two of whom have one of 0.9. Under majority voting, the group's positive and negative tracking reliability on 'p' turns out to be 0.87, which is below that of each of its most reliable members, namely 0.9. If majority voting and a dictatorship are the only contenders for the group's aggregation function in this case, the group is better off making one of its most reliable members a dictator.

However, a weighted form of majority voting can still outperform a dictatorship here. Suppose, for example, we give one vote to each of the three less reliable individuals but three votes to each of the two more reliable ones. We can then apply majority voting in a 'virtual' nine-voter group, where each of the two more reliable individuals plays the role of three voters and the other three each play that of one voter. Under this arrangement, the group's positive and negative tracking reliability goes up to 0.93 and thus exceeds that of both majority voting and a dictatorship.

More generally, weighted majority voting maximizes the group's positive and negative tracking reliability if each individual's judgment is given a weight depending on the individual's reliability on the proposition in question, namely a weight proportional to the logarithm of $r/_{1-r}$, where r is the individual's reliability as before (Shapley and Grofman 1981; Grofman, Owen, et al. 1983).[84] To get an intuitive sense of what this means, note that the logarithm of $r/_{1-r}$ is positive when r is above a half, with a value approaching infinity as r goes to one; negative when r is below a half, with a value approaching minus infinity as r goes to zero; and zero when r is exactly a half. This means that individuals whose judgments are positively correlated with the truth get a positive weight; ones whose judgments are negatively correlated with the truth get a negative weight; and ones whose judgments are equivalent to an unbiased coin toss get a weight of zero – as they obviously should, since they are randomizers. When an individual's reliability is one or zero, that is, his or her judgment is perfectly correlated or perfectly inversely correlated with the truth, the individual gets a weight of infinity or minus infinity and thus becomes a dictator or inverse dictator.

In summary, even when different individuals have different levels of reliability, epistemic gains from democratization remain possible, but these are no longer achieved through ordinary majority voting, but through an aggregation function under which different individuals have different weights, depending on their reliability.

Inadequate propositional decomposition

We have seen that, when there are multiple propositions, individuals do not generally have the same tracking reliability on all of them, and it may be epistemically beneficial to decompose a larger judgmental task into several smaller ones. This may involve identifying relevant premises and conclusions and applying a premise-based procedure, under which the collective judgments on the conclusions are derived from the majority judgments on the premises.

Decomposing a larger judgmental task into several smaller ones, however, is not always beneficial. What matters is the right level of decomposition. Suppose, for example, an expert committee has to make a judgment on whether there will be a global temperature increase of 1.5 degrees Celsius over the next three decades. This proposition, in turn, is true if and only if at least one of several possible causes for such a temperature increase is in operation. Given the complexities of the climate, a temperature increase can be driven by a large number of different mechanisms. The following is a plausible scenario in our hypothetical committee (List 2006b). If there will be no temperature increase – that is, none of the relevant causes is in operation – then each committee member has a probability above a half of ruling out an increase and all its causes. But if there will be a temperature increase – that is, at least one cause is in operation – then each committee member also has a probability above a half of judging this to be the case but only a probability below a half of identifying the correct cause. It may be a lot easier to figure out whether there will be a temperature increase than to figure out the correct underlying causal mechanism, which, as noted, may be extremely complicated. Under these conditions, the conclusion-based procedure, that is, majority voting on whether or not there will be a temperature increase, is better at truth-tracking than the premise-based procedure, which requires majority voting on each of the possible causes of global warming. Individuals meet Condorcet's competence condition on the conclusion here, but not on the premises.

The key to choosing the right level of decomposition within a judgmental task lies in identifying, and designating as premises, those propositions on which individuals meet Condorcet's competence condition. Any decomposition that is too fine-grained or too coarse-grained by this criterion may undermine the group's ability to track the truth.

Interdependent individual judgments

Just as successful information pooling requires the reliability of individual judgments, so it requires their independence. If different individuals' judgments are perfectly correlated with each other, to give an extreme example, then pooling them cannot possibly provide us with any new information. Whether or not aggregating different individuals' judgments enhances truth-tracking in the presence of less extreme interdependencies between them depends on the nature of these interdependencies (Boland 1989; Ladha 1992; Estlund 1994; Dietrich and List 2004; Berend and Sapir 2007).

To illustrate this point, recall that the Condorcet jury theorem has two parts. The first part states that the group's truth-tracking reliability under majority voting on a given proposition exceeds that of any group member, and the second that this reliability approaches one as the group size increases. Some interdependencies between different individuals' judgments leave both parts of the theorem intact and only reduce the rate at which the group's tracking reliability approaches one with increasing group size. Thus more individuals are required to achieve any desired level of reliability in a group with interdependent judgments than in one with independent ones. Those relatively mild interdependencies arise, for example, when individuals make their judgments partly based on their own private information about the truth and partly based on information obtained from others (Ladha 1992; Estlund 1994).

Other interdependencies, however, limit the benefits of information pooling more significantly. Arguably, and unfortunately, these interdependencies are quite common, and hence they deserve a closer look (for a detailed analysis, see Dietrich and List 2004). Condorcet's original independence condition states that, once the truth of the matter about proposition 'p' is given, the individuals' judgments about 'p' are mutually independent. Under this condition, different individuals' judgments – call them J_1, $J_2, \ldots, J_n$ – are separate causal descendents of the truth of the matter about 'p', as shown in Figure 4.9.

If group members play the role of independent eye-witnesses to the truth about proposition 'p', each having his or her own separate channel of access to it, then this condition is indeed satisfied. But if, for example, there is an intermediate shared body of evidence on which all individuals' judgments on 'p' depend, as illustrated in Figure 4.10, the independence condition is violated.

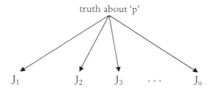

Figure 4.9 Condorcet's independence condition

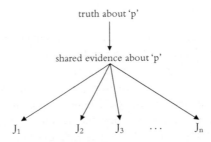

Figure 4.10 Interdependencies created by a shared body of evidence

In this case, different individuals' judgments are no longer independent from each other once the truth of the matter about 'p' is given, but only once the shared body of evidence is given. Only a 'conditional' form of independence is satisfied here, not Condorcet's 'unconditional' one. More precisely, Condorcet's original condition stipulates independence of individual judgments *given the state of the world*, whereas the revised condition stipulates their independence *given the shared evidence*. Arguably, this is precisely the situation we find in many court rooms, expert or parliamentary committees, company boards, and so on, where individuals are constrained in their access to the state of the world by a shared body of evidence. In most legal systems, for example, jurors are obliged by law not to use any evidence other than the shared one presented to them in the courtroom. They may even be physically prevented from getting access to any other evidence, for instance by having to stay in a hotel for the duration of the trial, with limited contact to the outside world.

It can be shown that, under this revised independence condition, only the first part of the Condorcet jury theorem continues to hold, while the second part breaks down (Dietrich and List 2004). That is, while the group's truth-tracking reliability under majority voting still exceeds that of any group member, it no longer approaches one as the group size increases. Instead it is bounded above by some threshold – a maximal feasible level of reliability – which in turn depends on the quality of the evidence. If the evidence is noisy, there is no way of filtering out that noise, regardless of the group size and the competence of the individual group members.

Concluding remarks

We have seen that, under favorable conditions, a group agent can succeed at tracking the truth, but the group's aggregation function and, more broadly, its organizational structure play an important role in determining its success. Three principles of organizational design may help a group to satisfy the epistemic desideratum: the group may benefit from democratization, from decomposition, and from decentralization. Whether or not each of these design principles is helpful, and to what extent, depends on the group agent and epistemic task in question, and there may not be a 'one size fits all' organizational design that is best for all group agents and all epistemic tasks. But the mere possibility of the three types of benefits reinforces the potential of epistemic gains through group agency.

Despite some of the complications we have discussed, the present results give a fairly optimistic picture of a group's capacity to perform as an epistemically well-functioning agent. There has been much research on failures and inefficiencies in the performance of epistemic tasks by groups. In addition to the paradoxes of majoritarian aggregation and the challenges to information pooling already discussed, several other effects are known to threaten a group's performance. We turn to some of them – incentive incompatibility and informational cascades – in the next chapter. The details of our more optimistic results clearly depend on a number of favorable conditions and change with changes in these conditions. But our primary aim has been to establish a possibility result, showing that a group agent can indeed live up to the epistemic desideratum, and identifying organizational design principles that can help it turn that possibility into a reality.

5

The Incentive-Compatibility Desideratum

This chapter, like the previous one, concerns a particular desideratum of good organizational design of a group agent. So far we have examined an epistemic desideratum, asking how a group agent must be organized to form true rather than false beliefs about the world. We now turn to what we will call an 'incentive-compatibility' desideratum.

It is not enough for a well-functioning group agent to work only under maximally favorable conditions, such as when its members are unconditionally truthful, cooperative, and sincere. Individuals will often pursue their own advantage rather than that of the group, or at least act in ways that appear rational to them individually. A well-functioning group agent must therefore cope with the basic fact that individuals are themselves rational agents. Their individual rationality can show up in something as innocent as merely acting rationally according to their own beliefs and desires, or in something as explicitly strategic as lying or otherwise deliberately misrepresenting their attitudes or intentionally withdrawing their cooperation with others to promote their own interests. Accordingly, the group's organizational structure must be designed not for maximally well-behaved or idealized group members but for real people, who behave strategically when this is expedient.

Consider the government of a country or the board of a company. If the members of such a body vote strategically against the group's interests, misrepresent or withhold certain information, or defect from the pursuit of collective goals, this can seriously compromise the group's performance as a whole. Cases of corruption or the explicit pursuit of a private agenda against the interests of the group are the most flagrant instances of this, but individual strategic actions can also compromise the group's overall performance in more subtle and surprising ways, as this chapter will illustrate.

We call a group agent's organizational structure 'incentive compatible' if it is resilient to individual strategic behavior. But what precisely does this mean, and how can a group agent achieve it? Our discussion of these questions is divided into three sections. In the first, we formulate the incentive-compatibility desideratum. In the second, we discuss several challenges to it and sketch some responses to these challenges. In the third, we conclude with a few general remarks about available strategies for achieving incentive compatibility in a group agent.

5.1 Formulating the incentive-compatibility desideratum

The concept of incentive compatibility

The concept of incentive compatibility is relevant to a much wider range of contexts than that of group agency alone. It is relevant to practically all areas of society in which there are social or economic institutions – particularly when these have to be designed or reformed – ranging from constitutions and voting procedures to tax systems, auction mechanisms, and arrangements for the provision of public goods in a group or society. Recently, the theme of incentive compatibility received a lot of media coverage when the 2007 Nobel Prize in Economics was awarded to three pioneers in the field of 'mechanism design', Leonid Hurwicz, Eric Maskin, and Roger Myerson (for a survey, see Royal-Swedish-Academy-of-Sciences 2007). To introduce the relevant ideas, let us begin by considering a generic social mechanism, which could be anything ranging from a tax system or an arrangement for the provision of public goods to a voting procedure or an auction mechanism. What does incentive compatibility mean in relation to such a mechanism?

To answer this question, we need to introduce some preliminary concepts. Any social mechanism allows certain choices by the relevant individuals: the group members, citizens, voters, or traders. We call each individual's possible choices his or her possible 'actions'. In the case of a tax system or public-goods-provision mechanism, the alternative actions between which individuals can choose may be cooperation and defection in paying or participating, perhaps at different levels of contribution. In the case of a voting procedure, they may be, for example, voting for the conservative candidate or voting for the liberal. In the case of an auction mechanism, each individual's possible actions are the possible bids he or she can make for the goods on offer, say for a price of $100, $200, or $500. In the case we are most interested in – that of a group agent – each individual can act, for example, by performing some task on behalf of the group or not doing so; or by expressing one particular set of judgments or preferences to the group rather than another. For example, speaking in favor of a 'guilty' verdict is one action an individual may take in a jury, speaking in favor of an 'innocent' verdict another.

Now the actions taken by the individuals may or may not be cooperative, if they are practical acts; and they may or may not be truthful, if they are expressive ones. For example, citizens may or may not pay the taxes they owe; voters may or may not vote sincerely; and bidders in an auction may or may not reveal their true valuation for a good when bidding for it. A property such as cooperativeness or truthfulness is called 'incentive compatible' under a given social mechanism if it is rational for the individuals to take actions with that property.

It is worth pausing for a moment and dissecting this definition carefully. First of all, incentive compatibility is always something that applies to a particular 'target property' of the actions taken under the given social mechanism. Cooperativeness and truthfulness are prominent examples of such properties. But the target property could also be something altogether different, such as maximizing the total revenue generated by the social mechanism. According to the definition just stated, the target property is said to be incentive compatible under the given mechanism *if it is rational for the individuals to take actions with that property*. What does this if-clause mean?

Imagine a form of social organization in which, by acting in accordance with their own beliefs and desires, individuals are naturally led to act *un*cooperatively with others. This is precisely what we would ordinarily describe as a bad social arrangement. In this case, the target property of cooperativeness is not incentive compatible, since it is not rational for the individuals to take cooperative actions. A tax system in which there is no monitoring or policing may be an example of this. Assuming that people are no angels, they are unlikely to cooperate in paying their taxes under such a system. By contrast, a carefully devised tax system, with the right monitoring, rewards, and sanctions, may very well make it individually rational for people to pay their taxes as required. Thus cooperativeness may well be incentive compatible in such a case. In short, incentive compatibility requires the social mechanism to achieve a happy alignment between individually rational behavior on the one hand and the desired target property on the other.

Using this terminology, we say that cooperativeness is incentive compatible under a given tax system or public-goods-provision mechanism if people will rationally cooperate rather than defect in making their contributions. Similarly, truthfulness is incentive compatible under a group agent's organizational structure if, when it comes to the formation of the group's attitudes, individuals will rationally express their judgments or preferences truthfully. And truthful bidding is incentive compatible in an auction if bidders will rationally express their true valuation for the goods they are bidding for.

To complete our definition of incentive compatibility, we finally need to make explicit two further elements: first, the individuals' preferences over different possible outcomes of the given social mechanism, and second, the criterion of rationality. Let us briefly look at each of these in turn.

The individuals' preferences over outcomes can vary in many ways: they can be narrowly or broadly defined, self-regarding or other-regarding, driven by purely material considerations or also non-material ones, focused solely on outcomes or also on histories of events leading to those outcomes, and so on. Thus it makes little sense to say that individuals will rationally pursue certain actions without saying what their preferences are. Similarly, there can be more or less demanding criteria of when an action or set of actions counts as 'rational'. A very demanding criterion is that of 'dominance'. An action is 'dominant' for an individual if he or she prefers, or is indifferent to, the outcome of taking that action, compared to the outcome of taking any other action, regardless of what other individuals do. A less demanding criterion is that of 'Nash equilibrium'. A combination of actions across individuals is a 'Nash equilibrium' if every individual prefers, or is indifferent to, the outcome of taking that action, compared to the outcome of unilaterally deviating from it, assuming others do not deviate.

Before giving some concrete illustrations, it is useful to relate the present ideas to the standard terminology of game theory. In game theory, what we have called a social mechanism, such as a particular organizational structure, voting procedure, or auction mechanism, is called a 'game form' and is formally defined as a specification of possible actions for each individual, together with a mapping from combinations of such actions across individuals to resulting outcomes. The social mechanism *together with the individuals' preferences* is called a 'game'. A fully specified game thus consists of a game form *and* associated individual preferences. The relevant criterion of when an individual action or set of actions across individuals counts as rational is called the 'equilibrium concept' (or sometimes 'solution concept'). The concepts of dominance and Nash equilibrium, which we have mentioned, are two prominent examples of equilibrium concepts.[85] Economists have developed many others, applicable to different contexts and background conditions.

Some illustrations

No example can better illustrate the concept of incentive compatibility than the well-known prisoner's dilemma. Suppose two individuals interact, perhaps in the pursuit of some collective project. Each individual has a choice between two actions, 'cooperation' and 'defection', and his or her material pay-off depends on his or her own choice and that of the other individual. As shown in Table 5.1, if both cooperate, each receives $3; if both defect, each receives $1; if one cooperates and the other defects, the defector receives $4 and the cooperator nothing.

This specifies the social mechanism governing the individuals' interaction and thus the game form. Suppose we are interested in whether the individuals will cooperate. Is cooperativeness incentive compatible here?

To answer this question, we first have to say what the individuals' preferences are, so as to specify a fully defined game. As an initial case, let us assume that the individuals' preferences over the four possible outcomes are simply determined by their own material pay-offs: the higher an individual's pay-off, the more preferred the outcome.

Table 5.1: Pay-off structure of a prisoner's dilemma

| | | Individual 2 | |
		Cooperate	Defect
Individual 1	Cooperate	$3 / $3	$4 / $0
	Defect	$0 / $4	$1 / $1

Note: In each cell of the table the bottom left entry is individual 1's pay-off; the top right entry is individual 2's pay-off.

Thus individuals are purely self-regarding. For individual 1, defect-cooperate is the most preferred outcome, cooperate-cooperate the second most preferred one, defect-defect the third most preferred one, and cooperate-defect the least preferred one. Individual 2's preferences are analogous. The resulting game is the classic 'prisoner's dilemma'. Under the criterion of dominance, the only individually rational action is to defect. Each individual receives a higher pay-off by defecting than by cooperating, regardless of what the other individual does, and therefore always prefers to defect. Consequently, cooperativeness is not incentive compatible here.

But now suppose the individuals' preferences are different. Suppose that each individual's preference over outcomes is determined not by his or her own material pay-off, but by the sum total of pay-offs across the two individuals; perhaps the individuals are group-oriented rather than purely self-regarding. Thus preferences are utilitarian: for both individuals, cooperate-cooperate is the most preferred outcome, cooperate-defect and defect-cooperate are tied for second most preferred one, and defect-defect is the least preferred outcome. The resulting game is different from the previous one, although it shares the same game form. Now the only rational action for each individual is to cooperate, again under the criterion of dominance. Regardless of what the other individual does, each individual prefers the outcome of cooperating to that of defecting, since it leads to a higher sum total of pay-offs. Cooperativeness *is* incentive compatible here.

These two variants of the original game form of the prisoner's dilemma already illustrate that whether or not a property such as cooperativeness is incentive compatible depends crucially on the individuals' preferences, not just on the social mechanism. To see that it also depends on the criterion of rationality, consider another variant of the example. This time suppose that each individual's preference over the four outcomes is driven solely by how equally or unequally pay-offs are distributed. The two individuals are thus pure egalitarians. In this hypothetical example, cooperate-cooperate and defect-defect are tied for most preferred outcome for both individuals – those outcomes give rise to an equal distribution of pay-offs – and cooperate-defect and defect-cooperate are tied for least preferred outcome – they give rise to an unequal distribution. As a result, neither individual has a dominant action. The game is now a 'coordination game': which action each individual prefers depends on the other individual's action. Two combinations of actions across the two individuals constitute Nash equilibria: cooperate-cooperate and defect-defect. Each individual prefers to cooperate when the other cooperates, and to defect when the other defects. Under the demanding criterion of dominance, cooperativeness is not incentive compatible here, whereas under the less demanding criterion of Nash equilibrium it is.

In summary, incentive compatibility is such an important concept because the alignment it captures between individual rationality and a collective target property is a key prerequisite for any successful pursuit of social goals. If truthfulness is incentive compatible under a social mechanism involving the expression of individual judgments or preferences, we can be confident that rational individuals will indeed reveal their judgments or preferences truthfully. If cooperativeness is incentive compatible, we can be confident that they will indeed cooperate.[86] Without this alignment between individual rationality and the relevant target property, a group's ability to achieve its goals may be seriously compromised. In a world of rational individuals, incentive compatibility is therefore a central desideratum of good organizational design, and it is time to apply it more explicitly to the context of group agency.

5.2 Satisfying the incentive-compatibility desideratum

We have argued in earlier chapters that a group can successfully perform as an agent if it has a suitable organizational structure for forming intentional attitudes and for putting them into action. So far, however, we have said nothing about whether, in the process of forming the group's attitudes, it will be rational for members to be truthful, and further, whether it will be rational for them to cooperate when those attitudes are to be enacted. Are truthfulness and cooperativeness incentive compatible here?

In what follows we discuss four challenges to incentive compatibility in a group agent. These challenges are only illustrative: real-world group agents are bound to be more complex, and incentive compatibility is likely to be harder to achieve in the real world than in our simple examples. Nonetheless, despite their simplicity, the four challenges point to some general lessons for the organizational design of a group agent.

Before presenting the details, it is useful to summarize the four challenges informally. The first challenge arises when opinionated group members each want the group to adopt their own preferences or judgments. Imagine, for instance, that each member of a committee – say, a selection panel for a job – wants to impose his or her opinion on the rest of the committee. One might think that in such cases it is rational for group members to reveal their own preferences and judgments truthfully, if forcefully. But it turns out that they may still have an incentive to misrepresent them. Of course, this observation will not be too surprising on reflection, since the strategic incentives in this case can be traced to conflicts of interest between different group members wanting the group to adopt different attitudes.

The second challenge, however, shows that, even in the absence of any conflicts of interest between group members, strategic incentives can still persist. Surprisingly, there can be strategic incentives even when, for example, all group members share a strong preference for the group to track the truth in its judgments. But we also identify necessary and sufficient conditions under which a group can avoid these problems and ensure that truthfulness will be incentive compatible among its members.

The next two challenges are harder to answer than the first two. The third challenge occurs when group members, despite strongly preferring the group to track the truth in its judgments, also have a very slight preference to conform with the majority of their peers. It is a familiar phenomenon that people prefer to be in the majority rather than in the minority. In this case, unfortunately, our earlier recipes for ensuring the incentive compatibility of truthfulness break down. Thus peer-group conformism introduces a much trickier challenge to achieving incentive compatibility of truthfulness than do some of the more self-regarding strategic incentives discussed earlier.

The fourth, and final, challenge to be discussed concerns the enactment of a group agent's intentional attitudes. We have seen in Chapters 2 and 3 that it is a constant possibility in a group agent that the group's intentional attitudes may come apart from those of its members. Just as this possibility underlies the surprising autonomy of group agents, so it may also generate incentives for group members not to cooperate with what is required of them by the group, leading to a phenomenon we describe as 'corporate akrasia' (Pettit 2003a). A group needs to find ways to overcome such collective weakness of will in order to get its act together and to achieve its goals.

Our discussion of the four incentive-compatibility challenges will be more technical than the material presented elsewhere in the book – and some readers may wish to skip to section 5.3 – but we think that this technical work is warranted, as it yields some insights that would be hard to attain without it.

Strategic incentives when individuals want the group to adopt their own attitudes

Our discussion of the first challenge is based on Dietrich and List's (2007c) work on strategy-proof judgment aggregation, which in turn draws on a large literature on strategic manipulation in social choice (Gibbard 1973; Satterthwaite 1975; Barberà, Gul, et al. 1993; Nehring and Puppe 2002). Recall the example of the three-member court making a decision in a breach-of-contract case, where the defendant is liable (the 'conclusion') just in case two premises are jointly met: firstly, the defendant had a contractual obligation not to do a particular action (the 'first premise'), and secondly, he or she did that action (the 'second premise'). The judges' individual judgments are restated in Table 5.2.

As before, the court's majority judgments are inconsistent relative to the legal doctrine which says that obligation and action are jointly necessary and sufficient for liability. The majority holds that the defendant had an obligation not to do the action, that he or she did the action, and yet that there is no liability.

We have argued that the court can avoid this inconsistency by using a premise-based procedure. Here a majority vote is taken on each premise, and the collective judgment on the conclusion is derived from the majority judgments on the premises. Applied to the judgments in Table 5.2, this leads to the acceptance of both premises, and hence to a 'liable' verdict, assuming the judges express their judgments truthfully.

Table 5.2: The three-member court

	Obligation?	Action?	Liable?
Judge 1	True	True	True
Judge 2	True	False	False
Judge 3	False	True	False
Majority	True	True	False

THE INCENTIVE-COMPATIBILITY DESIDERATUM III

But is it rational for them to do so? Suppose that each judge is convinced of the truth of his or her own opinion and wants to bring about a collective verdict on the liability issue that agrees with his or her individual judgment. Thus the first judge wants to hold the defendant liable and the second and third want the opposite. Call these preferences 'outcome-oriented'. Given such preferences, how will the judges act?

The first judge, who wants to bring about a 'liable' verdict, obviously has an incentive to support both premises in order to produce the preferred verdict. So judge 1 will be truthful. But what about the other two judges? Let us assume, for the sake of argument, that judge 2 will also be truthful, which means that he or she will vote in support of the first premise but against the second. Now consider the third judge. By voting truthfully in support of the second premise and against the first, judge 3 would bring about the majority acceptance of the second premise while failing to prevent the majority acceptance of the first premise resulting from the other judges' votes. Consequently, the premise-based procedure would lead to the acceptance of the conclusion, that is, a 'liable' verdict, and thereby to judge 3's dispreferred outcome.

If, on the other hand, judge 3 were to vote strategically, rejecting the second premise contrary to his or her truthful judgment, the majority judgment on it would change from a positive to a negative one, and the premise-based procedure would lead to the rejection, rather than the acceptance, of the conclusion: a 'not liable' verdict. So, by voting untruthfully, judge 3 can bring about his or her preferred outcome. The same reasoning would apply to judge 2 if judges 1 and 3 were truthful. This shows that if the judges have outcome-oriented preferences, truthfulness is not incentive compatible here: it fails to be a dominant action for two of the three judges, namely judges 2 and 3, and it is not a Nash equilibrium.

Can we find an aggregation function for the court that does not run into this problem? Let us formalize the requirement of incentive compatibility of truthfulness (List 2004b; Dietrich and List 2007c):[87]

Incentive compatibility of truthfulness. At every profile of individual attitudes, every individual prefers, or is indifferent to, the group attitudes that would result from expressing his or her individual attitudes truthfully, compared to those that would result from misrepresenting them, other individuals' expressions of attitudes remaining fixed.

Our example shows that the premise-based procedure violates this desideratum when individuals have outcome-oriented preferences. In particular, the example shows the existence of a profile of individual attitudes, namely the one in Table 5.2, for which some individuals, specifically judges 2 and 3, prefer the group attitudes that would result from misrepresenting their individual attitudes (here leading to a 'not liable' verdict) to those that would result from expressing them truthfully (here leading to a 'liable' verdict). This, in turn, violates incentive compatibility of truthfulness.

As already noted, whether or not truthfulness is incentive compatible depends on the individuals' preferences.[88] In our example, each judge's preference was to reach a collective verdict on the liability issue that agrees with his or her individual verdict. We

Table 5.3: The concept of 'closeness' illustrated, where 'p', 'q', and 'r' are the propositions of concern

	'p'	'q'	'r'
Individual	True	False	False
Group in situation A	True (match)	True (mismatch)	False (match)
Group in situation B	False (mismatch)	True (mismatch)	False (match)

described these preferences as 'outcome-oriented': what any judge was concerned about most was to bring about a collective judgment on the relevant outcome proposition that matches his or her individual judgment on it. More generally, let us call the propositions that the individuals care about most – the propositions that they are 'oriented towards' – their 'propositions of concern'. In our example there was only one proposition of concern, namely the one about liability, but there could also be several. To keep things simple, we assume that all individuals have the same propositions of concern, but of course they will often disagree in their judgments on them.

In order to describe the nature of individual preferences in this more general case, going beyond the special case of 'outcome-oriented' preferences, we need to introduce one preliminary definition. Consider any individual, who holds certain individual attitudes, and let us compare the group attitudes in two alternative situations, A and B, as for instance in Table 5.3. We say that the group attitudes in situation A are 'equally close or closer' to the individual's attitudes than the group attitudes in situation B if, for any proposition of concern on which the group attitude in situation B matches the individual's own attitude, the group attitude in situation A does so too.

In the example of Table 5.3, this definition is met. The group attitudes in situation A are closer to the individual's attitudes than those in situation B, since in situation B there is an agreement between the individual and the group only on proposition 'r', while in situation A there is also an agreement on proposition 'p'. Now the general idea is that whenever the group attitudes on the propositions of concern in one situation, such as A, are closer to the individual's attitudes than in another situation, such as B, the individual prefers situation A to situation B. Thus the assumption about individual preferences can be stated as follows:

Individuals want the group to adopt their own attitudes. Whenever the group attitudes on the propositions of concern in one situation, A, are equally close or closer to an individual's attitudes than in another, B, this individual prefers, or is indifferent to, the group attitudes in situation A, compared to those in situation B.[89]

We are now able to look at how incentive compatibility of truthfulness can be achieved. It turns out that an aggregation function satisfies this desideratum whenever it simultaneously satisfies two conditions. The first is 'independence on the propositions of concern', a weakened version of the condition of systematicity that we discussed extensively in Chapter 2. It requires that the group attitude on each proposition of concern – but not necessarily on other propositions – should depend only on the individuals' attitudes towards it (and not on individual attitudes towards other propositions). The second is 'monotonicity on the propositions of concern'. This is the requirement that a positive group attitude on any proposition in that set never change into a negative one if some individuals rejecting it change their attitudes towards accepting it. Intuitively, the group attitude on each proposition should be an increasing function of the individual attitudes on it. Majority voting, for example, satisfies both conditions – independence and monotonicity on the propositions of concern – irrespective of what those propositions of concern are. The premise-based procedure, by contrast, violates them if the conclusion is among the propositions of concern. The following theorem formally states the connection between the two conditions and incentive compatibility of truthfulness (related to Barberà, Gul, et al. 1993; Nehring and Puppe 2002; proved in this form by Dietrich and List 2007c):

Theorem. For individuals who want the group to adopt their own attitudes, an aggregation function satisfies incentive compatibility of truthfulness if and only if it satisfies independence and monotonicity on the propositions of concern.

The theorem immediately confirms the earlier observation that truthfulness is not incentive compatible under the premise-based procedure when individuals have outcome-oriented preferences. The reason is that the propositions of concern include (in fact, consist precisely of) the conclusion here – that is, the liability issue – and the premise-based procedure violates independence on the propositions of concern in this case. The theorem also implies that, for the same individual preferences, truthfulness *is* incentive compatible under the conclusion-based procedure, which satisfies independence and monotonicity on the propositions of concern when these are restricted to the conclusion alone. The price to pay for this is that no group attitudes are generated on the premises at all, and we thus fail to achieve group rationality in the full sense.

The general strategy for making truthfulness incentive compatible should now be clear. The group must use an aggregation function that satisfies independence and monotonicity on the propositions of concern. In the terminology of the first part of this book, the group must ensure that its attitudes supervene in a proposition-wise way *at least on those propositions that the individuals are concerned about most*, which is entirely consistent with violations of proposition-wise supervenience elsewhere.

There are at least two ways of achieving this. The first is to take the propositions of concern as given, thereby assuming that individuals' preferences are fixed, and then to choose an aggregation function that satisfies independence and monotonicity on those propositions. The second is to try to change the individuals' preferences by persuading or convincing them that they should care about a different set of propositions of concern.

How well does the first strategy work? In the lucky scenario in which the propositions of concern are mutually independent and fit to serve either as premises or as conclusions, a suitable premise-based or conclusion-based procedure can work. For example, if the only proposition of concern is a single conclusion, as in our example of the three-member court, a conclusion-based procedure ensures incentive compatibility of truthfulness. Similarly, if the only propositions of concern are some mutually independent premises, then a premise-based procedure can do the job.

If the set of propositions of concern exhibits richer logical interconnections, however, then incentive compatibility of truthfulness becomes impossible to achieve in a non-degenerate way. Why is this? Suppose the set of propositions of concern involves a number of logical connections, such as conjunctions and disjunctions, and forms a (sub) agenda to which the impossibility theorems of Chapter 2 apply. Then the only aggregation functions satisfying independence and monotonicity on those propositions of concern (together with universal domain and collective rationality) are degenerate ones, which either violate unanimity preservation or are dictatorial. Since independence and monotonicity on the propositions of concern are necessary for incentive compatibility of truthfulness, it follows that this desideratum cannot be satisfied in a non-degenerate way (Nehring and Puppe 2002; Dietrich and List 2007c).

This failure of the first approach towards achieving incentive compatibility of truthfulness leads us to the second approach. Rather than taking the propositions of concern as fixed, the group might seek to change them in a beneficial way: for example, by making group members more 'reason-oriented' than outcome-oriented, that is, leading them to consider relevant premises rather than conclusions as their propositions of concern. For example, judges could be persuaded that, rather than manipulatively promoting a collective verdict on the liability issue that agrees with their individual verdicts, they should try to convince the court of their sincerely held judgments on the premises. Attempts to create a deliberative ethos in a group can be seen as instances of this second approach. It remains an open question how widely applicable this approach is, but the limitations of the first approach should be enough to lead us to consider this second one more seriously.

Strategic incentives when individuals want the group to track the truth

One may think that the incentive *in*compatibility of truthfulness in the cases just discussed stems from the fact that different individuals' interests conflict with each other: each individual is firmly convinced of the correctness of his or her own attitudes and wants the group to adopt them, even if this involves strategic misrepresentation. By contrast, if each individual accepts the fallibility of his or her own attitudes − in particular, his or her judgments − and believes that the attitudes of others may be important sources of information, then one might expect that truthfulness will naturally become incentive compatible. Surprisingly, however, this need not be the case. Even more surprising is the fact that the conditions that were sufficient for incentive compatibility of truthfulness in the earlier case, where individuals wanted the group to adopt their own judgments, are no longer sufficient in this new case, where individuals want the group to track the truth. Even when the aggregation function is independent and monotonic on all the propositions of concern, truth-seeking individuals may still have an incentive to misrepresent their attitudes to the group. Our discussion of this problem is based on Austen-Smith and Banks's (1996) and Feddersen and Pesendorfer's (1998) seminal works on strategic voting in information-pooling contexts.

Consider a jury in a criminal trial, and suppose jurors satisfy Condorcet's competence and independence conditions, as introduced in the last chapter. Specifically, suppose each juror has a positive and negative tracking reliability of 0.6 on the guilt of the defendant, and different jurors' judgments are mutually independent. Suppose, further, the prior, unconditional probability of guilt is 1/2. We have seen that if the jury uses majority voting – setting aside, for the moment, any real-world requirements of unanimous or supermajoritarian jury verdicts – the jury's positive and negative tracking reliability exceeds that of each individual and approaches certainty in a sufficiently large jury. Moreover, the jury's positive and negative indicating reliability has similar properties, and it is therefore exceedingly likely, in a large jury, that the defendant will be convicted if and only if his or her guilt is beyond reasonable doubt. Both of these points are immediate consequences of the Condorcet jury theorem, as we have seen. But crucially, all of this assumes that jurors will be truthful. Is truthfulness rational, though?

Suppose that each juror is 'introspective' in the sense that he or she knows that his or her initial opinion about the guilt of the defendant has a positive and negative tracking reliability of 0.6. And suppose that jurors are 'truth-seeking', in the following illustrative sense:

Individuals want the group to track the truth. Each juror prefers the group to convict the defendant if and only if, by the juror's lights, the probability of guilt exceeds some threshold of reasonable doubt, say 0.9.

Given what we have just said about the jury's high positive and negative indicating reliability under majority voting, we might expect jurors to reveal their judgments truthfully. In particular, they should be confident that their truth-seeking preferences will be satisfied by the jury's majority verdict. Contrary to this assumption, however, rational truth-seeking jurors may still decide to be untruthful. The reasoning goes as follows.

In deciding whether to cast a 'guilty' or 'not guilty' vote, each juror must consider two cases. Either he or she is pivotal – meaning that the other jurors' votes are equally divided between a 'guilty' and a 'not guilty' verdict – or he or she is not. If the juror is not pivotal, his or her vote makes no difference to the majority verdict, and so it does not matter for the outcome how he or she votes. The only case in which the juror's vote can make a difference to the majority verdict is the case in which he or she is pivotal. In this case, there is an equal number of 'guilty' and 'not guilty' votes among the other jurors.[90] Assuming the others' votes reflect their truthful judgments, the posterior probability of guilt of the defendant can now be calculated using the formula discussed in the previous chapter. It is

$$\frac{t\ r^{x-y}}{t\ r^{x-y} + (1-t)(1-r)^{x-y}},$$

where t is the prior probability of guilt, r the individual reliability of each juror, x the total number of 'guilty' judgments and y the total number of 'not guilty' judgments. In our example, we can set t = 1/2 and r = 0.6. Given that the juror under consideration is pivotal — meaning that there is an equal split among the others — notice that x–y equals 1 just in case he or she judges the defendant to be guilty and −1 otherwise. Therefore the posterior probability of guilt equals

$$\frac{0.5 \times 0.6^1}{0.5 \times 0.6^1 + (1-0.5) \times (1-0.6)^1} = 0.6$$

if the pivotal juror judges the defendant to be guilty, and

$$\frac{0.5 \times 0.6^{-1}}{0.5 \times 0.6^{-1} + (1-0.5) \times (1-0.6)^{-1}} = 0.4$$

if he or she judges the defendant to be innocent. In either case, the posterior probability of guilt is well below the illustrative threshold of reasonable doubt, which was 0.9, and thus too low to support a 'guilty' verdict according to the juror's truth-seeking criterion. A juror with truth-seeking preferences will therefore prefer to vote for 'not guilty', regardless of his or her own individual judgment, assuming others are truthful. This shows that truthfulness is not incentive compatible under majority voting in the present example.

Is unanimity rule any better? After all, the requirement of unanimous jury decisions is common in criminal trials. Here, again, each juror must consider two cases in deciding how to vote. Either his or her vote is pivotal, or it is not. A juror's vote is pivotal under unanimity rule if and only if all the other jurors cast a 'guilty' vote, so that he or she can either bring about or block a unanimous agreement. If his or her vote is not pivotal, then it makes no difference to the outcome how he or she votes. If it is pivotal, however, the juror must consider the posterior probability of guilt, taking into account the other jurors' judgments and his or her own. Again, assuming the others' votes are truthful, the formula above applies, with the same prior probability of guilt t= 0.5 and the same individual reliability r = 0.6. When the juror under consideration is pivotal under unanimity rule, x–y equals n just in case he or she judges the defendant to be guilty and (n−1)−1 = n−2 otherwise, where n is the total number of jurors. Thus the posterior probability of guilt equals

$$\frac{0.5 \times 0.6^n}{0.5 \times 0.6^n + (1-0.5) \times (1-0.6)^n} = \frac{1}{1 + (2/3)^n}$$

if the pivotal juror judges the defendant to be guilty, and

$$\frac{0.5 \times 0.6^{n-2}}{0.5 \times 0.6^{n-2} + (1 - 0.5) \times (1 - 0.6)^{n-2}} = \frac{1}{1 + (2/3)^{n-2}}$$

otherwise. It is easy to calculate that, as soon as the jury size n is 8 or higher, both figures are above the illustrative threshold of reasonable doubt, which is 0.9 in the example, and therefore high enough to support a 'guilty' verdict according to the juror's truth-seeking criterion. A juror with truth-seeking preferences will thus prefer to vote for 'guilty', regardless of his or her own individual judgment. As in the case of majority voting, truthfulness is not incentive compatible here. Under the assumption that other jurors are truthful, a rational juror may have an incentive to misrepresent his or her judgment, despite being truth-seeking, and thus truthfulness is not sustained in Nash equilibrium. Unanimity rule may even give jurors the perverse incentive to convict the innocent, even when jurors individually have doubts about the defendant's guilt, as Feddersen and Pesendorfer (1998) have pointed out in a by-now classic article.

We have seen that neither majority voting nor unanimity rule generally ensure incentive compatibility of truthfulness when jurors want the group to track the truth. This is particularly surprising since there is no conflict of interest between jurors here – they all want the group to track the truth – and majority voting and unanimity rule are also both independent and monotonic on all propositions and therefore fulfill the sufficient condition for incentive compatibility of truthfulness in the earlier case, where individuals wanted the group to adopt their own judgments.

How can we ensure incentive compatibility of truthfulness for truth-seeking individuals, then? As we have seen, requiring merely independence and monotonicity on some, or all, propositions on the agenda is not enough; we need to require something else. The reasoning above has revealed that a truth-seeking individual's voting decision depends only on the case in which he or she is pivotal. Therefore, *if* we can give each individual an incentive to be truthful in the case of pivotality, *then* he or she will prefer to be truthful in all cases (or at least be indifferent), and truthfulness will be dominant.

To see how we can meet this challenge, let us consider the class of 'generalized majoritarian aggregation functions'. An aggregation function falls into that class if there exists some required margin between the number of 'guilty' votes and the number of 'not guilty' votes that is deemed necessary and sufficient for a 'guilty' verdict. Majority voting is the special case in which the required margin is one vote, and unanimity rule the special case in which it is all votes. When is an individual pivotal under such an aggregation function? He or she is pivotal precisely if the difference between the number of 'guilty' votes and the number of 'not guilty' votes among the others together with an additional 'guilty' vote is just at or above the required margin, while the same difference among the others together with an additional 'not guilty' vote is just below it. As before, an individual can calculate the posterior probability of guilt, conditional on the event of being pivotal. Reusing our earlier illustrative figures and assuming, as before, that the number of jurors n is odd and that the required margin – call it m – is specified by an even number, the posterior probability of guilt equals

$$\frac{0.5 \times 0.6^{m+1}}{0.5 \times 0.6^{m+1} + (1 - 0.5) \times (1 - 0.6)^{m+1}} = \frac{1}{1 + (2/3)^{m+1}}$$

if the pivotal juror judges the defendant to be guilty, and

$$\frac{0.5 \times 0.6^{m-1}}{0.5 \times 0.6^{m-1} + (1 - 0.5) \times (1 - 0.6)^{m-1}} = \frac{1}{1 + (2/3)^{m-1}}$$

if the pivotal juror judges the defendant to be innocent. If truthfulness is to be incentive compatible for a truth-seeking individual, the first of these two probabilities must be above the threshold of reasonable doubt, and the second below it. To achieve incentive compatibility of truthfulness, we must therefore adjust the required margin m such that those constraints on the two probabilities are satisfied. Call the resulting aggregation function 'well-calibrated'.

In the present example, a required margin of 6 will do the job. When a juror is pivotal, then, the posterior probability of guilt is 0.944708 if he or she judges the defendant to be guilty, and 0.883636 if he or she judges the defendant to be innocent. Since 0.944708 is above 0.9 and 0.883636 below it, a truth-seeking juror will indeed prefer to reveal his or her judgment truthfully in the case of pivotality and by implication in all cases. The following theorem summarizes this observation:

Theorem. For individuals wanting the group to track the truth, a generalized majoritarian aggregation function satisfies incentive compatibility of truthfulness if and only if it is well calibrated.[91]

How feasible is this route to incentive compatibility of truthfulness? Well-calibration is a very demanding condition on an aggregation function. In its present form, it requires an equal reliability across all individuals. When different jurors have different levels of reliability, the posterior probability of the defendant's guilt conditional on a juror's being pivotal may differ significantly across jurors and may therefore fail to lie at, or near, the threshold of reasonable doubt for all jurors in the required manner. Similar complications can arise when different jurors assign different prior probabilities to the guilt of the defendant, or when they use different criteria of reasonable doubt. Furthermore, the actual level of individual reliability may differ across groups and across judgmental tasks, and an aggregation function that is well calibrated for one group and one judgmental task may not be well calibrated for others. To achieve incentive compatibility of truthfulness, groups must therefore adjust their aggregation functions in a highly context-sensitive manner. Finally, the condition of well-calibration places heavy informational demands on a group's organizational design. To determine what the required margin between positive and negative judgments must be for the collective acceptance of a proposition, a large number of parameters has to be known, ranging from the precise reliability of all individuals to the precise prior probability of all propositions under consideration. Our discussion should therefore make it clear how hard it is to achieve incentive compatibility of truthfulness, even under the relatively benign assumption of rational, truth-seeking individuals.

Strategic incentives when individuals want to conform with others

Now let us suppose a group has successfully met the first two incentive-compatibility challenges. Specifically, suppose individuals use an aggregation function that is not only independent and monotonic on the propositions of concern but also well calibrated. They may use majority voting, for example, to make a judgment on the truth or falsity of a single proposition to which they all assign a prior probability of 1/2 and which they all want to accept just in case it is more likely to be true than false. Here majority voting has all the properties required to ensure incentive compatibility of truthfulness for rational, truth-seeking individuals. Could individuals still have an incentive to be untruthful?

Let us continue to assume that individuals overwhelmingly prefer a correct group judgment to an incorrect one, but let us add one complication. The individuals are no longer exclusively truth-seeking; they are also very slightly conformist, in the following sense.

Individuals have a slight conformist preference. While still strongly preferring a correct group judgment on each proposition to an incorrect one, individuals very slightly prefer being in the majority to being in the minority.

Individuals might, for instance, derive a very small benefit from being in the majority or suffer a very small cost for being in the minority. Crucially, this small conformist preference by no means replaces the stronger preference for a correct group judgment. The conformist preference can be arbitrarily small – in a sense to be made precise – compared to the preference for a correct group judgment. This assumption is still a fairly benign one, as it continues to depict individuals as primarily truth-seeking, and yet it is slightly more realistic than the earlier assumption. It concedes that, when other things are equal, individuals very slightly prefer to be on the winning side.

What is the effect of such a small conformist preference? First, truthfulness may cease to be incentive compatible, and second, even more dramatically, the situation in which all group members unanimously vote in support of an incorrect group judgment can become a Nash equilibrium, even when they all individually think that this judgment is wrong. Moreover, this can happen irrespective of how reliable the individuals' judgments are. The incentive structure resulting from the slightest conformist preference can prevent the truthful revelation of individual judgments even when these are maximally reliable. Our discussion of this problem is based on unpublished work by Christian List.

To explain the problem formally, suppose that each individual makes an independent judgment on some proposition 'p', as before in accordance with Condorcet's competence and independence conditions introduced in the last chapter. Suppose

Table 5.4: The truth-seeking component of each individual's preferences

	'p' is true	'p' is false
majority judges that 'p'	1	0
majority judges that 'not p'	0	1

Table 5.5: The conformist component of each individual's preferences

	majority judges that p	majority judges that not p
Individual votes for 'p'	ϵ	0
individual votes for 'not p'	0	ϵ

Table 5.6: Each individual's overall utility

	individual is in the majority	individual is in the minority
correct group judgment	$1 + \epsilon$	1
incorrect group judgment	ϵ	0

further that each individual's preferences over various situations are captured by a particular utility function: the higher the individual's utility, the more he or she prefers a given situation. We assume that the individual's utility function can be expressed as the sum of two components, a truth-seeking component and a conformist component. The truth-seeking component represents the utility the individual gets from whether or not the majority judgment is correct. As shown in Table 5.4, we assume that the individual gets a utility of 1 from a correct majority judgment and a utility of 0 from an incorrect one.

The conformist component represents the utility the individual gets from whether or not he or she is in the majority. As shown in Table 5.5, we assume that he or she gets a utility of ϵ from being in the majority and a utility of ϵ from being in the minority, where ϵ is a small but positive amount; let us say $\epsilon = 0.01$.

Crucially, the utility from conforming can be much smaller than that from a correct group judgment, since the value of ϵ can be arbitrarily small. If we add up the truth-seeking and conformist components of the individual's utility function, the individual will still prefer a correct group judgment to an incorrect one, regardless of whether or not he or she is in the majority. The individual's overall utility is represented in Table 5.6. He or she most prefers a correct group judgment together with being in the majority, second most prefers a correct group judgment while being in the minority, third most prefers an incorrect group judgment together with being in the majority, and least prefers an incorrect group judgment while being in the minority.

How will individuals with such preferences vote? Will they reveal their own judgments truthfully to the group or do something else? Strikingly, we can easily identify at least three Nash equilibria under the assumptions just introduced. The first involves all individuals voting in support of proposition 'p', regardless of their own individual judgments. The second involves all individuals voting against proposition 'p', also regardless of their own individual judgments. Only the third involves all individuals revealing their judgments truthfully, but this equilibrium is arguably the most fragile one among the three. In other words, two of those three equilibria involve a voting behavior that is utterly unconnected to the individuals' own truthful judgments. Let us explain this result.

Recall that a combination of actions across individuals is a Nash equilibrium if every individual prefers, or is indifferent to, the outcome of taking that action, compared to the outcome of unilaterally deviating from it, assuming others do not deviate. How could the situation in which all individuals vote for proposition 'p', regardless of their individual judgments, be a Nash equilibrium? To sharpen the case, suppose an overwhelming majority of individuals (perhaps all of them) judge that not p, their individual judgments are highly reliable (perhaps even $r = 1$), and they are known to be so. To see that the situation in which everyone votes for 'p' could nonetheless be a Nash equilibrium, consider one particular individual, and ask how this individual should rationally vote, assuming the others vote for 'p'. The majority will then support 'p', no matter how the given individual votes, since 'p' is supported by at least $n-1$ other individuals (assuming the group size n is greater than two). Thus the given individual is not pivotal, which means that the truth-seeking component of his or her utility is completely unaffected by his or her voting decision. What about the conformist component of the utility? Since the value of ϵ, the strength of the conformist preference, is positive, the individual will derive a benefit of ϵ from joining the majority by voting for 'p', as compared with no benefit from voting against the majority. Given that all others vote for 'p', it is therefore rational for the individual in question to vote for 'p' too, despite his or her truthful judgment to the contrary. Since the same reasoning applies to all individuals, the situation in which everyone votes in favor of 'p', even if no one agrees with this judgment, is a Nash equilibrium. Analogously, the situation in which everyone votes in favor of 'not p', regardless of anyone's judgments, is also a Nash equilibrium. We turn to a third equilibrium in a moment. The following theorem summarizes the finding so far:

Theorem. For individuals with slight conformist preferences, the situation in which everyone votes in favor of 'p' and the one in which everyone votes against 'p' are both Nash equilibria, irrespective of anyone's individual judgments.

By implication, truthfulness is not incentive compatible, in the sense of dominance defined above. But it can also happen – in Nash equilibrium – that all individuals reveal their judgments truthfully. In the absence of any information about how others are going to vote, it may be rational for an individual to reveal his or her own judgment truthfully. If there is no independent indication as to how the majority will vote, an individual's best guess about the likely majority judgment may indeed be his or her own individual judgment. Thus the situation in which every individual reveals his or her own judgment truthfully, not knowing the other individuals' judgments, can be a Nash equilibrium as well.

But even here – assuming an individual has no special reason to expect pivotality – the individual's voting decision is driven not by an incentive to bring about a correct group judgment, but by an incentive to be in the majority. It just so happens that an individual's own judgment is his or her only available cue about what the judgments of others are likely to be and thus how the majority is likely to vote. Moreover, it should be clear that this reasoning works only in the case of maximal uncertainty. As soon as individuals have slightly more information about how the majority is likely to vote, they will be rationally driven to vote the same way, regardless of their individual judgments. For this reason, the more benign Nash equilibrium in which individuals are truthful appears to be rather fragile.

The phenomenon of conformism identified here is distinct from an informational cascade (Bikhchandani, Hirshleifer, et al. 1992). In an informational cascade, a plurality or majority that accidentally emerges in support of some proposition is mistakenly interpreted by others as evidence for the truth of that proposition and consequently keeps growing, although few if any individuals initially judged the proposition to be true. But in an informational cascade, unlike in the case of conformism, agents genuinely update their judgments based on the expressed judgments of others and thus really change their minds, albeit based on mistaken evidence. Conformism, by contrast, requires no belief change at all and can sustain a majoritarian or unanimous judgment which everyone believes to be wrong. If it is costly to be the lone dissenter who says that the emperor is without clothes, then people may refrain from saying so, even if everyone agrees with the proposition.

Strategic incentives in action

The incentive compatibility problems discussed so far all concern the formation of intentional attitudes – preferences and judgments – at the group level. In concluding this section, it is therefore worth illustrating some incentive compatibility problems that may arise when a group seeks to put those attitudes into action. When individuals participate in the activities of a group agent, which may involve taking certain actions on the group's behalf, they may face difficult choices between whether to act in pursuit of their own beliefs and desires, or in pursuit of those of the group. Incentive compatibility would require an alignment between what they are led to do individually and what is required of them by the group.

Incentive compatibility of cooperativeness. At every profile of individual attitudes, every individual prefers, or is indifferent to, the outcome of taking the action required of him or her by the group, compared to any other action.

The difficulties of achieving incentive compatibility of cooperativeness are well known from social-scientific work on the design of organizations and social mechanisms. The literature on so-called 'principal-agent problems' is full of examples of situations in which the interests of a 'principal', such as an employer, a firm, or an organization, may come apart from those of its 'agent', such as its employee, member, or representative. So it should come as no surprise that such problems can arise in any context of group agency too.

Let us give one illustrative example. Take a non-commercial academic journal with a three-member editorial committee that initially tries to decide all the policy decisions it faces by majority vote but relies on the sequential priority procedure described in Chapter 2 to resolve any problems. Suppose that the committee votes in January for promising subscribers that there will be no price rise in the next five years (proposition 'p'). Suppose that it votes in July that it is prepared to publish papers involving technical symbolism and color diagrams that are costly to produce (proposition 'q'). And suppose that in December it faces the issue of whether it should accept fewer papers overall (proposition 'r'), since the increase in the proportion of technical papers with color diagrams together with the price freeze would otherwise force the journal out of business. (Thus the background constraint is 'if p and q, then r'.) By the sequential priority procedure, the majority acceptance of the first two propositions necessitates the collective acceptance of the last, even if this involves overruling the majority verdict on it, as shown in Table 5.7.

So far so good. The journal may even decide at its editorial meeting in December to make it an official policy to accept fewer papers, following the sequential priority procedure. But the policy also needs to be put into action, and it is the editors who decide whether to accept or reject submitted papers. We may suppose, as is common practice with many journals, that each submitted paper is editorially handled by one member of the editorial committee. The first editor will have no difficulties enacting the new policy and rejecting more papers, since he or she individually agrees that the journal should accept fewer papers. But the other two editors are individually opposed

Table 5.7: The three-member editorial committee

	Price freeze	Publish technical papers with color diagrams	Accept fewer papers
Editor 1	Preferred	Preferred	Preferred
Editor 2	Preferred	Dispreferred	Dispreferred
Editor 3	Dispreferred	Preferred	Dispreferred
Majority	Preferred	Preferred	Dispreferred

to this new policy and did not vote for it in the first place. The second editor would have preferred to secure the journal's financial viability by refusing to publish technical papers with costly color diagrams, and the third by increasing the journal's subscription charge. The second and third editors may therefore find themselves torn between acting in accordance with their own preference, thereby continuing to accept a large number of papers, and going along with what is required of them by the group as a whole. Unless they are sufficiently group-minded and able to change or overrule their individual preference, they may well stick to their private viewpoints and refuse to cooperate with the journal's policy; cooperativeness is not incentive compatible here. In the terminology of the philosophical literature on failures of agency, we may describe this phenomenon as 'corporate akrasia' (Pettit 2003a). The group agent is subject to a sort of civil war that Plato's Republic represented as a permanent danger for the soul as well as for society (Adams 1985; Korsgaard 1999).

Such violations of incentive compatibility of cooperativeness are a constant possibility in any group in which the group's intentional attitudes may come apart from those of its members. But as we have seen in Chapter 3, the achievement of robust group rationality usually requires violations of proposition-wise supervenience. That is, the group attitudes on some propositions are not a function of individual attitudes on those propositions, suggesting that almost any group agent may be subject to the problems we have identified.

In a related vein, Nehring (2005) has shown that, for a large class of aggregation functions generalizing the premise-based procedure, it is inevitable that even unanimous individual preferences on certain practical conclusions are sometimes overruled in order to ensure collective rationality (for a related result, see Mongin 2008). This, in turn, opens up the possibility of incentives for group members to act against the preferences of the group as a whole.

The area is too broad to allow the statement of a single general theorem. Our discussion should be sufficient, however, to illustrate the challenges that incentive compatibility of cooperativeness raises for the design of a group agent's organizational structure.

5.3 Two routes to incentive compatibility

We have seen that whether or not truthfulness or cooperativeness is incentive compatible depends not only on the social mechanism in place – here the group agent's organizational structure – but also on the individuals' preferences and the criterion of rationality. This observation points us to two distinct ways in which incentive compatibility can be achieved; they have already been implicit in our discussion up to this point. The first is to take the individuals' preferences and the criterion of rationality as given, and to adjust the group's organizational structure so as to make truthfulness or cooperativeness incentive compatible for those given preferences and rationality criterion. We call this the 'organizational route'. The second involves changing the individuals' behavior, perhaps through persuading, educating, or otherwise inducing them to change their preferences or behavioral dispositions, while holding the group's organizational structure largely fixed. We call this the 'behavioral route'. We now discuss the two routes in turn.

The organizational route

The organizational route towards incentive compatibility rests on the well-established fact that, for the exact same preferences and behavioral dispositions of everyone involved, one social mechanism may give individuals an incentive to be truthful and/or cooperative while another doesn't. We have seen, for example, that when judges are outcome-oriented – meaning they each care primarily about achieving a collective judgment on the liability issue that agrees with their own individual judgment – then the conclusion-based procedure gives them an incentive to vote truthfully while the premise-based procedure does not. Similarly, in a jury whose members are truth-seeking, only some but not all aggregation functions ensure the incentive compatibility of truthfulness. Majority voting or unanimity rule, for example, may fail to induce jurors to reveal their private judgments truthfully except in special cases, while a well-calibrated aggregation function makes truthfulness incentive compatible.

If a problem of incentive incompatibility arises in a group agent, the general idea is therefore to adjust the group's organizational structure in such a way as to achieve incentive compatibility. In our examples, the court might switch to the conclusion-based procedure and the jury to a well-calibrated aggregation function. Similarly, many real-world organizations whose success depends upon their members' willingness to participate – whether they are firms, trade unions, or other purposive groups – often try to solve collective-action problems, which are paradigmatic incentive-compatibility challenges, by reforming their organizational structures and adjusting their procedures.

However, the limitations of this approach should be clear. Although in some cases it is possible, happily, to find an organizational structure that guarantees incentive compatibility, in others such an organizational structure demonstrably fails to exist, even in principle. One example of this difficulty is given by the impossibility results that apply when group members care not only about a single conclusion or multiple independent propositions but about several propositions which are interconnected. Here it is simply impossible to find a non-degenerate aggregation function – one that doesn't violate basic democratic desiderata – which satisfies the conditions for incentive compatibility of truthfulness, namely that the group's intentional attitudes on these issues depend in an independent and monotonic way on the members' attitudes.

Another, perhaps milder example of the same difficulty is given by the case of conformist preferences. Here truthful expression of individual judgments, although not dominant, constitutes at least a Nash equilibrium, along with several other Nash equilibria involving blind conformism with what the majority is expected to do. Unfortunately, however, the equilibrium in which individuals are truthful is more fragile than the other equilibria, and it is therefore difficult to come up with purely organizational measures that would favor the 'good' equilibrium over the 'bad' ones. Perhaps anonymous voting would be one such measure, and reducing the amount of communication or signaling among the group members another. But these measures are neither guaranteed to avoid the problems of conformism, nor are they free from other problems of their own. A side-effect of reducing the opportunities for conformist behavior might be the suppression of various benefits of communication, for example. Moreover, anonymity might reduce conformist pressures on individuals at the expense of encouraging more opportunist voting decisions, since individuals would no longer build up a publicly known track record of their voting behavior.

Similarly, as is well known from the literature on principal-agent problems, it can be extremely difficult to get individuals to cooperate with what is required of them, purely on the basis of organizational reforms that leave underlying preferences and behavioral dispositions in place. It is no surprise that many organizations seek to improve cooperative behavior among their members, not by adjusting their organizational structure alone but by seeking, in addition, to change their organizational *culture*, thereby presumably inducing individuals to develop more group-minded preferences or behavioral dispositions. This leads us to the behavioral route towards achieving incentive compatibility.

The behavioral route

We have seen that truthfulness or cooperativeness cannot always be made incentive compatible through organizational measures alone. The basic insight underlying the behavioral route towards incentive compatibility is that the same social mechanism – permitting the same possible actions by the individuals and generating the same possible outcomes – may violate incentive compatibility relative to one particular set of preferences and rationality criterion, and satisfy it relative to another. Think of the game form of the prisoner's dilemma, captured by the pay-off structure in Table 5.1 above. When individual preferences are purely self-interested – that is, driven solely by individual pay-offs – cooperativeness is not incentive compatible here, but when they are utilitarian – that is, induced by the sum total of pay-offs across individuals – it is.

If a group runs into an incentive-compatibility problem, a possible response might therefore be to try to transform the members' preferences from those that generate strategic incentives into those that make cooperativeness or truthfulness incentive compatible. The group might try to achieve this through educational, communicative, or social measures that change the group's informal norms and culture as opposed to its formal mechanisms and procedures.

Let us revisit our three-member court example in light of this idea. If the court seeks to achieve incentive compatibility through the organizational route, as we have already seen, it has no choice but to adopt the conclusion-based procedure; the premise-based procedure will not generally lead the judges to reveal their views truthfully, given their outcome-oriented preferences. The drawback of this approach is that the court will reach no judgments on the reasons behind its overall verdict, generating only an incompletely theorized decision.[92] Suppose, therefore, that the court wishes, or is externally expected, to use the premise-based procedure. Can the behavioral route towards incentive compatibility help in this case? If the judges' preferences remain purely outcome-oriented, we will have reached an impasse: truthfulness will simply not be incentive compatible. But if the court succeeds at changing its culture, making judges reason-oriented rather than outcome-oriented, then the judges' objective will no longer be just to reach an overall verdict they personally like; instead, they will seek to convince the court of their sincerely held judgments on the premises, and truthfulness will become incentive compatible.

Similarly, if a jury or expert committee uses a well-calibrated aggregation function and yet faces an incentive-compatibility problem due to conformism, it may seek to bring about a culture in which dissent is not penalized but made socially acceptable, insofar as it serves the truth. Thus the group may try to transform its members' conformist preferences into truth-seeking ones. The consequence would be that the very same aggregation function that previously gave rise to conformist equilibria, with individuals disregarding their individual judgments, will make truthfulness incentive compatible.

In both cases, of course, it is a difficult question whether the required cultural change is empirically possible, but under the given assumptions, it is the only logically possible route towards incentive compatibility.

A particularly persistent incentive-compatibility challenge arises in a group agent when it comes to ensuring that the group's intentional attitudes are put into action. Members may find it difficult to take the actions required of them by the group, because the group's intentional attitudes supporting those actions may be at odds with their own individual attitudes. Conflicts between group attitudes and individual ones are unavoidable in a group agent because of inevitable failures of proposition-wise supervenience. As we have shown in Chapter 3, the group attitudes on some – possibly many – propositions will not be a function of individual attitudes on those propositions, and may sometimes even contradict unanimously held individual attitudes on them.

Given the nature of this challenge, it may be difficult to tackle it through purely organizational measures alone, although a group might try to introduce selective rewards, say financial ones, to encourage members to enact the group's attitudes even in light of their pre-existing individual preferences. Generally, a change in the members' preferences or behavioral dispositions may be needed to overcome the present incentive-compatibility problem. Members may sometimes need to be motivated to temporarily suspend their own individual preferences and judgments and to identify with those of the group, so as to take the required actions, at least when there is no overriding reason – for instance, a moral reason – for them not to cooperate with the group.

How can the required identification with the group's attitudes be made to work? In Chapter 9, we discuss this issue in greater detail. We notice that, just as an individual agent may experience a rationality breakdown consisting in a failure to identify with, and enact, his or her own intentional attitudes, so a group agent may experience a similar rationality breakdown when its members fail to identify with, and enact, the group's attitudes. One way to bring about the behavioral changes required to avoid such rationality breakdowns in a group agent is to get members to adopt a 'we-frame' of thinking rather than an 'I-frame' (see, for example, Bacharach 2006). Again, it is a difficult empirical question how such a we-frame can be brought into effect among group members.

A possible psychological mechanism leading people to think in we-terms – or more generally, to behave in a socially 'virtuous' way – rests on the fact that people care about the opinion or esteem in which they are held by others, seeking to be held in high esteem and shrinking from the prospect of being held in low (Lovejoy 1961; McAdams 1997; Brennan and Pettit 2004). If in a given context the standards of social virtue are clear and the performance of individuals on these standards is generally detectable by others, then the desire to be considered virtuous can lead the non-virtuous to behave as if they were virtuous, and the virtuous to be reinforced in their virtue, not to have their virtue 'crowded out' (Frey and Jegen 2001). If this mechanism is effective in a group, then members can lead one another into adopting a we-frame just by being around to observe one another's behavior. They can each 'regulate' others just by manifestly observing and assessing what they do – just, as John Locke (1975, pp. 353–4) put it in 1690, by 'thinking well or ill, approving or disapproving of the actions of those whom they live amongst and converse with'.

We suggest in Chapter 9 that apart from some natural psychological mechanisms that lead individuals to identify with groups they belong to, activist group members may also play an important role. When a group agent suffers from corporate akrasia due to identification failures, activist members may remind their peers of their shared identity and move them back into a we-frame in which they individually endorse, and by implication enact, the relevant group attitudes.[93]

6

The Control Desideratum

In the last two chapters, we have examined two desiderata that a well-organized group agent may be expected to satisfy: an epistemic desideratum and an incentive-compatibility one. According to the former, a group agent should form true rather than false beliefs about the world, and according to the latter, it should cope with its members' tendencies to act strategically when the opportunity arises.

In this chapter, we introduce a third desideratum of good organizational design of a group agent: a control desideratum. Given that group agents can be potentially powerful entities, they should be organized in such a way as to respect their members' rights and freedoms, or, as we shall say, to give their members certain 'spheres of control'. Members may be entitled to these spheres of control for a number of reasons, for instance because certain issues affect them privately in ways that merit individual self-determination, or because of their expertise on certain issues. How can a group agent be made to respect such individual spheres of control?

Our discussion of this question is divided into three sections. In the first, we formulate the control desideratum. In the second, we discuss some of the difficulties that arise in designing an organizational structure for a group agent that satisfies it. And in the third, we outline some broader lessons about collective organization that emerge from this discussion.

6.1 Formulating the control desideratum

The need for control

The fact that group agents, particularly those that are effective in the pursuit of their goals, can be powerful presences in the social world should be fairly evident. The power of group agents may stem from their political, cultural, economic, or civic roles, from their financial and other assets, or simply from the fact that what they do can greatly affect the lives of their members and others. A much-discussed documentary film, 'The Corporation' (2003) (see also the book by Bakan 2004), graphically portrays the power of group agents, in the form of commercial corporations, and the way they often act like steamrollers in the social world, ruthlessly pursuing their own goals and disregarding the interests of their members and others. The film's central claim is that if we view corporations as persons and assess their social behavior according to the criteria employed by clinical psychologists, then many corporations exhibit precisely the characteristics usually associated with psychopathy. Going through a diagnostic checklist, the film suggests that a corporation's personality may display self-interest, amorality, callous and deceitful behavior, a willingness to breach social and legal norms to advance the organization's interest, a lack of any feelings of guilt, and at the same time the ability to mimic empathy and altruism.

Whether or not real-world group agents generally conform to this bleak picture, the importance of imposing certain constraints on them should be clear. We will say more about the relationship between group agents and the outside world in the third part of this book. For now, let us focus on their power vis-à-vis their members. Think of the grip a state has on its citizens, a corporation on its employees, a university on its students and faculty, a church on its members, and so on. What, then, is required if we want to ensure that the members of a group agent retain a certain degree of control?

There is one sense in which members always have control over the group agent on our account: what the group agent thinks and does is always determined by what the members think and do. According to the supervenience thesis we have defended, the group's attitudes and actions are a function of the members' attitudes and actions. This, however, is not the sense of control we have in mind when we talk about *protecting* the members' control in relation to the group agent. First of all, as we have seen, the supervenience relation between the members' attitudes and actions and those of the group can be so complex that the group agent may sometimes think or do something that few, if any, members individually support. And secondly, the supervenience of the group's attitudes and actions on those of its members is entirely consistent with some individuals being systematically overruled on issues that matter to them a lot. Accordingly, the kind of control that individual members must be able to exercise in order to enjoy effective protection has to be stronger. It is not enough for individuals to be able to *contribute* to what the group thinks or does on the issues that particularly matter to them. They must be individually *decisive* on those issues. Roughly speaking, we say that an individual is 'decisive' on a particular issue if he or she is able to determine fully – and not merely in conjunction with other individuals – how this issue is settled.[94] We give a more precise definition below.

What are the kinds of issues on which it is plausible to grant individuals such control? We can distinguish between at least two such kinds of issues (see also Dietrich and List 2008b). First, there are those issues that significantly affect the personal opportunities of some individuals, for example whether those individuals are required, allowed, or forbidden, to do certain things that fall intuitively into their private spheres. Here one might require that, in order to protect those individuals' personal autonomy, the issues in question should belong to their individual spheres of control. And second, there are those issues on which some individuals have a special expertise, for example something on which they have exclusive information or insight. Again, one might require that these issues should belong to those individuals' spheres of control, this time in the interest of taking their expertise into account. In the first case, the individuals' spheres of control can be justified in terms of what we often call their 'autonomy rights'; in the second, in terms of what we may describe as their 'expertise rights'. The precise assignment of issues to each of these categories would of course require a more detailed account, which is outside the scope of this book.

Clearly, both kinds of issues on which there are grounds for giving individuals control – those on which the individuals' personal autonomy is at stake, and those on which some individuals have special expertise – can be frequently found in group agents, though the details depend on the group and context in question. There are also important connections between the two justifications for individual control: autonomy and expertise. On the Austrian approach to economics, associated with Hayek (e.g. 1945) and others, for example, a key justification for respecting the autonomy of individuals on a number of issues – such as whether to engage in certain private market transactions – is that individuals are regarded as experts on issues concerning themselves.

So far, we have seen that on certain issues within the realm of a group agent's attitudes and actions there can be good reasons – such as autonomy and expertise – for granting some group members individual control, in the sense of making them individually decisive. How can we express this desideratum more formally?

The definition of control

As noted, we employ a definition of control in terms of 'decisiveness'. Given that a group agent's actions are usually mediated by its attitudes – its preferences and judgments – we take those attitudes, rather than the group's actions themselves, to be the targets of the relevant individuals' control. But, with suitable modifications, a similar analysis to the one we are about to give could also be framed in terms of direct control over the group's actions. With this qualification in place, what is our definition of control? We say that an individual 'exercises control' on the group's attitude on proposition 'p' just in case he or she is decisive on it, where decisiveness is understood in terms of the conjunction of two conditions:

Positive decisiveness. If the individual has a positive attitude on 'p' – that is, he or she judges that p, or prefers that p, depending on whether we are dealing with judgments or preferences – then the group also has a positive attitude on 'p'.

Negative decisiveness. If the individual has a negative attitude on 'p' – that is, he or she does not judge that p, or does not prefer that p, again depending on whether we are dealing with judgments or preferences – then the group also has a negative attitude on 'p'.

If an individual exercises control on 'p', under this definition, the group's attitude on 'p' will coincide with his or her individual attitude: The group accepts – judges, prefers – 'p' if and only if the individual does. Thus control, at the very least, ensures a 'match' between the individual's attitude on a given proposition and that of the group.

Notice, however, that this definition still leaves many important questions open. Perhaps an individual is decisive on a particular issue only when circumstances are favorable – e.g. when others are well disposed towards this individual – but not more generally. Or perhaps an individual is decisive on a particular issue only when he or she holds a certain set of individual attitudes – in the most extreme case, those attitudes that would have prevailed anyway – but not otherwise. Until we answer these questions in more detail, our initial definition of control will remain only a definition scheme, which requires further spelling out.

The 'content-' and 'context-independence' dimensions of decisiveness

So how can we spell out our definition of control more precisely?[95] First of all, our two conditions for control – positive and negative decisiveness – each involve a conditional of the form 'if the individual has such and such an attitude on "p", then so does the group'. We thus need to say more about the interpretation of this conditional: Should it be interpreted narrowly as a material conditional, or more demandingly as a subjunctive one?[96] On the material interpretation, the conditional is true whenever, in actual circumstances, its antecedent is false or its consequent is true, whereas on a subjunctive interpretation, it is true only (and precisely) if the consequent is true in *all* nearest possible circumstances in which the antecedent is true. Clearly, the subjunctive interpretation is much more demanding than the material one.[97]

Secondly, even when the conditionals in the definitions of positive and negative decisiveness are true (on whichever interpretation we adopt), this may be the case only contingently, under actual background circumstances, or more robustly, across a broader range of counterfactual as well as actual circumstances. This raises the question of which of these – the contingent or robust truth of the conditionals – is required for control.

These two questions – on the material versus subjunctive interpretation of the relevant conditionals, and on their contingent versus robust truth – correspond very roughly to two dimensions of decisiveness:[98] first, whether or not an individual's decisiveness on 'p' depends on the *content* of his or her attitude on 'p', such as whether the attitude is actually a positive or a negative one; and second, whether or not his or her decisiveness depends on the external *context* of the attitude, as given, for example, by the attitudes (and actions) of others.

To see the connection, let us begin by looking at our first question about the interpretation of control: whether to interpret the conditionals in our definition of positive and negative decisiveness as material conditionals, or as subjunctive ones. On the material interpretation, one of the two conditionals is always vacuously true. The individual either has a positive attitude on 'p', or a negative one. If the individual has a positive attitude on 'p', the conditional in the definition of negative decisiveness is vacuously met, since its antecedent – 'the individual has a negative attitude on "p"' – is false, making the conditional automatically true on the material interpretation. And if the individual has a negative attitude on 'p', the conditional in the definition of positive decisiveness is met for similar reasons: this time, its antecedent is false. Thus, on the material interpretation of the conditionals, an individual can be said to be 'decisive' on the group's attitude on proposition 'p' even when the match between the individual's attitude and that of the group is entirely dependent on the actual content of the attitude – for example, its being a positive attitude rather than a negative one.

Suppose, on the one other hand, we take decisiveness to require that even if the content of the individual's attitude were different – say, he or she had a negative rather than a positive attitude on 'p' – the individual's attitude would still prevail at the group level. Then we must adopt a subjunctive interpretation of the two conditionals, requiring us to look not only at what happens when the individual holds his or her *actual* attitude on 'p' but also at what would happen if the individual's attitude on 'p' were different. Call this the 'content-independence' dimension of decisiveness (Pettit 2001a; List 2004a).

If we were to affirm the view rejected by Berlin (1969) – albeit in the language of 'freedom' rather than 'decisiveness' – that someone can make themselves 'decisive' on some issue simply by adapting his or her attitude on it, then we would have a reason for not requiring content-independence, and we would be justified in adopting the material interpretation of our two conditionals. If, on the other hand, we agree with Berlin (1969) that, to be genuinely decisive on some issue, one has to be decisive on it independently of what attitude one actually holds, then we must impose the content-independence requirement and interpret the two conditionals subjunctively. Just as Berlin would say that adaptive preferences cannot make an agent free when he or she is in fact externally constrained, so it seems plausible to say that an individual cannot gain control on some issue simply by adjusting his or her attitudes on it.

Next, consider our second question about the interpretation of control: whether it is enough for control that our two conditionals – the positive and the negative one – are true contingently, in actual circumstances, or whether they must be true robustly, across a broader range of actual and counterfactual circumstances. Suppose we demand only the contingent truth of these conditionals. This means that in the actual or nearest possible circumstances in which the individual has a positive attitude on 'p', so does the group, and in the actual or nearest possible circumstances in which he or she has a negative attitude on 'p', so does the group as well. There is no implication as to what would happen if circumstances were different from these actual or nearest possible ones, such as if other individuals were to change their attitudes or certain other contextual factors were different. On this interpretation of positive and negative decisiveness, an individual can count as 'decisive' on the group's attitude on proposition 'p' even when his or her decisiveness is entirely contingent on the attitudes or goodwill of others, or on the presence of other favorable conditions.

If, on the other hand, we think that decisiveness requires more than this, namely decisiveness even in the face of adversity in the general context, we must require not merely the contingent truth of our two conditionals but their robust truth across a broader range of circumstances. Call this the 'context-independence' dimension of decisiveness (Pettit 2001a; List 2004a).

Again, an example from the discussion of freedom is helpful to illustrate the idea. Imagine a slave who happens to have a particularly benevolent master. The master lets the slave do as the slave pleases, thus allowing the slave's attitudes to prevail on a large number of issues. We certainly find that the slave is *content*-independently decisive here: If he or she forms a positive attitude on some relevant issue, this positive attitude prevails; and if he or she forms a negative one, it prevails too. But all of this is contingent on the master's goodwill. The master still owns the slave and is entirely free to change his mind at any time, and to suppress the slave's attitudes and actions at his discretion. The slave clearly lacks *context*-independent decisiveness. If we are nonetheless prepared to say that the slave is 'in control' over the relevant issues, despite his or her lack of context-independent decisiveness, we are thereby committing ourselves to the contingent interpretation of positive and negative decisiveness. By contrast, if we believe that control would require decisiveness in a stronger, context-independent sense, which the slave lacks, this speaks in favor of the robust interpretation.

It should be clear that different accounts of control differ in where they locate the notion of decisiveness on the dimensions of content- and context-independence. As we explain below, we adopt a relatively demanding interpretation of control for the purposes of our analysis, making not only content-independence but also some degree of context-independence a requirement of control. However, we also show that giving multiple individual members of a group agent control in this sense is harder to achieve than one might initially expect, and we are faced with some difficult trade-offs between satisfying the control desideratum and achieving other objectives. But before we turn to these questions, it is useful to say a few words about the relationship between the notion of control, as employed here, and the notion of freedom, as discussed in political philosophy. We have already hinted at this relationship briefly in our discussion of content- and context-independent decisiveness.

Control and freedom

The different interpretations of control we have identified are closely related to different interpretations of freedom in political philosophy. Let us begin with the weakest interpretation of control, according to which neither content- nor context-independent decisiveness is required for control. From our discussion above, it seems that this interpretation does not really merit the label 'control' in any ordinary sense, but if we set this linguistic point aside for the moment, we find that the present limiting case of control has a counterpart in the debate on freedom: freedom most narrowly construed as (actual) opportunity. Here the idea is that someone is free to do whatever they can actually do in current circumstances. On this extremely narrow definition, someone is free to do x simply if he or she is able to do x here and now. It does not require that he or she is also able not to do x, or to do x in different circumstances. Most political philosophers agree that, just as the weakest definition of control does not really merit the label 'control', so freedom in this extremely narrow, actual-opportunity-based sense does not really merit the label 'freedom'. Yet, the concept is useful – perhaps even indispensable – for a number of theoretical and applied purposes, for instance if we want to assess someone's actual opportunities in a precisely specified situation, as conceptually distinct from his or her freedom in a broader sense.[99] For this reason, the interpretation of freedom as opportunity is employed extensively in the literature on the measurement of freedom (for an overview, see, e.g. Carter 1999). Among political theorists, it may only have been endorsed by Hobbes (Pettit 2008b, Ch. 6).

Once we include the requirement of content-independent decisiveness in our definition of control, however, its natural counterpart becomes the negative interpretation of freedom, as famously introduced by Berlin (1969): freedom as non-interference. According to this conception, someone is free, for example in the choice between x and not-x, if he or she is not subject to any interference in this choice, meaning that, irrespective of whether he or she wants to do x or not-x, there are no external obstacles in the way – or at least no deliberate, intentional ones.[100] As in our definition of control in terms of content-independent decisiveness, the agent's freedom here is not dependent on whether he or she actually chooses to do x or not-x, but it may depend on other contextual factors. Like control as content-independent decisiveness, negative freedom, in Berlin's sense, need not be robust. Provided the master in our earlier example is sufficiently benevolent, the slave may indeed count as negatively free.

Finally, if we also add the requirement of context-independent decisiveness to our definition of control, we are in a conceptual terrain that corresponds roughly to the republican interpretation of freedom (Pettit 1997; Skinner 1998; Pettit 2001a; List 2004a; 2006c; Pettit 2008b). On this interpretation, neither the opportunity to do something in actual circumstances, nor the absence of interference is sufficient for freedom. Rather, freedom is taken to require non-domination, the absence of anyone else's *capacity* to interfere – specifically, to interfere arbitrarily – whether or not they actually choose to exercise this capacity. This means that someone's freedom to do x or not-x must be independent not only of the actual content of his or her choice but also of any favorable circumstances or the goodwill of others.[101] The agent in question will count as free in the republican sense only if the freedom is sufficiently robust; say, it is entrenched in some constitutional arrangements (on the conceptual connection between republican freedom and the rule of law, see also List 2006c).

This sequence of different interpretations of freedom, like that of different interpretations of control, ranges from most contingent to most robust. Since we are interested in finding an organizational structure for a group agent that respects the desideratum of individual control, it makes sense to ask for control in an organizationally entrenched, robust sense; and the use of a demanding interpretation of control, which corresponds broadly to republican freedom, seems warranted. Let us now turn to the question of how individual control in this sense can be secured.

6.2 Satisfying the control desideratum

The framework

As before, we use the theoretical framework developed in the first part of this book, and ask what the organizational structure of a group agent must look like in order to satisfy the control desideratum along the lines formulated in the first section of this chapter. Since our definition of control has taken the group's attitudes, rather than its actions themselves, to be the targets of the individuals' control – the reason being that the group's actions are usually mediated by its attitudes – we can focus, once more, on the part of the organizational structure that is easiest to model theoretically: its underlying aggregation function. Accordingly, our question is the following: what aggregation function must a group agent implement in order to satisfy the control desideratum, together with other desirable conditions?

To answer this question, let us explicitly restate the control desideratum as a condition on the aggregation function, adapting our definition of positive and negative decisiveness above. For each individual member of the group, we define the individual's 'sphere of control' to be the set of those propositions on the agenda over which the individual is to be given control (typically, together with their negations). This definition by itself does not imply anything about how large or small each individual's sphere of control is supposed to be. This needs to be specified later. For some (in principle also all) individuals, it could even be empty. We say that the aggregation function meets the 'control desideratum' just in case it satisfies the following condition:

> **Control desideratum.** For every admissible profile of attitudes across group members, every individual group member, and every proposition 'p' within that individual's sphere of control, the following two conditionals hold:
>
> - If the individual has a positive attitude on 'p', then so does the group.
> - If the individual has a negative attitude on 'p', then so does the group.

Thus formulated, the control desideratum requires that every individual's sphere of control – whatever it is – be respected, in the sense that the individual is both positively and negatively decisive on every proposition in his or her sphere of control. The quantification over *all* admissible profiles of attitudes across group members – crucially, including ones in which both the content and the context of each individual's attitudes vary – ensures a strong (that is, robust and subjunctive) interpretation of positive and negative decisiveness.

In the next few subsections, we discuss what is involved in satisfying this desideratum. The technical results to be presented are based on Dietrich and List's work on

'A Liberal Paradox for Judgment Aggregation' (2008b), generalizing Sen's classic work (1970b) to the case of attitude aggregation.

Reconciling individual control with group agency

We begin by asking whether satisfaction of the control desideratum is at least in principle consistent with the achievement of group agency. As before, we take the conjunction of two conditions on the aggregation function – namely universal domain and collective rationality – to be baseline conditions for group agency. Following the terminology of Chapter 3 in a slightly reworded but equivalent form, let us again call this conjunction 'robust group rationality':

> **Robust group rationality.** The aggregation function is defined so as to produce consistent and complete group attitudes on the propositions on the agenda for any possible profile of consistent and complete member attitudes on these propositions.

Can the control desideratum be satisfied in the presence of robust group rationality?

> **Theorem.** There exists an aggregation function satisfying robust group rationality and the control desideratum if and only if the spheres of control across all the individuals are mutually consistent (Dietrich and List 2008b).

What does 'mutual consistency' of different individuals' spheres of control mean? Informally, it means that, whatever attitudes any individual holds on the propositions within his or her sphere of control, these do not logically conflict with the attitudes held by any other individuals on propositions within their own spheres of control. More formally, the spheres of control across individuals are called 'mutually consistent' just in case they are given by mutually logically independent sets of propositions.

The result is quite intuitive. If, for example, proposition 'p' is in one individual's sphere of control, then proposition 'p and q' cannot consistently be in that of another. If it were, then it could happen that the first individual held a negative attitude on 'p' while the second held a positive one on 'p and q', so that, to respect both individuals' spheres of control, the group would have to affirm 'p and q' and reject 'p', a violation of robust group rationality. On the other hand, if different individuals' spheres of control are given by mutually independent sets of propositions, then there cannot be any conflicts between different individuals' exercise of their control. In the philosophical literature on freedom and rights, constraints of this kind have become known as constraints on the 'compossibility' of different individuals' rights and freedoms (e.g. Steiner 1994).

However natural the present result may seem, it poses a significant challenge for the satisfaction of the control desideratum by a group agent. After all, it may be difficult to assign propositions to different individuals' spheres of control in such a way as to avoid the occurrence of any interdependencies whatsoever, as required in order to achieve the mutual consistency of these spheres of control. In the interconnected world we inhabit, it can easily happen that some of the issues that intuitively fall into one individual's sphere of autonomy, for example, are connected with issues that equally intuitively fall into the spheres of others. Exceptions may be relatively trivial private issues such as whether someone sleeps on their back or on their side at night, but these are usually outside a group agent's agenda anyway. Similarly, in an epistemic setting in which some individuals' expertise is to be respected, it is not guaranteed that different individuals' spheres of expertise can be neatly demarcated in such a way as to ensure their complete mutual independence.

One response to the existence of interdependencies between different individuals' spheres of control might be to lower the standards of control, by making each individual's control conditional upon certain configurations of attitudes among the other individuals (in the contexts of rights and freedoms, Dowding and van Hees 2003 made a proposal along these lines). But to do so would be to weaken substantially the requirement of context-independence which – we have suggested – is an important ingredient in the idea of control; we revisit this point in the last section of this chapter.

Another response might be to shrink the individuals' spheres of control so as to avoid any interdependencies between them. But this will not necessarily respect our normative criteria for the assignment of issues to the individuals' spheres of control on the grounds of their autonomy or expertise; we also say more about this in the last section of the chapter.

It should be clear, then, that we are faced with a significant challenge. As we show in the next subsection, this challenge is even amplified if we impose a further plausible condition on the aggregation function.

An impossibility result

The conditions on the aggregation function we have required so far in this chapter are still rather minimal. We have only required robust group rationality, which seems non-negotiable in the context of group agency, and the control desideratum, albeit interpreted in a very robust manner. What happens if we add a further, seemingly plausible condition to these two conditions, demanding responsiveness of the group's attitudes to those of the members on propositions on which there is unanimous agreement?

Proposition-wise unanimity preservation. If all individuals hold the same attitude on proposition 'p', then this unanimous agreement is preserved at the group level.[102]

Proposition-wise unanimity preservation can be seen as a requirement of collective democratic control. While the majority principle may be too strong – as we have seen, the group's attitudes cannot generally be determined by majority voting if we wish to ensure collective rationality – proposition-wise unanimity preservation might at first sight be regarded as a bottom-line democratic principle. If even unanimous agreement among the group members could be overruled, this would appear to go against the idea of a democratically organized group. Surprisingly, however, proposition-wise unanimity preservation is inconsistent with the control desideratum together with robust group rationality, as soon as there are certain logical connections between the propositions on the agenda and more than one individual has a non-trivial sphere of control. Formally, let us call the group's agenda 'conditionally connected' if any two propositions on it are conditionally interdependent. (Roughly speaking, this means that, for any 'p' and 'q' on the agenda, one of 'p' or 'not p' is inconsistent with one of 'q' or 'not q', conditional upon some other subset of the agenda that by itself is consistent with each member of the pair.)

Theorem. Suppose the propositions on the group's agenda are conditionally connected, and two or more individuals each have at least one proposition–negation pair in their spheres of control. Then there exists no aggregation function satisfying robust group rationality, proposition-wise unanimity preservation, and the control desideratum (Dietrich and List 2008b).

Some examples will help to illustrate this result, though the proof of the theorem (in Dietrich and List 2008b, from which the examples are drawn) is entirely general and independent of the examples. The first example concerns an expert committee giving advice on the health risks of air pollution in a big city. Suppose that the experts have to make judgments on the following propositions (and their negations):

- The average particle pollution level is above 50 micrograms per cubic meter air (proposition 'p').
- If the average particle pollution level is above this amount, then residents have an increased risk of respiratory disease (proposition 'if p then q').
- Residents have an increased risk of respiratory disease (proposition 'q').

All three propositions are complex factual propositions on which the experts may reasonably disagree. Furthermore, the propositions relate to different areas of expertise. Proposition 'p' is a matter for scientists specializing in the physics of air pollution, while proposition 'if p then q' falls into the area of medicine and physiology. Proposition 'q', finally, draws on both of these areas. In a committee with representatives of these different areas, it therefore seems plausible to give the physicist (or perhaps several of them) the expertise right to determine the committee's judgment on 'p' and to give the medical researcher (again perhaps several of them) the expertise right to determine the collective judgment on 'if p then q'. Since 'q', finally, is not restricted to either of these areas of expertise, respecting the experts' unanimous judgment on 'q' seems reasonable as well.

Notice, however, what can happen: if the experts' individual judgments are as shown in Table 6.1, each of 'p' and 'if p then q' are collectively accepted in virtue of the appropriate expertise rights, while 'q' is collectively rejected, and its negation collectively accepted, in virtue of the experts' unanimous judgment on it. The resulting collective judgments – the collective acceptance of 'p', 'if p then q' and 'not q' – are clearly inconsistent.

Of course, one might object that the conflict arises only for this particular combination of individual judgments and that it would go away if judgments were different. Further, one might argue that the physicist(s) on the committee ought to defer to the

Table 6.1: A simple illustration of a conflict between expertise rights and proposition-wise unanimity preservation

	Pollution above 50 micrograms per cubic meter air? ('p')	If pollution above this amount, then increased risk of disease? ('if p then q')	Increased risk of disease? ('q')
Physicist(s)	True	False	False
Medical researchers(s)	False	True	False

medical researcher(s) on the proposition within the other's area of expertise, rather than disagree with them, and vice versa; we return to this point when we discuss escape routes from the impossibility. However, our claim is not that expert judgments on some propositions will *always* conflict with unanimous judgments on others – indeed, the conflict will not arise in more favorable circumstances. Our claim is only that robust group rationality, proposition-wise unanimity preservation, and the control desideratum, in its present robust form, are mutually inconsistent. Once we are prepared to relax robustness, either of the group's rationality or of the control desideratum, the impossibility can be avoided, albeit at some cost, as discussed below.

The second example concerns the case of autonomy rights rather than expertise rights and is inspired by Sen's classic example (1970b) of the liberal paradox (developed in the present form by Dietrich and List 2008b). A book lovers' club seeks to take a coherent stand on how to deal with a book that runs the risk of causing outrage, such as *Lady Chatterley's Lover* or something more recent that the reader may wish to substitute. For expositional simplicity, suppose the club has two members, whom, following Sen, we call Lewd and Prude, though the example easily generalizes. The club seeks to form preferences in the sense introduced in Chapter 2, on three propositions (and their negations):

- Lewd reads the book (proposition 'l').
- Prude reads the book (proposition 'p').
- If Lewd reads the book, then so does Prude (proposition 'if l then p').

It is reasonable to assume that proposition 'l' should fall into Lewd's sphere of control, while proposition 'p' should fall into Prude's. Can the club as a whole simultaneously satisfy robust group rationality, proposition-wise unanimity preservation, and the control desideratum? Consider the individual preferences shown in Table 6.2.

Lewd prefers to read the book himself, as he expects to derive pleasure from its graphic nature. But his pleasure will be further increased by the thought of Prude reading the book as well; and so he prefers that, if he, Lewd, reads the book, then so should Prude. Prude, by contrast, abhors the idea of reading the book and prefers that neither of the two should read it. But in the event of Lewd reading the book, Prude

Table 6.2: A simple illustration of a conflict between autonomy rights and proposition-wise unanimity preservation

	Lewd reads the book ('l')	Prude reads the book ('p')	If Lewd reads the book, then so does Prude ('if l then p')
Lewd	Preferred	Preferred	Preferred
Prude	Dispreferred	Dispreferred	Preferred

wishes to have an idea of what dangerous material Lewd is exposed to, and so he prefers that, conditional on that event, he, Prude, should read it too.

What should the club as a whole prefer? Lewd's autonomy rights would dictate a collective preference in favor of 'l', Prude's autonomy rights a collective preference against 'p', and proposition-wise unanimity preservation a collective preference in favor of 'if l then p': an overall inconsistent set of propositions, which cannot be simultaneously realized. Once again, we have identified a profile of individual attitudes that illustrates the conflict between robust group rationality, the control desideratum, and proposition-wise unanimity preservation.

The same disclaimers as in the earlier example apply. In particular, background conditions are not entirely favorable here, as the two individuals' preferences are in an intuitive (and also technical) sense 'meddlesome': each individual has preferences that directly affect the other's sphere of autonomy. But arguing that it would be sufficient to satisfy the control desideratum only in more favorable circumstances would be to weaken the requirement of robustness. Let us therefore turn to the more general question of how the present impossibility result can be avoided.

Escape routes from the impossibility

We have seen that the control desideratum is surprisingly difficult to satisfy, even if the only other condition imposed on the aggregation function is robust group rationality. And once we add the further condition of proposition-wise unanimity preservation, we are faced with an outright impossibility, assuming that the propositions on the agenda are conditionally connected and two or more individuals have a non-trivial sphere of control.

In principle, of course, each of the conditions generating this impossibility could be relaxed. As already noted, however, robust group rationality seems non-negotiable in the context of group agency, although there may be special cases in which the universal-domain component of robust group rationality could be replaced with something less demanding, as discussed in Chapter 2. But in the context of group agency we certainly wouldn't wish to drop the demand for group rationality altogether. So let us focus on the other escape routes from the impossibility.

First route: Relaxing proposition-wise unanimity preservation and thereby
reducing control in the democratic, unanimitarian sense

Although proposition-wise unanimity preservation appears to be a plausible desideratum of democratic control, the impossibility result we have identified may prompt us
to reconsider it. If we try to resolve the problem by relaxing proposition-wise
unanimity preservation while keeping the control desideratum, we are thereby privileging individual control over democratic, unanimitarian control. If the individual
spheres of control thus protected represent individual autonomy rights, this solution
may seem compelling, especially from a liberal perspective with its emphasis on
individual autonomy.

The present escape route from the impossibility corresponds roughly to a response
given by Nozick (1974) and others to Sen's classic liberal paradox (1970b): the idea of
rights as side constraints. According to this idea, a liberal form of social organization
must first respect individual rights, here individual autonomy rights, before turning to
other values, in the present example, those of democratic, unanimitarian control.
Ultimately, it is a normative question which kind of control matters more: individual
or unanimitarian; and different normative theories give different answers to this
question.

If, on the other hand, the individual spheres of control represent expertise rights, the
issue becomes an epistemic one. The precise details of the judgmental task at hand, the
nature of the agenda and the epistemic context of the individuals will determine
whether the group can achieve more reliable judgments by respecting expertise rights
or by respecting unanimous judgments across the group as a whole – or perhaps by
opting for some mixed approach. There is no general one-size-fits-all answer to the
question of whether or not it is epistemically advantageous to keep proposition-wise
unanimity preservation; the answer will vary from case to case.

Second route: Relaxing the control desideratum and thereby making individual
control less robust

We have already pointed out that the profiles of individual attitudes illustrating
the conflict between the control desideratum and proposition-wise unanimity preservation in our examples capture less than favorable circumstances. By contrast, if the
control desideratum is restricted to cases in which individual attitudes are relatively
favorable – that is, if a certain amount of context-*dependence* within individual control is
permitted – the conflict goes away. One example of a favorable context is given by the
possibility that whenever a proposition is in some individual's sphere of control, then
all other individuals defer to that individual's attitude on the proposition in question,
rather than forming their own attitudes on it that might deviate from it. Such attitudes
can be described as 'deferential' (in the expertise case) or as 'empathetic/respectful' (in
the autonomy case) (Dietrich and List 2008b).[103]

Another example of a favorable context is given by something less demanding than deferential or empathetic/respectful attitudes on the part of the whole group: namely by the possibility of 'agnosticism' or 'tolerance'. Here the individuals do not form any attitudes on propositions that lie within others' spheres of control, and, equally crucially, they make sure that their attitudes on other propositions do not logically constrain the attitudes on the propositions on which they reserve judgment.

It is clear that if the control desideratum is restricted to such more favorable circumstances, it no longer creates any difficulties in the presence of proposition-wise unanimity preservation and robust group rationality (for a formal proof, see Dietrich and List 2008b). The cost of this solution is a certain sacrifice of robustness. Control in the original content- and context-independent sense cannot be fully attained within a group agent on this approach. However, we return to this route in the last section of this chapter and suggest that the sacrifice in formal robustness that it involves need not always compromise robustness in a more substantive sense. In short, under the right conditions, the present escape route from the impossibility may be consistent with the spirit of the republican interpretation of freedom.

Third route: Shrinking the individual spheres of control or 'disentangling' the agenda

A third, though only rather hypothetical escape route from the impossibility, consists in shrinking the individuals' spheres of control or 'disentangling' the agenda, so as to remove the relevant conditional dependencies between propositions. As we have seen, a necessary condition for the impossibility result to arise was that the propositions on the group's agenda are conditionally connected, and that two or more individuals each have at least one proposition–negation pair in their spheres of control. Clearly, if all but one individual have an empty sphere of control, the impossibility goes away.

But we have already noted in response to our first compossibility problem that shrinking the individuals' spheres of control so as to avoid interdependencies between them will not generally respect our normative criteria for when certain propositions ought to belong to someone's sphere of control, for instance for autonomy reasons or expertise reasons. Now if we tried to shrink the individuals' spheres of control even further – not only eliminating any interdependencies between them but effectively eliminating the control of all but one individual altogether – we would clearly run into frequent violations of those normative criteria. After all, the mere fact that there is a conflict between the control desideratum and other formal conditions does not make the need for individual control go away.

Similarly, redefining the agenda so as to ensure that there are no conditional connections between any two propositions cannot generally be a viable solution to our problem. If all individuals lived on separate Robinson Crusoe islands, each faced with his or her own agenda that is wholly disconnected from anyone else's agenda, then such a solution might be a possibility. Again, if each individual's sphere of control is restricted to those private matters that can be completely insulated from the rest of society, such as the earlier example of sleeping on one's back versus sleeping on one's side, the present route may have some plausibility.[104] But we do not need to say much in order to persuade the reader that the context of a group agent is not generally like this, and so this third escape route is only of limited help.

6.3 Broader lessons

What broader lessons about collective organization can we learn from this discussion? Satisfying the control desideratum within a group agent – that is, ensuring that its individual members retain certain 'spheres of control' – is harder to achieve than one might have expected. Even if we do not insist on securing control in the democratic, unanimitarian sense as well, we have seen that the control desideratum can be reconciled with robust group rationality only if the members' spheres of control exhibit no mutual interdependencies – a difficult requirement in the interconnected setting of a group agent. And if we do insist on the additional requirement of unanimitarian control, we are faced with a full-blown impossibility result, typically forcing all but one individual's spheres of control to be empty.

This problem – albeit unfortunate – may be tolerable in voluntary associations, that is, group agents that people can freely join or leave. To the extent that members retain a genuine option of exit from such a group, they may be taken to consent implicitly to whatever loss of control their membership entails (Hirschman 1970). But the option of exit is not available in all group agents, particularly in the kind of group agent that the state constitutes and similarly in other organizations that members have only limited opportunities to leave. Although a state may formally allow members to leave, this right of exit is not generally effective, since the earth is exhaustively occupied by states and other states may not admit those who have permission to leave. Thus we are bound to be concerned about whether the results of the last section mean that membership in a powerful group agent such as a state entails a serious loss of individual control.

We address those concerns, though only briefly, in this final section. We attempt to show that the political implications of the results discussed are not quite as dire as they may seem. Specifically, the results depend on a very demanding notion of individual control and do not rule out individual control in a less demanding sense, which still preserves the basic idea of control. In particular, we look at two plausible strategies by which the citizens of a state can enjoy such less demanding control under suitable democratic arrangements; in principle, those strategies carry over to other group agents as well. While associated with independent bodies of informal political thought – in particular, republican thought – they represent ways, broadly, of exploring the second and third escapes routes from the impossibility discussed in the last section.

Firstly, there are ways of weakening the 'formal' robustness of the control desideratum in such a way as to avoid an impossibility result without weakening its *de facto* 'substantive' robustness. And secondly, the desideratum of individual control can be achieved in a looser, more indirect manner, through securing the non-arbitrariness, transparency, and democratic accountability of the group's decision making – in short, through securing the 'contestability' of the group agent vis-à-vis its members. We now address these strategies in turn.

Ensuring substantive robustness while relaxing formal robustness

As we have mentioned, the requirements of content- and context-independence in our account of control are associated broadly with the republican interpretation of freedom. Under this interpretation, freedom in a choice between x and not-x requires the absence of any interference, regardless of whether x or not-x is chosen: regardless of the content of the choice. And equally it requires the absence of any interference, regardless of certain variations in the context. So far, we have taken context-independence to require independence of the attitudes of others, capturing the idea that an individual should be decisive on the propositions in the relevant sphere, regardless of the attitudes held by others. But while this conception of context-independence is clear and attractive for technical reasons, it is perhaps stronger than what is strictly required in republican thought.

Suppose someone has a choice between x and not-x. The agent's freedom in that choice certainly requires that he or she be able to choose x, if disposed to do so, and equally able to choose not-x, if this is what he or she is disposed to do. This is the requirement of content-independent control. Each option, in a metaphor from Isaiah Berlin (1969, xlviii), should be an open door: there should be no one who locks it and – to allow for the case of obstacles that do not actually prevent the choice – no one who jams it. When republicans argue that the choice should in addition be independent of certain contextual variations, what they have in mind is the following. Not only should the door be open, or the options accessible. Whether the door remains open – that is, unlocked and unjammed – should not depend on the goodwill of others. There should be no doorkeepers who can lock or jam the door if they wish to do so.

The context-independence thereby required is intuitively quite substantive, ensuring that when someone exercises his choice between x and not-x, he or she does so without having to depend on anyone else's explicit or implicit permission. It means that in this choice the agent is not subject to the will of another, in particular, their will as to what he or she should do. But while this context-independence is substantive, it falls well short of the stronger kind of context-independence supposed earlier: the requirement of robust control across *all* possible combinations of attitudes held by others. The republican understanding of context-independence – expressed in suitably refined terms – requires only that a person's control be robust over variations in others' attitudes *towards this person*, but not that it be robust over the attitudes that members of society hold more generally.

Suppose, for example, that x is an act of voting for a particular party in an election – say a socialist party. Clearly, this option will be available to a given voter only insofar as the attitudes of people in society are sufficient to ensure that this party remains in electoral contention. Republican freedom and control do not require that this option remain accessible even in the event that attitudes change so that the party in question ceases to exist. Similarly, suppose that x is an act of buying shares in a particular corporation. This option will be available only insofar as the attitudes of others in society are such as to support the continued existence of a stock market. But republican freedom and control do not require that this option remain accessible even across variations of context in which people's attitudes shift and there is no longer a stock market.

Republican freedom and control are robust in a substantive sense, guarding individuals against the ill will of others, including those others who are currently well disposed and are likely to remain well disposed. It means, in a traditional way of speaking, that individuals are not at the mercy of others. But this substantive robustness does not require the full formal robustness that would guard individuals equally against the endless number of ways the attitudes across society might change, any more than it has to guard individuals against the endless number of ways the natural world might turn hostile.[105]

If republican freedom and control do not require full formal robustness over variations in people's attitudes, then that means that the negative findings of the last section are not as threatening as they may have seemed. As we have noted, the identified impossibility result goes away if the control desideratum is required to hold not for every logically possible profile of rational attitudes across group members but only for a more limited range of profiles. While requiring 'respectful' or 'deferential' attitudes among others may amount to the kind of goodwill republicans would not like an individual's control to depend upon, the weaker requirement of what we described as 'tolerant' or 'agnostic' attitudes, or other even less demanding such requirements, may cause no particular problems from a republican perspective. This is especially so if, along with the group's formal organizational structure, the group – in particular, the state – manages to nurture an informal organizational culture that reliably promotes the kinds of general attitudes needed for securing individual control.

In this case, one can plausibly say that, even though the formal robustness of the control desideratum has been weakened – in the sense that the individuals' decisiveness on the propositions in their spheres is not guaranteed across all possible counterfactual circumstances – its *de facto* substantive robustness is still secured. Individuals will be decisive on the relevant propositions across those circumstances that matter: namely those that are likely to arise given the group's reliable organizational culture. And in exercising their control, individuals are unlikely to depend on the goodwill of others.

How could a group agent be organized so as to bring about that outcome? In particular, how could a state be organized so that individuals do not depend on anyone's goodwill for making choices on propositions in their spheres of control? How could such a powerful organization not have the status of a doorkeeper that could lock or jam the door against its members?

The traditional republican response to this challenge has been to institute a separation and sharing of powers among different authorities: different individual and corporate agents. Let it be the case that someone's control can be denied only in the event that such different agents combine against him or her. Then he or she does not depend on the goodwill of any single one of them. And let there be further arrangements in place that make it unlikely, at least in suitable circumstances, that these agents will combine against the individual. Then it will be unlikely that he or she will have to depend on the goodwill of any coalition they form.

Ensuring the contestability of the group agent vis-à-vis its members

While the first strategy for securing the members' control within a group agent preserves the basic structure of the original control desideratum, albeit in a formally somewhat weakened form, the second strategy involves the protection of individual control in a looser, more indirect way. Like the first, it also turns on ideas associated with the republican tradition.

The driving idea behind republican freedom is that if someone depends on the goodwill of another for being able to do x, then the will of the other rules in his or her life. The second person may be content with the choice of the first and refrain from interfering. But he or she may do so only because the choice is to his or her taste. Had the choice been different, he or she might have interfered. Thus even in the absence of interference the one person is 'dominated' by the other. Nor is that all. If someone is subject to domination, he or she is likely to second-guess what the other wants and to adjust his or her behavior accordingly – and all this without anyone's actual interference (Pettit 2008c).

The republican interpretation of freedom requires the absence of domination of this kind. But republican freedom has an important implication besides the lesson that domination does not require interference: just as one can suffer domination without interference, so one can suffer interference without domination. This can happen when the interference is practiced with the genuine license or acquiescence of the person at the receiving end. If this condition is met, the interference is said to be 'non-arbitrary', in the old sense of not being the product of the will or *arbitrium* of the interferer.

Non-arbitrary interference does not impose the will of another, since it is guided by the will of the person interfered with. Therefore it does not imply a loss of freedom. Suppose that x and not-x are the options of having an alcoholic drink after dinner or just taking coffee and that someone, for fear of his alcoholic weakness, has asked another to hide the key to the alcohol cupboard and only let him have it at twenty-four hours' notice. When the other refuses to hand over the key, even upon begging, this is certainly an act of interference. But the interference is clearly licensed and non-arbitrary and does not reduce the person's freedom. It is a means whereby that person self-imposes his or her own will, not a case of a will imposed from outside.

This second aspect of republican freedom suggests a second way in which the citizens of a state – the paradigmatic group agent for the purposes of this discussion – might soften the loss of control to which membership in it exposes them. The state will inevitably interfere in the lives of its members, levying taxes, imposing coercive laws, and punishing offenders. And even if the state gives its citizens a formal right of exit, as we have seen, this cannot ensure that the interference is non-arbitrary. But citizens can reduce the arbitrariness of state interference in another way. They can look for an informal, equally shared form of popular control over the state. To the extent that they are able to achieve such control, they will each feel that the state is not an alien will in their lives but a will over which they have maximal control consistent with their living on equal terms with others.

Here is one way in which such equally shared, informal control might be achieved (Pettit 2009). Deliberation about government policy is a key characteristic of open societies, occurring in homes, cafés, and workplaces, in the media, and in public forums. Let us assume, as is common in a variety of theories, that such deliberation will generate a recognition of considerations that are accepted commonly on all sides as being relevant to the choice of public policy. Now suppose that the state's constitutional and democratic constraints require it to justify its policies in terms of such common considerations. Policies inconsistent with them are taken off the table. And the selection of the successful policy from the remaining ones is made under processes supported by those considerations. If a society's political institutions operate like this, then citizens will have an important form of informal control over the state.

The relevant institutions must guard against 'false negatives' and 'false positives': that is, against the failure to identify policies that are supported by mutually acceptable considerations and against the error of selecting policies that are inconsistent with them. The ordinary processes of competitive, open elections might help to achieve the first aim, since they provide incentives for politicians and parties to come up with popular policy proposals. And a battery of familiar constitutional and popular processes ought to help with the second. These restrict the ways in which the state can make decisions and the things it can do; impose a regime of transparency and deliberation; and expose those in government to potentially effective challenge and review in a variety of contexts: in parliament, in the courts, in commissions of inquiry, in the press, even on the streets.

The informal control envisaged here would make the state effectively contestable by its citizens, individually and collectively. It would provide citizens with the means for holding government accountable against the standard of mutually acceptable reasons that can be generated and sustained in popular deliberation. And it would thereby prevent the state from exercising domination over its citizens. At least when things go well, citizens would be in a position to contest any proposal or policy that threatens to treat them in a discriminatory manner: in a manner that cannot be justified, substantively and procedurally, in commonly acceptable terms.

One of the difficulties discussed in the last section was that of identifying spheres of control that members of a group agent might be given without problems of compossibility. It should be clear that a central role for the state is to identify and protect such spheres (Pettit 2008a). The republican state would seek to protect its citizens' freedom in the same range of choices, and on the same legal and cultural basis. That the state is subject to the informal control of its people – in particular, that it is contestable in the things it does – means that citizens will have control over how those spheres are defined. But it also means that the state should have a capacity to overcome some of the problems of compossibility that we have discussed.

Suppose a state identifies spheres of individual control on an initial basis and that the society then operates on the assumption that these are to be protected for each individual. And now imagine that after a certain time it becomes clear, perhaps as a result of legal suits, that the original demarcation of those spheres generates some serious conflicts between individuals. That revelation can prompt a judicial or legislative exercise, under the discipline of commonly accepted reasons, of adjusting the demarcation of spheres so as to guard against the problem that arose. Or if a readjustment is not feasible it can at least identify *ad hoc* ways in which the rival claims can be reconciled; it can achieve a more or less satisfactory compromise.

There may be serious difficulties with identifying compossible spheres of individual control in a once-for-all manner that is secure against all possibilities of conflict. But what this observation shows is that an organizational structure that allows for continuing adjustment and compromise may go some way towards resolving those problems. It can provide for a dynamic, continuing exercise of identifying and reconciling individual spheres of control and mitigate some of the implications of the formal impossibility results.

We saw in the first part of the book that the organizational structure associated with a straw-vote procedure can get over some serious formal problems of collective rationality. Although majority voting can give rise to inconsistency in group judgments, the group can avoid this problem by resort to a procedure in which every majority vote is checked for whether it is inconsistent with prior commitments and, if it is, the vote is nullified or the prior commitment revised. The organizational structure associated with contestable government can serve the same role in dealing with the kinds of compossibility problems we have considered here. It can enable the members of a state to assign individual spheres of control in a reliable manner, being prepared to deal with any problems that may arise just as a straw-vote procedure enables a group to deal with problems of inconsistency in group judgments.

Concluding remarks

We have seen that, despite the impossibility result we have discussed, there are strategies available for ensuring that a paradigmatically powerful group agent such as a state respects its members' rights and freedoms and that members retain certain spheres of control. The first strategy we have considered – preserving the substantive robustness of the control desideratum while relaxing its formal robustness – highlights the need for a suitable organizational culture within a group agent, along with a suitable organizational structure. And the second strategy – achieving control in a looser, more indirect manner, through securing the non-arbitrariness, transparency, and democratic accountability of the group's decision making – underlines the importance of a thoroughly democratic organizational structure. With both components in place – a suitable organizational culture and a transparent, democratic organizational structure – a group agent is well placed to protect its members' control.

PART III

The Normative Status
of Group Agents

7

Holding Group Agents Responsible

While in the first part of the book we have looked at the case for thinking that group agents exist and in the second at how their organizational structure affects their performance on several fronts, we turn in this final part to issues concerning the normative status of group agents. In this chapter we discuss how far group agents can be held responsible in the way in which we hold individual human beings responsible; in the next, how far they count as persons, displaying the capacities associated with personhood; and in the final chapter, the extent to which they offer members a novel object of identification, leading individuals to think in a we-frame in addition to an I-frame.

This chapter is divided into three sections.[106] In the first section, we look at what responsibility means and at the conditions that make an agent fit to be held responsible. In the second, we argue that group agents can satisfy these conditions and deserve to be held responsible for what they do. And in the third section, we review several issues involving the relation between individual responsibility and the responsibility of the group agents they constitute: their 'corporate responsibility'.

The issue of corporate responsibility goes back a long way and is at the heart of many discussions of group agents. That discussion often focuses on whether group agents count as persons, a topic to which we turn in the next chapter. The classical connection between corporate responsibility and personhood was made in a debate about the exposure of a group agent or *universitas* to excommunication. In 1246 Pope Innocent IV argued against the excommunication of any such corporate entity on the grounds that although it might be a person – this important concession was made in passing – it was a *persona ficta*, a fictional or artificial person, and did not have a soul (Eschmann 1946, pp. 29–36; Kantorowicz 1997, pp. 305–6). In arguing that group agents are fit to be held responsible, contrary to the gist of Innocent's message, we lay the ground for the claim, discussed in more detail in the next chapter, that they can count as institutional or juristic persons: artificial to be sure, but not fictional.

7.1 Fitness to be held responsible

Holding responsible and related attitudes

There are many ambiguities in the notion of holding someone responsible and it is useful to guard against these from the outset. First, holding an agent responsible for something in the intended sense does not mean just assigning causal responsibility for what was done. We might hold the dog causally responsible for soiling the carpet but we would not hold it responsible in the sense we have in mind; not at least by our understanding of canine capacities. Holding responsible in our sense implies that, if what was done is something bad, then the agent is a candidate for blame; if it is something good, then the agent is a candidate for approval and praise. We may be angry at the dog, or frustrated at the failure of the training regime, but by most lights it makes little more sense to treat the dog as blameworthy than it does to treat the weather in that way.

But while our sense of holding someone responsible is a moral rather than just a causal one, it should also be distinguished from two other moral senses.[107] It is distinct from merely holding an agent accountable, identifying that agent as the one who carries the can, the one who occupies the desk where the buck stops. We might hold agents accountable in that sense, and apportion blame or approval, without thinking that they were responsible in the sense intended here. The parent might be accountable for how the twelve-year-old child behaves in certain domains, for example account-able before the law. But we would not hold the parent responsible in the sense in which we might hold the child responsible – or in which we might hold the parent responsible, had he or she been the agent. The grounds on which someone can be held accountable are much less demanding than those on which they can be held responsible.

Holding someone responsible is also distinct from just thinking the agent respons-ible. Holding an agent responsible requires thinking that the agent is responsible but it also involves something else. We think someone responsible when we think they satisfy conditions sufficient for being a candidate for blame or approval; we hold them responsible when we go one further step and actually blame or approve. The agent who forgives an offender will have to think that the offender was responsible for what was done, and a candidate for blame, else forgiveness would not be in place. But what the forgiveness presumably involves is an eschewal of the blame itself. Similarly, the therapist may believe that a patient was responsible for some deed, yet put blame aside. The therapist might say: 'We both know, of course, that you were fully responsible for that action but we are not concerned with blame; our task is to understand why you did it.'

How can we understand the blame that is put aside in such cases, or the comple-mentary approval? We need not go into that question in detail, but, to focus on the negative case, we assume that blaming involves adopting or identifying with the stance of a creditor: someone to whom at least an apology is owed. Adopting such a stance typically means indulging in resentment, identifying with the stance means indulging in indignation (Strawson 2003). Adopting the stance towards oneself, as in blaming oneself, means indulging in a sense of guilt.

Three conditions for fitness to be held responsible

Almost everyone is likely to agree that it is often appropriate to hold a group agent causally responsible for certain actions and their effects. Almost everyone will also agree that it is often appropriate to hold a group agent accountable for various deeds and effects: for example, those brought about by their employees in corporate business. Certainly no one who goes along with our account of group agency will demur at either of these ways of treating a group agent. But the question is whether it can also be appropriate to hold a group agent responsible in the richer sense intended here: to think the group is responsible and, in the case of blame, to adopt or identify with the stance of a creditor – someone to whom a debt is owed. Is a group agent a suitable candidate for blame or approval by the criteria of ordinary practices?

We think that three conditions must be satisfied, under ordinary practices, for someone to be fit to be held responsible in a choice. These conditions correspond to the requirements outlined in some Christian catechisms as necessary and sufficient for a deed to constitute a serious sin. There must have been 'grave matter', it is said; there must have been 'full knowledge of the guilt'; and there must have been 'full consent of the will'. The first condition stipulates that the agent faced a morally significant choice; the second that the agent was in a position to see what was at stake; and the third that the choice was truly up to the agent: it was within the domain of the agent's will or control. Regimenting these ideas a little, we lay down the following three conditions for an agent to be fit to be held responsible in a choice.

> **Normative significance.** The agent faces a normatively significant choice, involving the possibility of doing something good or bad, right or wrong.

> **Judgmental capacity.** The agent has the understanding and access to evidence required for making normative judgments about the options.

> **Relevant control.** The agent has the control required for choosing between the options.[108]

Why accept these conditions? We think it is clear that they are individually necessary for responsibility, since no agent who violated any of them could be reasonably held responsible for what is done. Let the agent not face a normatively significant choice, and no question of responsibility arises. Let the agent not be in a position to make normative judgments about the options, say because of being denied understanding or evidence on these matters, and again there is no basis for holding the agent fully responsible. Genuine incomprehension or unavoidable ignorance is a perfectly good excuse when something bad is done. Finally, let the agent not have full control over what is done, and there is no basis for expecting the agent's normative judgment to have a strong enough effect on the action in question, for example, and so no basis for regular fault-finding; the agent will have a full or partial excuse for having behaved in that way.

These considerations suggest that the three conditions are individually necessary for fitness to be held responsible. But are they are also jointly sufficient? We think they are, since it is hard to see why someone should not be held responsible for a deed if they satisfied all the conditions at once. We assume in what follows that the conditions are both necessary and sufficient.

Holding responsible and regulation

Before turning to the responsibility of group agents, it is worth making two further observations. Both bear on the connection between holding agents responsible and acting so as to regulate their performance. The one concerns 'instrumental regulation', the other 'developmental regulation'.

Instrumental regulation consists in the imposition of sanctions, whether rewards or penalties, with a view to shaping the choices agents make. The most salient form is the penal regulation of the law, which seeks to shape the behavior of citizens by the threat of legal penalty. Holding someone responsible in law, say in the criminal law, for having committed a certain offense is distinct from punishing them, say by imposing a fine or prison term or whatever. This is important to recognize because discussions about criminal justice often run the two together, setting up a false contrast between backward-looking 'retributivism' and forward-looking 'consequentialism'.

The retributivist theory rules that offenders should be held responsible and punished in accordance with their desert, where this is a function of their fitness to be held responsible, by the criteria of ordinary practice, and the gravity of the offense. The consequentialist alternative argues that they should be held responsible and punished in whatever manner promises to yield the best results overall. But this dichotomy is false, as it runs together the issue of how far to hold someone responsible and how far, in light of that responsibility, to impose penalties that may regulate their future behavior or the behavior of others. If this distinction is easily missed, that may be because the fact of holding someone responsible for doing good is in itself a reward, and the fact of holding them responsible for doing evil a penalty; a long tradition holds that we bask in the good opinion of others, and smart under their implied censure (Brennan and Pettit 2004).

How far someone is fit to be held responsible for having committed an offense is certainly to be determined, as retributivism holds, by looking backwards to the measure in which the agent satisfies conditions like those mentioned here; those conditions are deemed relevant within our familiar practice of finding fault and assigning credit. It would be grotesque to think that whether someone deserves to be held responsible should be determined by whether holding them responsible has desirable consequences. That would be like thinking that whether a proposition deserves to be believed depends on whether believing it would have desirable consequences.

But where retributivism wins on that first issue, it loses out on the second. It is implausible to think that the same criterion would tell us how various offenses should be punished. Retributivism, or at least a more general theory of fairness, might dictate some constraints on the practice of punishment but the shape taken by the penal regime should surely be affected by the consequences it promises to deliver: consequences in deterrence and protection, for example, but also more general consequences for the quality of the society as a whole. To think otherwise would be to give credence to a doctrine in the vicinity of the *lex talionis*: an eye for an eye, a tooth for a tooth.

Our concern in this chapter is with how far group agents can be held responsible, not with how they can be best regulated, penally or instrumentally. We argue that corporate bodies are fit to be held responsible in the same way as individual agents and this entails that it may be appropriate to make them criminally liable for some things done in their name; they may display a guilty mind, a *mens rea*, as in intentional malice, malice with foresight, negligence, or recklessness. But we say nothing on the practical considerations relevant to determining the best sanctions to impose in criminal law, tort law, the law of contract, or any other branch of jurisprudence. There is a voluminous literature on this subject and, while our argument makes criminal liability a sensible option with group agents, it does not provide a clear line through the thicket of related practical problems (Laufer 1994; Colvin 1995; Grantham 1998).

So much for holding agents responsible and regulating them instrumentally. The other form of regulation is developmental rather than instrumental in character. To introduce this idea, think of the way parents often deal with their growing children in domains of behavior where the children may not be fully fit to be held responsible. While recognizing this lack of fitness, parents may yet announce that they will hold the children responsible for the good or the bad they do; and they may reinforce this attitude with appropriate sanctions. They may allow the teenage son to host a party but insist that they will hold him responsible for any damage done by his friends. Or they may allow the teenage daughter to stay out late but hold her responsible for not missing the last bus. And they may do these things, while being conscious that the children do not yet have the capacities required for reliably achieving the desired results.

Why do this? The most plausible answer is that by treating the children as if they were fit to be held responsible, the parents may help to induce in them the self-awareness and self-regulation such fitness requires. The practice has a developmental rationale. It makes sense as a way of encouraging in the children those very habits that may one day underpin their fitness to be held responsible. This has been described as a practice of 'responsibilization'; the word is cumbersome but the idea clear (Garland 2001; Pettit 2001c).

As holding someone responsible for an action is distinct from punishing or rewarding them, thereby seeking an instrumental regulation, so it is distinct from the responsibilizing initiatives in which we seek to regulate agents developmentally. This is important, as we can imagine initiatives designed to achieve a developmental effect in group agents, not to reflect a prior conviction that the groups are truly fit to be held responsible. Just as children can be educated to mature and grow in the abilities that make them fit to be held responsible, so we might think that the same is true of some groups. We return to this thought at the end of the chapter.

7.2 The fitness of group agents to be held responsible

Applying our three conditions for responsibility to the corporate case, a group agent is fit to be held responsible for doing something to the extent it satisfies these requirements:

First requirement. The group agent faces a normatively significant choice, involving the possibility of doing something good or bad, right or wrong.

Second requirement. The group agent has the understanding and access to evidence required for making normative judgments about the options.

Third requirement. The group agent has the control required for choosing between the options.

The first condition

The argument of the opening part of this book shows that the first of these conditions is easily met by group agents. As we have argued, a group can be organized for agency and act so as to pursue a collectively endorsed body of desires according to a collectively endorsed body of beliefs. There can be little doubt that such a group is liable from time to time to face normatively significant choices, in which the options differ on the good–bad or right–wrong axis. And so we have every reason to think that the first condition for fitness to be held responsible can be satisfied by a group agent.

Things are not so straightforward, however, with the second condition; and they are decidedly less straightforward with the third. But there are still good grounds for maintaining that those conditions can also be fulfilled by group agents – at least by group agents formed on the basis of the joint intentions of their members.

The second condition

To satisfy the second condition for fitness to be held responsible, a group agent must be able to form judgments on propositions bearing on the relative value of the options it faces – otherwise it will lack normative understanding – and it must be able to access the evidence on related matters. While it is a difficult issue what exactly is required for access to evidence – what makes ignorance of evidence invincible and blameless, and what does not – this issue is not distinctive of the group case and raises no special problem for us (Rosen 2004). Thus we can focus on the question of whether group agents are able to form judgments on normative propositions.

The notion of agency itself certainly does not imply the ability to form judgments on normative propositions, as the second condition requires. A simple agent like the robot considered in Chapter 1 gets along perfectly well with beliefs about the location and orientation of the cylinders in its environment, given its desire to keep them upright. It does not form any judgments about the value of the options it faces. Propositions about their value are sophisticated in character, as we put it in Chapter 1. Their expression requires the use of operators like 'it is desirable that' or 'it is right that' or the use of a metalanguage in which the propositions that are the contents of different options have desirability or rightness predicated of them. Simple intentional systems need not have intentional attitudes over such sophisticated propositions.

Is there any reason, then, why we should expect group agents to be able to form judgments over normative propositions? The answer is short: it depends very much on the group agent in question. A group forms a judgment or other attitude over a certain proposition when the proposition is presented for consideration – it is included in the agenda – and the group takes whatever steps are prescribed in its organizational structure for endorsing it. As we have discussed, these steps may involve a vote in the committee-of-the-whole, a vote in an authorized subgroup, or the determination of an appointed official. Since the members of any group are able to form judgments on normative propositions in their individual lives, there is no principled reason why they should not be able to propose such propositions for group consideration and resolution – that is, for inclusion in the group's agenda.

The ability of members to make such proposals in principle, however, does not imply that they will do so in practice. The procedures of a group may even restrict its agenda to propositions of a purely descriptive kind, in which case the members can put normative propositions onto the agenda only if they are able to change the established procedures. Although it may be possible for members to change those procedures, this may still be difficult, so that the group's ability to make normative judgments remains only a remote one.

These considerations need not be disturbing from our point of view, for two reasons. First, few group agents are likely to impose procedural restrictions against forming normative judgments about the options they face, even if they are not in the habit of making such appraisals. And second, it would seem to be a serious design fault, at least from the perspective of society as a whole, to allow any group agents to avoid making judgments of this kind. Why should any group of individuals be allowed to incorporate under an organizational structure that deprives the group of the ability to assess its options normatively, thereby making it unfit to be held responsible for its choices?[109] We might propose that society should regulate group agents so as to ensure fulfillment of the second condition: groups seeking to be incorporated would thus be legally required to have procedures in place whereby they give due consideration to evaluative matters and form collectively endorsed judgments on them.

A problem with the third condition

The question raised by the third condition is whether a group agent is in control over the actions it takes so that we might expect its normative judgments, for example, to be capable of impacting on its behavior. The notion of control needs analysis in any full theory of agency, but since the issue arises with individual agency as much as with group agency, we need not provide that analysis here (Pettit and Smith 1996; Pettit 2001c; 2005). The challenge for us is not to explain what an agent's control is but rather to show that there is no special reason why such control, whatever it involves, shouldn't be instantiated in a group agent as much as in an individual.[110] By almost all accounts, an agent's control comes in degrees. It may be reduced or eliminated by factors like obsession or compulsion, low impulse-control, inconstancy over time, or any of the less florid failures associated with underperformance. These problems are likely to affect group agents too but, being common to individuals and groups, they need not concern us here. What we focus on is a group-specific consideration that seems to suggest that corporate agents lack control.

This difficulty has long been registered in philosophy and theology. Arguably, it lies behind Innocent IV's insistence that a *universitas* cannot be excommunicated, being a purely artificial or fictional person. As one commentator points out, the argument rests on 'the old and solid truth that only individuals can act and, more especially, that only individuals can commit a delict and become guilty' (Eschmann 1946, p. 35). Building on this view, St Thomas Aquinas defended Innocent's line, arguing that something done by a group agent is usually done only by some members, in which case the fault lies with them. Sometimes an action is performed by all members together and we can speak of the responsibility of the group agent as a whole but the Thomist view is that even then the fault is divided up among members as individual agents; it does not belong independently to the body corporate (Eschmann 1946, p. 11).

Put abstractly, the problem is the following:

(1) Whatever a group agent does is done by individual agents.
(2) Individuals are in control of anything they do, and so in control of anything they do in acting for a group.
(3) One and the same action cannot be subject both to the control of the group agent and to the control of one or more individuals.

Therefore:

(4) The group agent cannot be in control of what it does; such control always rests exclusively with the individuals who act for the group.

This argument is clearly valid; so, if we are to reject its conclusion, we must find fault with one or more of its premises.[111] But the first two premises are compelling, as we have assumed or argued throughout this book. Thus the question is whether we have to accept the third premise, which denies the possibility that control over an action might be exercised at once by the group and by the members acting on its behalf.

At first sight that premise might not seem plausible at all. Those who act for group agents typically act on the instructions of the group, or by the commission of the group. But in that case both the group and the members can each have control over the action: the group as the agent that gives the relevant instructions, and the members as the agents who carry out those instructions. This line doesn't work, however. Just as anything the group does is done by its members, so any instructions the group gives are given by one or more members. And so the problem recurs one stage earlier. How can the group be in control of the instructions given, if those instructions are already under the control of the members issuing them?

The problem parallels a classic problem in the philosophy of mind, or more generally, in the theory of 'multi-level causality' (e.g. Kim 1998; for a recent general discussion, see List and Menzies 2009). The general issue is how causal control can be exercised simultaneously at different levels: say, by the neurons and the intentional attitudes of an individual human being. The actions of an individual are mediated by the neuronal activities in his or her brain, just as the actions of a group agent are mediated by the activities of its members. And so the mediating neurons in the individual human being threaten to rob that individual of causal control, in the same way in which the mediating members in a group agent threaten to rob that agent of causal control.

If the problem raised is parallel to this classic problem, however, then in what sense is it a group-specific difficulty? The specificity comes from the connection with responsibility. Even if his or her neurons rob an individual of control – and philosophers are divided over whether it is correct to say they do – these neurons will not count as morally responsible for the individual's actions, since they will not satisfy the first two conditions for fitness to be held responsible. But if its members rob a group agent of control, they can count as morally responsible for the group's actions; typically, they will satisfy the required conditions. Hence the problem in the group case is sharper. It is not merely a metaphysical difficulty for the assignment of responsibility to agents but a specific difficulty about why we should count group agents responsible, and not just their members.

We develop an approach to the problem of control in a group agent that draws on the more general issue of multi-level causality. We hold that, even in the case of an individual, it is wrong to think that the neurons rob the agent of control and we argue that, equally in the case of a group agent, it is wrong to think that the members rob the group of control. Hence we see no problem with the group's meeting the third condition for fitness to be held responsible.

A general perspective on the problem

The issue of multi-level causality arises in non-agential contexts as well as in agential ones. It is that of how there can be higher-level and lower-level factors that are causally relevant to one and the same event – and this, despite the fact that neither factor causes the other, and that neither combines with the other as part of a larger cause. We look at that more general problem, and at a plausible way of dealing with it, before returning to the group case.

Consider a natural process in which water in a closed flask is brought to the boil and, as a consequence, the flask breaks. Let us assume, to take a simplified story, that what happens in the process is that as the water boils – as the mean motion of the constituent molecules reaches a certain level – it becomes nearly inevitable that some molecule will have a position and momentum sufficient to break a molecular bond in the surface of the flask; and that this actually happens, leading to the collapse of the flask. What causes the flask to break in such a case?

At one level the molecule that actually triggers the break in the surface causes the collapse. Yet, the fact that the water is boiling is also causally relevant to the event. The boiling temperature of the water consists in the mean molecular motion being at such and such a level and so is constituted by the motion of the triggering molecule together with the motion of the other molecules. While the boiling of the water cannot be described as 'causing' the motion of the triggering molecule – the motion is a constitutive part of the boiling – or as combining with that molecule under the umbrella of a larger cause, its causal relevance consists in the fact that the boiling makes it more or less inevitable that there will be *some* constituent molecule, maybe this, maybe that, whose position and momentum are sufficient to induce a crack in the surface of the flask.

The relationship between the causally relevant temperature and the causally relevant molecule might be described in terms of a metaphor from computing (Jackson, Pettit, and Smith 2004, Part 1; see also Macdonald and Macdonald 2007, and Pettit 2007a). The higher-level event – the water being at boiling point – 'programs' for the collapse of the flask, and the lower-level event 'implements' that program by actually producing the break. The facts involved, described more prosaically, are these. First, the higher-level event may be realized in many different ways, with the number, positions, and momenta of the constituent molecules varying within the constraint of maintaining such and such a mean level of motion. Second, no matter how the higher-level event is realized – no matter how the relevant molecules and motion are distributed – it is almost certain to involve a molecule that has a position and momentum sufficient to break the flask. And, third, the way it is actually realized does have a molecule active in that role.

Given the fulfillment of these conditions, we can say that the water's being at boiling temperature 'programs' for the breaking of the flask, whereas the molecule's behaving as it does 'implements' that program, playing the immediate productive role. Both programming and implementing are ways, intuitively, of being causally relevant and so it makes sense, depending on context, to invoke one or the other in causal explanation of the effect. Information about either antecedent, higher-level or lower-level, is significant for the causal history of the event (Lewis 1986a). (For an alternative argument for the possibility of higher-level causation in a multi-level system, see List and Menzies 2009.)

Resolving the problem with the third condition

The analogy with the water gives us a helpful angle on our problem with a group agent's control over its actions. Suppose that an individual member of a group does something in the group's name, exercising control in the usual manner. Is there any sense in which the group also exercises control over what is done? The answer is that it can share in that control so far as it relates as a 'programming cause' to the 'implementing cause' represented by the enacting individual (Pettit 1993).

The temperature of the water controls for the breaking of the flask so far as it ensures, more or less, that there will be some molecule, maybe this, maybe that, which has a momentum and position sufficient to trigger the breaking; the molecule itself controls for the breaking so far as it ensures that this particular crack materializes in the surface of the flask. Things may be perfectly analogous in the case of the group agent. The group may control for the performance of a certain action by some members, maybe these, maybe those. It does this by maintaining procedures for the formation and enactment of its attitudes, arranging things so that some individuals are identified as the agents to perform a required task and others are identified as possible back-ups. Consistently with this group-level control, those who enact the required performance also control for what is done; after all, it is they and not others who actually carry it out.

Under this story, the group agent is fit to be held responsible for ensuring that one or more of its members perform in the relevant manner. At the same time, the enacting members of the group are not absolved of their own responsibility. Other things being equal, they are still fit to be held responsible for the fact that it is they who actually help to get the action performed. The members have responsibility as enactors of the corporate deed so far as they could have refused to play that part and didn't. The group agent as a whole has responsibility as the source of that deed, the 'planner' at its origin.

This line of thought resolves the problem that seemed to prevent a group agent from satisfying the third condition for fitness to be held responsible. A group agent, so it now transpires, is as fit as any individual human being to be held responsible for what it does. The members of such an agent combine to form a single agent faced with normatively significant choices, capable of making a judgment on what is good and bad, right and wrong, and capable of ensuring that one or another option is chosen. The individuals who give life to such an agent have to answer, of course, for what they do in making corporate agency possible. But the entity they maintain also has to answer as a whole for what it does at the corporate level, drawing on the resources provided by its members. It has all the agential capacities to make this possible.

Conceptually, then, we have every reason to hold group agents responsible, given that they satisfy the conditions reviewed. Critics might wonder, still, whether there is a point to this exercise. Someone might maintain, after all, that so long as we hold members responsible for their individual contributions to the doings of a group agent, there is no practical gain, and there may even be a disadvantage, in holding the group as a whole responsible as well. This challenge gives us a question to address in the third section of this chapter.

7.3 Individual and corporate responsibility

Types of individual responsibility

The question we face is how far the responsibility of individuals for what is done in a group's name makes it unnecessary or redundant, perhaps even counter-productive, to hold the group corporately responsible. Individuals may bear three sorts of responsibility in relation to a group agent's behavior, and it is useful to ask which of these might compete with corporate responsibility. Individuals may be held responsible for what a group does as designers of the group's organizational structure, as members of the group, or as enactors of the group's deeds: that is, as the agents who carry out its wishes. Or they may bear responsibility under more than one of these headings. We argue that the question we are concerned with – how far individual responsibility makes corporate responsibility redundant – involves the responsibility of individuals as enactors, not in any other guise.

Individuals are responsible as designers of a group, so far as they determine the group's procedures for forming its beliefs and desires and taking its actions. The founders of any corporate entity, be it a church body, a political party, or a commercial organization, naturally bear some responsibility for how that group functions as a result of its design. Such responsibility is not very relevant to our question, however, since it leaves in place the responsibility of the group for doing what the designers made it possible to do. The designers' responsibility in relation to the group's later performance is like the parents' responsibility in relation to their grown-up children. As parents may have laid down formative habits in their children, so the designers will have laid down formative routines in a group they shape. But as the parents' impact normally does little to reduce their children's responsibility for their actions, so the same is true of the impact of designers on the group's behavior.

The responsibility that individuals have as members of a group is equally irrelevant for the question of how far individual responsibility competes with corporate responsibility. On our understanding, individuals have responsibility qua members only if the group is responsible for something. Member responsibility, as we define it, is the responsibility that individuals have as the members of a group agent that does good or bad. It is derivative from the group agent's responsibility, not something that competes with it. Individuals may have member responsibility for what a group does insofar as it is their group agent, their church, association, or company, which produces that result, although, importantly, their levels of member responsibility may vary with their roles in the group. Even if there is little those individuals could have done to stop the group behaving as it did, they may inherit a share in the group's responsibility to the extent that they continue to be members and explicitly or implicitly endorse the group's actions (see also Kutz 2001).

The third way in which individuals can be held responsible for a group's actions is as enactors of the group's plans. Other things being equal, enactors, as we have seen, are responsible for what they do in the group's name, to the extent that they could have refused to play that part. This responsibility is consistent with the group's responsibility overall for ensuring that someone plays that part. But the question is whether there is any point in ascribing responsibility to the group as a whole, given that this enactor responsibility may accrue to individual members. When we have identified the individuals who bear this responsibility, won't it be redundant to ascribe responsibility to the group as well? And mightn't it even be counter-productive, relieving the individual enactors of some of the responsibility that, intuitively, they should carry?

On the face of it, enactor responsibility may thus seem to compete with corporate responsibility, making the latter redundant if not counter-productive. Moreover, enactor responsibility comes in two forms, positive and negative. Those who act to carry out a group's wishes are enactors in a positive sense, those who fail to take some available steps to stop those wishes being carried out are enactors in a negative sense. It may well seem that when all enactor responsibility, negative and positive, is put in the scale, then there is no point in adding the responsibility of the group as a corporate agent.

Why group agents as well as individual enactors should be held responsible

We argue that even when all the relevant enactors in a group action have been identified and held responsible, it may still be important to hold the group agent responsible too. First of all, when the group agent satisfies the three conditions introduced in this chapter, which we have taken to be necessary and sufficient for responsibility, not holding it responsible would simply be to disregard that fact. And further, there can be situations in which there is ground for holding the group agent responsible, given that it satisfies these conditions, but not the same ground for holding individual enactors responsible. In such cases, not holding the group agent responsible would not only go against our conditions; it would also lead to a deficit of responsibility.

To argue for this view, it may be useful to consider first the more familiar case of individuals who do not incorporate as a group agent but happen to act for a common effect. Many people have argued that such unincorporated collections may act in ways that predictably bring about bad results, without the members being individually or distributively culpable, or at least not fully culpable (*pace* Parfit 1984). It may be that the individuals are blamelessly ignorant of the harm they bring about together. Alternatively, it may be that even though they are aware of the harm, they each take themselves not to make a pivotal difference to it, as in the awful case of a firing squad in which members each treat the behavior of the others as fixed. (Of course, lack of pivotality may not be enough to qualify as an excuse.) Or it may be that they take themselves to make a difference, but not the right sort of difference, in particular not the sort that increases the harm; for example, each driver in a group of dangerously speeding cars may see that he or she dare not slow down, for fear of making a bad outcome worse (Jackson 1987).[112] Finally, it may be that while each is aware of the harm done, and aware of making a difference, they each act under such felt pressure that they cannot be held fully responsible for their contribution to a bad outcome; they can each argue that the circumstances mitigate their personal control and responsibility (Werhane and Freeman 2003, pp. 523–4).

Individually, the members of an unincorporated collection are agents but in such cases they may not be fully culpable, insofar as each has at least a partial excuse for his or her behavior. But the members of the unincorporated group cannot be held corporately responsible either: that is, responsible as a group. The collection they constitute, being unincorporated, is not an agent and thus fails the most basic precondition for responsibility (Held 1970).[113]

The circumstances that would make the members of an unincorporated collection less than fully responsible for a collective effect can also arise in the case of a group agent. The members of a group agent, like those of an unincorporated collection, may be less than fully responsible if they are blamelessly ignorant of any harm collectively done, if they reasonably believe that they won't make the right difference to that harm, or if they act under duress or pressure from others.

Shortfalls of individual responsibility have a distressing aspect in the case of the unincorporated collection, since they mean that although the individuals do something bad together, no one is fully fit to be held responsible. But the failures of individual responsibility in the case of a group agent do leave us with someone to hold responsible: the group agent itself. The fact that the group agent can meet the three conditions for responsibility, as we have argued, is a clear reason to hold it responsible, in addition to holding the enactors responsible. To be sure, we should hold the enactors responsible, if circumstances allow, for any harm their voluntary acts and omissions produce. But we should also hold the corporate entity responsible for the harm that it arranges to have done, given the decisions it licenses and the procedures by which it channels those decisions.

Neglecting such corporate responsibility would mean allowing some responsible actions, as covered by our three conditions, to go undetected. Worse still, it would make it possible for individuals to incorporate, consciously or unconsciously, so as to benefit from this deficit of responsibility. They might seek to achieve a certain effect, say a certain bad and self-serving effect, while arranging things so that none of them can be held fully responsible for what is done; they are protected by excusing or exonerating considerations of the kind rehearsed earlier. We conclude that as it is possible to hold group agents responsible, so it is also desirable.

How likely is it that members might escape individual responsibility for a group action? The discussion in the first part of the book shows that this is a permanent possibility. We know that in forming its preferences and judgments, a group agent may break with the majority views of its members, perhaps under reflective consideration of how to ensure coherence, perhaps under the routinized application of some procedure like the sequential priority rule that may overrule unanimous views. But this means that a group's attitudes, including its intentions to take certain courses of action, may be formed without individual members actually voting for them or even being aware of their formation. Thus the group agent may end up doing something bad, or doing something good, where the members involved can reasonably claim not to have foreseen the effects of their actions. They may be able to invoke more or less blameless ignorance of the significance attaching to their individual contributions.

Take the case where a decision to be made rests, by group agreement, on the judgments made about certain premises. Let the premises be 'p', 'q', 'r' and let the decision be equivalent to endorsing 'p and q and r'. Suppose that the group votes on those premises and that the chair announces the decision resulting from those votes. The decision may be made along such lines that all individuals think it is mistaken – each rejects one of 'p' or 'q' or 'r' – though no one is aware of this. If the group acts on that decision, then those who contest it may find that each member can plead that his or her own view was against the action taken: 'Don't blame me; I didn't want this result'. If responsibility is to be assigned in this case, then, intuitively, the group as a whole had better be capable of being found responsible.

Not only is there a systematic basis for holding group agents responsible. There are real-world examples where the failure to do so generates a failure, intuitively, in justice. The 'Herald of Free Enterprise', a ferry operating in the English Channel, sank in the 1980s, drowning nearly two hundred people. An official inquiry found that the company running the ferry was extremely sloppy, with poor routines of checking and management. 'From top to bottom the body corporate was infected with the disease of sloppiness' (Colvin 1995, p. 17). But the Courts did not hold anyone responsible in what might seem to be appropriate measure, failing to identify individuals who were seriously enough at fault. As one commentator puts it, 'the primary requirement of finding an individual who was liable ... stood in the way of attaching any significance to the organizational sloppiness that had been found by the official inquiry' (Colvin 1995, p. 18). Without going into the details of this case, it seems plausible to say that the company as a whole ought to be held responsible for what happened, both in law and in ordinary moral discourse. Holding the company responsible would be quite compatible with holding the individual members responsible for any clear shortcomings in their performance.[114] And it would ensure that there is as much blame delivered as, on the face of it, there is blame deserved.

From corporate to collective responsibility

We should consider one final question before moving on to the topic of group personification. This concerns the much wider issue of collective as distinct from corporate responsibility. Does our discussion of corporate responsibility throw any light on that wider topic? Does the account given of how group agents can and should be held responsible tell us anything about whether looser groupings can and should be held responsible?

There are many cases of harms done by people in aggregate, where we have no inclination to think there is a group agent to be held responsible: an entity in respect of which we might feel resentment or indignation, as we contemplate the ill done. It may be, for example, that our species wiped out Neanderthal competitors about thirty thousand years ago. While we may regret that no members of that other species remain in existence today, it would be intuitively implausible to blame humankind, as if it were a group agent.

But there are cases where something close to holding a group responsible seems more appropriate, even when the group is not an agent in the ordinary mould. These are cases where – perhaps due to the special role played by the group's identity in the questionable actions – we are inclined to speak of a collective guilt, distinct from the guilt of the individuals in the collection. There is something about the group that seems to make it appropriate to adopt the stance that we normally reserve for agents that clearly satisfy the conditions for fitness to be held responsible.

The cases where this is so typically involve national peoples as distinct from governments, or religious congregations as distinct from their episcopacies, elders, or priests. Where the states and episcopacies would normally count as group agents, this is not clearly so with peoples or with congregations, yet we often attribute collective responsibility to these groupings as well. We sometimes speak of the collective responsibility of Christians for the treatment of Jews in western history or for the treatment of native populations in the colonial countries where they sought to proselytize. And similarly, we sometimes attribute collective responsibility to new world colonists and peoples, for example in America or Australia, for the shameful treatment of indigenous populations, or to the German people for its acceptance of Nazi atrocities.

Is the ascription of group-level responsibility in such cases sensible? We think it may be, at least to the extent that some of the groupings involved can be seen as rudimentary group agents, distinct from the group agents – the governments or episcopacies – that do the immediate harm. Those group agents pose as spokesbodies for the larger groupings, and to the extent that their claim to authority is unchallenged, they have the tacit authorization of the members of the larger groupings. In such a case the larger grouping may be seen as a group agent under an organizational structure that gives the spokesbody more or less dictatorial status in determining the attitudes and actions of the whole.

Still, it may seem that there is no point in holding the larger grouping responsible. When a group agent operates under dictatorial procedures, everything decided and done by the group is decided and done by the dictator. Having ascribed enactor responsibility to a dictatorial spokesbody and perhaps to its active or passive collaborators among the people or congregation, then, why is there any point in ascribing corporate responsibility to the group as a whole? The case is unlike those earlier examples in which there is a shortage of enactor responsibility among members and thus good reason to focus on the corporate responsibility of the group as a whole. Here the enactor responsibility of members, particularly of the dictatorial spokesbody, leaves no shortfall in responsibility.

What reason can there be for persisting in the ascription of corporate responsibility to a people or nation, or to a body of believers? We think that doing so can have a developmental rationale, to return to a thought from the beginning of this chapter. To refuse to ascribe responsibility to the group as a whole, on the grounds that the evil done was done entirely by the spokesbody, would be to miss the opportunity to put in place an incentive for members of the group to challenge what the spokesbody does, transforming the organizational structure under which they operate: making it into a structure under which similar misdeeds are less likely. By finding the group responsible, we make clear to members that unless they develop routines for keeping their government or episcopacy in check, they will share in member responsibility for what is done by the group and may also have a negative form of enactor responsibility for allowing it to be done. We may also make clear to the members of other similar groupings that they too are liable to be found guilty in parallel cases, should their collective body bring about one or another ill.

This developmental rationale for ascribing group responsibility is all the more powerful if the ascription of guilt is attended by a penal sanction of some kind. By way of parallel, think of the rationale for finding a commercial corporation responsible for some misdeed, rather than just finding the board or management responsible. Doing so is likely to provide an incentive for shareholders in that corporation, or in similar corporations, to establish checks on the board and on management. It is likely, then, to elicit the sorts of capacities that will truly equip the group as a whole to be fit to be held responsible. What is true in this respect of the large commercial corporation is true equally of the citizenry of a country and the faithful in a church.

Once we recognize the developmental rationale that may make sense in these cases of the ascription of collective responsibility, we can envisage its extension to other cases where the collection that is held responsible falls well short of being a group agent of any kind. Think of the school group who are told that they will all be held responsible if there is any sign of bullying in their midst; or the loose professional association that is held responsible for the misbehavior of any member; or the neighborhood that is held responsible in the public press when those who live there indulge in certain socially exclusionary acts, say of a racist character; or indeed the generation that is held responsible for the overuse and potential loss of antibiotics. It may not be strictly appropriate to hold such a loose grouping responsible, since some of the conditions necessary for fitness to be held responsible are missing. But holding it responsible may actually prompt the grouping to incorporate and organize against the condemned behavior.

We are naturally disposed to ascribe responsibility, it appears, not just to fully responsible agents but also to 'responsibilizable' entities; not just to agents that are already fit to be held responsible but also to entities that are capable of being made fit to be held responsible. Perhaps grounded in the role it plays in scaffolding the development of children, this disposition may serve us equally well in prompting social groupings to assume a corporate or quasi-corporate form.

8

Personifying Group Agents

When Innocent IV argued in 1246 that a corporate body, not having a soul, was not fit to be held responsible for things done in its name, he conceded, as we saw earlier, that nevertheless it was a person, or *persona*, albeit a *persona ficta*: a fictional or artificial person. In the years following his edict, the personhood theme became more and more prominent, as medieval lawyers and later thinkers began to take the theme seriously and to treat corporate agents as real, if artificial, persons. The emphasis on the reality of this personal status went hand in hand with the claim, defended in the last chapter, that group agents could be held responsible for their doings. But in addition it supported the idea that not only could group agents have responsibilities, they could also have rights; they could make demands, as well as having demands made upon them. In this chapter, we argue that group agents do constitute persons but maintain that this does not give them a standing akin to that of natural persons. They should be given rights, or allowed to command respect, only to the extent that this is in the overall interest of natural persons.

Our discussion is divided into three sections. In the first, we distinguish two conceptions of personhood, an 'intrinsicist' and a 'performative' one, and adopt the latter. In the second, we argue that group agents can be persons under the performative conception. In the third, we discuss how far their status as persons makes group agents worthy of respect.

8.1 The conception of personhood

Two conceptions of personhood

It is now a commonplace, at least among philosophers, that there are two fundamentally different conceptions of mind and mental states. One is that mind is distinguished by its intrinsic nature or character: by what it is in itself. It is different from matter because it is made out of different stuff, as with Descartes's *res cogitans*; or at least it has different intrinsic properties, such as being phenomenally conscious: that is, conscious in a way that cannot be explicated in terms of functioning alone (Chalmers 1996).

The other conception is that mind is distinguished, not by what it is intrinsically but by what it does extrinsically: by the roles it plays, the functions it discharges. On this conception, to have a mind is simply to function in a certain way. We gestured towards a functionalist account of mind in analyzing intentional states – beliefs and desires – in terms of the roles they play in directing the agent and guiding action (Lewis 1983, Chs. 6 and 7).

Just as there are two conceptions of mind, so there are two conceptions of person-hood. According to one, there is something about the 'stuff' that persons are made off that distinguishes them from non-persons: something that makes persons stand out. This is the 'intrinsicist' conception of personhood. According to the other, what makes an agent a person is not what the agent is but what the agent does; the mark of personhood is the ability to play a certain role, to perform in a certain way. We call this the 'performative' conception of personhood and later adopt it in our argument.

The history of the conceptions

The standard definition of a person within the philosophical tradition down to the seventeenth century was intrinsicist. It went back to Boethius, a Christian philosopher around AD 500, whom Dante described as the last of the Romans and the first of the scholastics. In a definition later endorsed by Aquinas, and given almost authoritative standing, Boethius had said that a person is an individual substance of rational nature: *naturae rationalis individua substantia*. Persons are necessarily substances or self-standing entities, on Boethius's definition, so what distinguishes them is their nature as distinct from their functioning, and particularly their rational nature. Rationality is understood here in a demanding sense, which does not apply to non-human animals. Perhaps because it is taken to include the capacity to reason, it is ascribed only to human beings and higher intelligences, angelic and divine.

The performative conception of personhood was first developed in legal thought rather than philosophical, especially in the reworking of Roman law during the Middle Ages. Under this approach a 'legal person' is an entity capable of legal rights and duties: an entity that can own, buy and sell, enter into contracts and sue for breach of contract, or otherwise have standing as a plaintiff or defendant in the courts (Duff 1938, Ch. 2). This legal sense of personhood focuses on what persons do rather than on what they are. It allows that an entity may be a legal person without being a natural person like an individual human being. When Innocent IV announced in 1246 that the corporation was only a *persona ficta*, and did not have a soul, it is natural to interpret him as saying that the corporation was not a person in Boethius's intrinsic sense but only in the extrinsic, performative sense of being able to operate in legal space.[115]

The performative conception was developed as a general theory of personhood only in the seventeenth century, after the rise of natural science. The outstanding figure here is Thomas Hobbes, who argued, against Descartes, that what gives an organism a mind, and what makes an agent a person, is not the presence of any non-material substance but the fact that the agent's material substance is organized in a manner that makes certain performances possible (Pettit 2008b). According to Hobbes, animals and humans have minds so far as they are capable of interacting with the environment on broadly the lines presented in the first chapter: on the lines that lead us to take an 'intentional stance' towards them (Dennett 1987). Human beings have the additional capacity to reason, through language;[116] and, given this capacity, they can constitute persons, developing the ability, as Hobbes describes it, 'to personate'.

Functioning as a person consists for Hobbes in giving one's word to others, claiming the ability to represent to others what one thinks and wants, and in living up to the expectations this representation supports under local conventions of honesty and fidelity. Thus it involves claiming to be disposed to act according to the attitudes one self-ascribes, provided there is no later reason for changing one's mind; and claiming to be disposed to act as one promises or contracts to act, without any such proviso.

To function as a person is to utter words as tokens of one's attitudes, then; to acknowledge the obligations incurred by these utterances, under local conventions one accepts; and, implicitly or explicitly, to provide a guarantee for one's addressees that one will act as those obligations require.[117] In a slogan, one will live according to any words given in self-description, and live up to any words given in self-commitment.[118]

The Hobbesian approach generalizes the performative conception of the person beyond the legal context, developing it as a rival to the intrinsicist view. To be a person, on this conception, does not depend on the stuff out of which one is made but only on one's performance, specifically one's performance in the space of social norms. A legal person is an agent who is able to claim standing in the law, as even Innocent IV might have argued. A person *simpliciter*, so Hobbes now maintains, is an agent who is able to claim standing in the law or in any system of social obligation. Personhood derives from the capacity to be a spokesperson for oneself that comes on stream once agents, particularly human beings, have access to a common currency of words and a common code of associated obligations.[119]

The performative core of Hobbes's view remains intact in a rather different picture of personhood later in the seventeenth century, in the work of John Locke. Locke is interested, as Hobbes is not, in personal identity over time: what it is that gives each of us a sense that it was he or she who had such and such an experience in the past, adopted such and such a position, made such and such a promise, or took such and such an action. This concern has commanded most attention among Locke's commentators, especially the suggestion that first-person memory and consciousness, not bodily continuity, is the criterion for personal identity. But from our perspective the important aspect of Locke's position is more basic than that.

Locke's interest in personal identity over time is related to a deeper concern he shares with Hobbes. He agrees with Hobbes, first, that being the same person with someone in the past means inheriting their obligations and entitlements vis-à-vis others and, second, that this is the essential feature of personhood (Rovane 1997). The concept of the person, as he puts it tellingly, is a 'forensic' concept that is used for tracking contracted obligations and entitlements, legal or otherwise, from the past to the present. His view comes out clearly in this passage from his *Essay Concerning Human Understanding* (1975, s. 26):

Where-ever a Man finds, what he calls *himself*, there I think that another may say is the same *Person*. It is a Forensick Term appropriating Actions and their Merit; and so belongs only to intelligent Agents capable of a Law, and Happiness and Misery. This personality extends it *self* beyond present Existence to what is past, . . . it becomes concerned and accountable, owns and imputes to it *self* past Actions, just upon the same ground, and for the same reason, that it does the present.

What makes an agent a person, then, is that he or she is capable of contracting obligations by entering into legal and other conventional arrangements with others. And what makes an agent the same person over time is that obligations and entitlements contracted earlier are inherited later.[120]

In favor of the performative conception

We think that while ordinary usage is relatively free, the best way to define personhood for the purposes of our theory is along broadly Hobbesian or Lockean lines. To be a person is to have the capacity to perform as a person. And to perform as a person is to be party to a system of accepted conventions, such as a system of law, under which one contracts obligations to others and, to add a point not explicit in Hobbes, derives entitlements from the reciprocal obligations of others. In particular, it is to be a knowledgeable and competent party to such a system of obligations. One knows what is owed to one, and what one owes to others, and one is able and willing to pay one's debts or to recognize that censure or sanction are reasonable in cases of failure. In short, a person is an agent who can perform effectively in the space of obligations.[121]

The conventions and obligations that people accept may take a variety of forms, some more attractive than others.[122] What matters is that there are some obligations under which people relate to one another, not that these have this or that content, nor even that they are egalitarian, fair, or best overall by our lights. The existence and acceptance of a system of obligations usually means that the parties to them share a common awareness (Lewis 1969) that they each have an 'addressive' power or status in relation to others (Darwall 2006). In domains where relevant obligations rule, the parties can address claims to others; expect others to comply; and in case of non-compliance, have a complaint others must endorse, on pain of having to reject the conventions. And in such domains, parties must acknowledge that others occupy a reciprocal status: they too may address claims, expect compliance, and make compelling complaints about failures. The claims associated with addressive status are claims to be treated in the way the conventions legitimize, and only in that way.

The performative conception of personhood maps the distinction between persons and non-persons onto the divide between agents who can be incorporated in a conventional system of mutual obligation and agents, such as non-human animals on the standard picture, that do not have this capacity.[123] Non-persons can be cajoled, charmed, or conditioned, tempted, inhibited, or intimidated, as persons can be. But non-persons cannot be moved by being made aware of obligations they owe to others, or of the force of any associated reasons they recognize in common, nor can they move others by making them aware of such obligations or reasons in turn. Persons are distinguished, under the performative conception, by the fact that they can access precisely those resources of mutual influence; they can call on one another as parties to a shared system of expectation and obligation and expect that call to be heard.

Perhaps the most persuasive observation supporting the performative conception of personhood is that we could scarcely deny the status of a person to any agent capable of an addressive performance towards us, assuming suitable obligations and entitlements, responsibilities and rights, under accepted conventions. Let the agent be a Martian, or a robot, or a chimp that has been trained or engineered to a higher level of performance. If it proves capable of engaging us on the basis of commonly recognized obligations, forswearing the resort to force, coercion, and manipulation, it is natural to treat it as a person. We cannot look at it as a mere stimulus–response mechanism. Nor can we treat it, in the way we tend to treat non-human animals, as an agent subject to training and conditioning, and capable of generating pleasure or frustration, but not deserving of gratitude or resentment, approval or indignation. We have every reason to incorporate it in the community of persons.

8.2 Group agents as persons

Established practice

Are group agents persons in the performative sense? The view that they are has been explicitly or implicitly present in western thought since the reworking of Roman law and the development of legal theory in the medieval period. Indeed, it may have had some presence in Roman thinking as well. There is now evidence that corporate entities were recognized, however informally, in the Roman practice of law, particularly in the republican period (Malmendier 2005). Such entities often came close to being treated as persons, with a suitable addressive standing. Roman law was summarized in the Digest issued by the Emperor Justinian in the sixth century, which includes this comment from Ulpian, a third-century authority: 'if anything is owed to a group agent (*universitas*), it is not owed to the individual members (*singuli*); nor do the individual members owe that which the group agent owes.'[124] This remark shows how close the Digest is to considering group agents as persons: agents with standing in the law, or legal persons. Although the term 'persona' was never clearly used of any group agent in Roman thought (Duff 1938, Ch. 1), that use fits comfortably with the approach taken in Roman law and became firmly established in medieval legal theory, at least from the time of Innocent IV's proclamation in 1246.

The strongest association of group agency with performative personhood was probably made by those fourteenth-century commentators on Roman law who adapted that body of law to contemporary purposes. They thought of the *universitas* or *collegium* – the group agent or *corporatio*[125] – as a *persona universalis* or group person (Canning 1987, p. 189). Thus Bartolus of Sassoferrato, followed by his pupil Baldus de Ubaldis, argued that the *populus liber*, the free people of a city republic, was a corporate entity or *universitas* on a par with the trade guild or monastic order, being organized through its *concilium* or council; that it was therefore a *persona*, implemented by those who acted for it, not as individuals (*singuli*) but as organizational agents (*universi*); and, more specifically still, that it was a self-governing person – a *sibi princeps* or prince unto itself (Woolf 1913; Canning 1983; Canning 1987; Ryan 1999). On these grounds, they maintained that city republics had the same status, and the same rights, as kings in relation to the emperor: the *dominus mundi* or lord of the world, as he was presented in Roman law.

Thomas Hobbes built on this background in arguing, on the basis of his explicitly performative conception of personhood, that the multitude of individuals who are suitably represented by a spokesperson or body are thereby 'made one person' (Hobbes 1994, 16,13). According to Hobbes, this will be so whether they are represented by one individual or a committee, or whether they represent themselves in a committee-of-the-whole that operates, as Hobbes wrongly thought it could, by majority voting. He emphasized the personhood of the latter sort of group, when he said: 'sovereign assemblies, if they have but one voice, though they be many men, yet are they but one person' (Hobbes 1990, 158; see also Pettit 2008b, Ch. 5).

The personification of group agents continues down to the present day. Commercial corporations, which appeared in full dress only in the nineteenth century, are routinely given the status and name of persons in contemporary law (Hager 1989). They are even protected as persons in the jurisprudence of the United States, under the fourteenth amendment to the Constitution. That amendment was designed after the Civil War to give emancipated slaves the standing and protection of other natural persons. From 1886, when the Supreme Court made its decision on *Santa Clara County versus Southern Pacific Railroad*, it was taken by the courts to give a comparable standing to corporations.

The issue in that decision was whether the railroad owed taxes to the county on certain property. The court found in favor of the railroad on independent grounds but the Chief Justice orally addressed a defense argument that the railroad was protected as a group person. He is quoted in the court report as saying: 'The court does not wish to hear argument on the question whether the provision in the Fourteenth Amendment to the Constitution, which forbids a State to deny to any person within its jurisdiction the equal protection of the laws, applies to these corporations. We are all of the opinion that it does' (http://supreme.justia.com/us/118/394/case.html). The report thereby established fourteenth amendment protection for group persons in American court practice and constitutional law.

This protection has been invoked in support of the right of corporations to express their views in the money they spend in political campaigns. That right was recently affirmed and extended in the 2010 decision by the US Supreme Court in *Citizens*

United versus FEC, a decision that was described by President Obama in his subsequent State of the Union address as disastrous for democracy. We comment later on the proper extent of such corporate rights, offering considerations that would support President Obama's stand in this case.

Not a misleading practice

But it is one thing to say that the personification of group agents is established practice in law and related thinking. It is another to consider this personification justified. For all that the existence of the practice shows, it may represent a legally useful fiction: it may involve a fictional treatment of corporations as if they were persons, though by common agreement they are not. And even if the practice of personification is seriously intended to represent corporate entities as persons, it may still be built on a straightforward, if legally harmless, error.

If we go along with the intrinsicist conception of persons, at least on its traditional interpretation, we are more or less bound to take such a line, that is, to be fictionalists or error theorists about the personification of groups. We may think that natural persons have souls, as Innocent IV thought, and depict corporate entities as bearers only of the trappings of personhood. Or we may think that natural persons are made of biological stuff and that only the simulacra of persons can be constructed institutionally or robotically, not persons proper.

But, following Hobbes and Locke, we have rejected the intrinsicist conception of personhood in favor of the performative one. What makes an agent a person on this conception is not what the agent is but what the agent can do; persons are agents capable of operating in the space of obligations. Should we thus consider group agents as persons? Should we accept the literal implications of the established practice? We think that we should, and reject the view that the personification of groups is fictional or built on error.

We argued in the last chapter that group agents – at least sufficiently sophisticated ones – are fit to be held responsible for what they do. More specifically, they are positioned to make normative judgments about the options they face and have the necessary control to make choices based on those judgments. The normative considerations group agents can recognize in this way include some that derive from obligations towards others, such as the obligations related to contracts. That means, then, that group agents can be held responsible by others based on such commitments and, given that contracts are reciprocal, that they can hold others responsible too. Thus group agents can relate to one another, and also to natural persons, as sources and targets of addressive claims.

If group agents can do this, then they have to count as persons, albeit ones of an institutional rather than a biological kind. To be sure, group agents are not flesh-and-blood persons. They are pachydermic and inflexible in various ways, and lack the perceptions and emotions of human individuals (but see Helm 2008). But they nonetheless have the basic prerequisites of personhood. Not only do they form and enact a single mind, as we have seen in earlier chapters, displaying beliefs and desires and acting on their basis. They can speak for that mind in a way that enables them to function within the space of mutually recognized obligations.

Not a honorific practice

But although it is not strictly misleading, calling a group agent by the name of person may still seem just a legal honorific, so that the group is not a person in the fullest measure (Hager 1989). The best way to counter this lingering appearance may be to emphasize that persons on the performative conception must have very distinctive capacities; their status as persons does not come cheap. We have defined a person as an agent who is capable of performing effectively in the space of obligations; and although there are thinner and thicker accounts of what this capacity requires, it is clear that only special agents meet it. Even on a thin account, it requires the ability to make judgments on normative propositions and to act rationally on their basis – something that our little robot, for example, lacks. On a thicker account, performing effectively in the space of obligations requires the ability to reason in the more demanding sense introduced in the first chapter of this book, which in turn presupposes a number of self-regulative abilities.

When one reasons theoretically, as discussed in Chapter 1, one asks oneself questions about the properties of various propositions, their logical relations to one another, and their relations to experience and action. As a result of this intentional self-interrogation, one forms metalanguage beliefs on the consistency and entailments between propositions, their evidential support, or the opportunity to realize one proposition by realizing another. And with such extra beliefs in place, one provides more inputs to one's rational processing and makes it more likely to discern any problems with one's first-order beliefs or desires. Suppose, unhappily, that one believes 'p', 'if p then q', and 'not q'. There is a better chance of exposing and correcting the inconsistency if by reasoning one forms the belief that the first two propositions entail 'q'. There will then be a further site at which the failure can come to light. That, as we presented it, is the rationale for reasoning.

While this account was designed to cover theoretical reasoning based on consistency and other logical properties, it clearly extends to practical reasoning based on normative considerations, such as the considerations agents have to take into account when operating in a system of obligations. It is natural to expect persons to be able to ask themselves about the normative properties of their options – that is, of the propositions they are consciously capable of realizing; to be able to recognize that a given option is required or forbidden under a relevant system of obligations; and to be able to let that recognition impact on their performance. Not only must they have the capacity to conform to the obligations that arise under the system. They must have the capacity to recognize those obligations – if only when others remonstrate with them – and to respond to that recognition in a manner characteristic of reasoning subjects.

To deserve the name of persons, on this thicker account, group agents must have all the abilities associated with the faculty of reason. And if this is not enough to emphasize the substantial requirements they must fulfill, we should add that the capacity to reason and to be guided by it presupposes a rich capacity for self-regulation.

All agents who reason can be described as self-regulating to the extent that they intentionally generate checks on themselves that are designed to guard against certain failures of rational or normative processing. But those who reason will almost all have to be self-regulating in a further way too. Suppose, for example, their reasoning makes them aware of the gambler's fallacy, letting them see that there is no good reason to bet on heads after a run of tails, if the coin is fair. They may still find that when they gamble, their instincts take over and they become driven to act as if the fallacy were no fallacy. Their only way to avoid this may be to take further regulatory steps through their practical dispositions (McGeer and Pettit 2002; McGeer 2008). They may decline to gamble altogether, or decline to gamble except when a friend is present to remind them of their weakness, or rule in advance that no bet of theirs is to be accepted if made in the wake of more than three heads or tails.

For group agents to perform as persons, on the thick account, they must have such a regulative competence; otherwise they will not be able to satisfy the addressive claims made against them. Moreover, they must be able to see themselves as having that capacity; otherwise they will lack the confidence to present themselves as addressable, addressive subjects. And they must also be able to see other individuals and groups as having these capacities too; otherwise they will not be able to engage them appropriately. This is no meager set of requirements. We hope that by drawing attention to them we can lay to rest any suggestion that there is little substantive content to the claim that group agents are persons in the performative sense, particularly if one takes the view that personhood requires the ability to reason.[126]

8.3 Group persons and respect

The ideal of respect

On our account, persons, natural or corporate, are distinguished by the fact that they can enter a system of obligations recognized in common with others, and limit their influence on one another to that permitted within the terms of that system. When persons seek and exercise such permissible influence on one another, and only such permissible influence, we say that they display 'respect' for one another. They may offer one another counsel or cooperation but they eschew force or violence, coercion or threat, deception or manipulation.

The fact that persons can exercise mutual respect, of course, does not mean that they always do so. Natural persons often try to influence one another coercively or manipulatively and the same is true, clearly, of their corporate counterparts. While group persons are able to achieve mutual respect in their relations with others, they may still fail to sustain such a regime.

Despite the fact that it is not invariably achieved, however, a regime of mutual respect has the attractions of a high ideal. It contrasts, for example, with how people often, and unfortunately, treat their enemies. Although the obligations on the basis of which people deal with others may not be symmetrical across different agents, even the respect they give under a hierarchical order contrasts favorably with certain other modes of influence. Mutual respect represents a form of relationship that can be grounded in the will of each, at least to the extent that the relevant obligations – the terms in which persons relate to one another – are accepted on all sides, as a matter of common awareness. These obligations may not have been the result of a consensual decision but they are contestable and have resisted or survived contestation.

The attraction of a regime of respect is palpable (Pettit 2008c). Whenever one deliberates over a set of options, one has to think 'I can do that' of each alternative; one has to realize the possibility it represents. And if the option is truly an option, then that can-do assumption must be true as well as thinkable. Respectful influence does not undermine the truth or the thinkability of such a can-do assumption in a choice situation, and that is its great attraction. If two agents reason with one another on the basis of commonly recognized obligations, and do nothing further to influence each other, then they leave all their can-do assumptions – at least those deemed true upon deliberation – in place. This is so, even if one agent makes the other a regular offer, indicating that he or she will reward the other for a particular choice. Since the offer is refusable, the second agent can ignore the reward and take any of the existing options, or take the new alternative, choosing the option-plus-the-reward.

Respectful influence thus preserves the agent's autonomy; it provides the agent with further feedback on the options available but leaves it up to the agent to decide how to act in response. The system of obligations it presupposes may involve sanctions for non-compliance with certain claims, but provided the obligations are commonly accepted, those sanctions can be seen as self-imposed costs, accepted as tokens of *ex ante* assurance to others. By contrast with respectful influence, force, coercion, and manipulation undermine some of an agent's can-do assumptions in a choice situation. They may remove one or more of the options, as with force, for example, or replace it with a penalized option, as in the case of coercion. Or they may mislead the agent about some of the options, as with the bluff threat or the strategic deception; they may undermine the thinkability rather than the truth of the relevant can-do assumptions.[127]

What are the implications of the ideal of respect for the standing of group persons in our society? Two questions stand out. One is whether group persons should be given equal standing and equal respect – equal rights – with individual persons. To that we answer, no, pointing out that individual human beings still enjoy a privileged position. The other question is whether the ideal of mutual respect requires group persons to be subjected to special disciplines and restrictions, deprived of rights that natural persons may enjoy. To that we answer, yes, again in order to protect individuals. Group persons are deserving only of a lesser range of rights, and should be disciplined in an especially strict manner.

In adopting this line, we plead guilty to the charge of taking back with one hand what we have given with the other. The intent of most thinkers who emphasize that group agents can be true and real persons has been to argue that such persons have important claims: for example, the claim of the medieval city republic against the Holy Roman Emperor or the claim of commercial corporations against government regulation. While we agree that group agents count as persons, and that they are inevitably given certain rights, we deny that the rights they enjoy are on a par with the rights of natural persons.

Should group persons be given equal standing? No

It is hard to see how one could morally justify a regime of less than equal standing among individual persons in society. Any system of obligations voluntarily accepted by a society of individuals is likely to permit them to talk with one another as advisors or collaborators on the basis of considerations each can recognize as relevant but no one is forced to act on. The obligations may give them an unequal standing in relation to one another but the fact that the parties relate to each other in a deliberative manner means that the terms of the system of mutual obligation should be open to question between them. While that exposure to interrogation may permit asymmetrical regimes in which rights vary across parties, it is not easily squared with the assignment of unequal standing in civil society at large.

Suppose that a number of us are debating about the terms under which we should operate on a mountain climb, in a political or social campaign, or in a military operation. We may conceivably agree to a system of obligations under which some of us are appointed to leadership posts with greater responsibilities and rights than others. But this is not readily imaginable when we are deciding on the basic structure of our society, as in a Rawlsian original position or other fundamental deliberative setting (Rawls 1971). Why would we be moved by arguments for privileging a particular class or caste, race or gender? Why would we settle for less than the equal status we already have as persons who can understand the force of common reasons?

Given this case for equal standing among individuals, our next question is whether group persons can claim the same standing as individual ones. We strongly believe that they cannot. There is nothing implausible about the idea that group persons should have only a limited range of rights and that other persons should have only a corresponding range of responsibilities towards them.

Before defending this claim, it is worth noticing that it is borne out in the main traditions of social thought and practice, which have given only limited rights to group agents. Indeed, in Chapter 6, we have already discussed an important desideratum of organizational design according to which a group agent must respect certain spheres of control of its individual members. The state is the most salient group agent of all, and from the days of classical Athens and the Roman republic, when it emerged as an agent distinct from any single prince or princely elite, the need to contain its power has been widely recognized. The causes the state was expected to promote, such as defense and social welfare, required it to have powers that outstripped those of any individual. But since those powers made it a danger to the very citizens it was meant to serve, it became standard to insist on not giving it the leeway of one person among persons. The Roman and neo-Roman tradition of republicanism held, for example, that there should be limits on the state's interference in private life, rule-of-law constraints on how it operates, checks on what it can do that are imposed by rotation in office and a separation of powers, and invigilation by an active citizenry for its conformity to those and other restrictions (Pettit 1997; Skinner 1998; List 2006c).

The same goes for the church, which, at least in liberal societies, has been consistently checked for what it may and may not do. The separation of church and state in those societies – though it comes in many varieties – has always imposed restrictions on the church's political and related activity. Since a majority church that is allowed to influence politics in certain ways may represent a threat to religious or secular minorities, it has become common to deny churches the presence and activity in politics that is usually accepted for individual persons.

The history of commercial corporations teaches a similar story. Commercial firms have had various kinds of responsibilities and rights over their history and continue to vary in the claims they can make, or have made against them, in different jurisdictions. But nowhere do they have equal rights and responsibilities with individual persons. Even in the United States, where their personal status is part of constitutional law since the *Santa Clara* decision of 1886 mentioned earlier, corporations are subject to a different regime of rights from that of individual persons. They may have the right to support political parties, as in a person's exercise of free speech, but they do not have the right to vote or stand for office. They may have the right to buy, sell, and own, as do individual persons, but they do not have the right not to be owned by others, even by other corporations; there is no prohibition against 'corporate slavery'.

Not only do group persons not command equal standing with individuals in most societies. Neither, plausibly, should they do so. The argument for equal standing that was based on what would be accepted in a decision on the basic structure of our society does not extend to group persons. Individual persons create and organize group agents and it is in the co-reasoning of individuals, not that of corporate bodies, that the case should be made for or against equal rights. On standard accounts, it must still be individuals, not groups, who deliberate about how to organize society. While the parties to such deliberation might be expected not to settle for less than the equal status of individuals in civil society, they can certainly be expected to agree to less than equal status for the corporate bodies they construct.

Could there be other arguments for the equal status of group persons? Some philosophers argue for the equal status of individuals by referring to their natural rights, others by reference to the benefits of equal respect, which may be measured in terms of utility or happiness, or by some other metric. But neither argument is likely to entail that group persons should enjoy equal standing with individual ones. No approach we know would accord natural rights to group persons – unsurprisingly, since we can create an unlimited number of them. And no approach we know suggests that group persons have morally commanding interests such that a corporate good or benefit would determine what should be done, independently of the good or benefit to individuals. Almost all approaches defend some variant of 'normative individualism' (Kukathas and Pettit 1990): the view that something is good only if it is good for individual human or, more generally, sentient beings.[128]

We think that normative individualism is more or less compelling. Whether or not a group person should exist, and whether it should function within this or that regime of obligation, ought to be settled by reference to the rights or benefits of the individuals affected, members and non-members alike. And it is extremely unlikely that giving group persons equal status with individuals could be in the interest of individuals. Normative individualism therefore seems to support a regime under which group persons have restricted rights as compared with individuals.

Is this downbeat attitude to the standing of group persons consistent with our demanding view about their responsibility? We think it is. When group agents exist – at least ones of sufficient complexity – there is every reason to hold them responsible in their own right. They can meet the conditions for responsibility, as we have seen, and not recognizing this would lead to intuitive and exploitable deficits of responsibility. That view about responsibility is fully consistent with thinking that what status group persons should enjoy ought to depend wholly on the returns promised for individuals. Both the view defended on corporate responsibility, and the view now upheld on corporate rights, make sense within the perspective of normative individualism.

Should group persons be especially checked? Yes

But even if their rights are drastically limited, group persons still raise a problem for the ideal of respect, particularly respect for individual persons. The problem does not derive from the abuses group persons actually commit. It comes from the fact that even if they do not practice any abuse, they retain relatively unconstrained powers of interference, which are not always subject to effective measures of prevention or deterrence.

When one agent has an asymmetrical power of interfering with force, coercion, or manipulation in another's choices, and when there are no inhibiting difficulties or costs, the regime of respect is compromised. And this is so even if that power is not actually exercised. Respect is possible between persons only if neither has an influence on the other that undermines the other's can-do assumptions in suitable choices, rendering them untrue or unthinkable. The existence of asymmetrical powers of interference, even unexercised ones, can undermine such assumptions.

Suppose an agent thinks he or she has a choice between options x, y, and z but another has a power of interfering with this choice. Then the first agent's choice is really between the options: x-if-the-other-allows-it, y-if-the-other-allows-it, and z-if-the-other-allows-it. When choosing, the agent chooses by the other's grace: *cum permissu*, as the old complaint put it. The very presence of the other means that the options are different from what they would be otherwise.

This problem is exacerbated if the agent becomes aware of the other's power to interfere. The thinkability as well as the truth of the original can-do assumptions is put in question: the agent knowingly faces not the simple options x, y, and z but only their modified counterparts. The knowledge that some of the options are subject to a threat, punishment, or other constraint may lead the agent to censor the preferred choice, acting so as to keep the other sweet and tolerant. And it may lead the agent to do something that he or she would otherwise shun, taking steps of self-ingratiation and servility to secure the other's favor. Those moves may reduce the probability of interference by the powerful agent but they will cause even greater problems for a regime of respect. The powerful agent will control the weaker in a way that makes a relationship of respect impossible.

The problem created by such asymmetrical power is one of 'domination': subjection to a master or *dominus* (Pettit 1997; Skinner 1998; List 2004a). There would be no problem if the interferee could control the interferer, whether by instruction, dismissal, or redress, direct or indirect. But where the interferee has no such control – where the interferer has the power of interfering arbitrarily – the powerful party is truly in the position of a master and the autonomy of the weaker is undermined. Such domination is as inimical to respect as actual force, coercion, or manipulation. And yet it does not require the dominating party to practice any interference, only to have the power of doing so.

It should now be clear why group persons create a special problem for the rule of respect. They often possess vastly more power than individuals, including a power of interfering in individuals' choices; and of course some group persons possess vastly more power than others. The great power of group persons is the reason the control desideratum discussed in Chapter 6 is so important. A group person's power derives from its financial assets, the network of clients it can summon in its support, the degree of dependency it can create in those who rely on it as an employer, customer, or financier, its mortality-free time-horizon, and the fact that it need not suffer any anxiety or related emotions (Bakan 2004).

The group persons that have vast power in relation to individuals include a variety of bodies, ranging from states and churches to trade unions, political parties, and commercial corporations. The problem arises in relation to any such bodies but is particularly salient with commercial corporations. This is because there is no tradition of guarding against their power. There is a long tradition of curtailing the powers of the state, churches, trade unions, and political parties. But, antitrust legislation notwithstanding, there is no similar tradition of guarding against the powers of commercial firms.

In early nineteenth-century Britain and the United States, a legislative act was required to establish a corporation; the corporation could only operate in territory and on terms laid down in the act; no corporation could control another; and the liability of shareholders was not limited to the resources they had invested in the corporation. All of that changed in the advanced, more or less democratic world over the course of the nineteenth century, so that the base was laid for the extraordinary proliferation of commercial corporations we see today. That proliferation was attended in the twentieth century by a gradual loosening of the conditions under which corporations could operate, as different polities competed for the investments of giant multinational corporations.

Group persons like corporations are clearly able to dominate those who depend on them. Customers may be protected by the fact that they can take their custom elsewhere or sue for redress of grievance. Again workers may be protected in some degree by the power of unions and by their rights against unfair dismissal. But those protections are limited, given the sheer financial resources of many corporations, and their ability to defend themselves under ever-escalating court costs.

Even protections of that kind are lacking on other fronts. Think of the small country where the corporation would trigger an enormous crisis by moving elsewhere, as it is always free to do. Or think of the community that has suffered serious environmental or other harm at the hands of a corporation and, even if it is successful in the courts, finds itself thwarted by endless appeals and other legally rigged delays in payment. Or think of those in government who depend on the financial support of corporations in their electoral campaigns and dare not get a corporation offside. This last problem has become particularly salient in the United States as a result of the Supreme Court's decision in *Citizens United* that many established restrictions on the corporate financing of politicians should be lifted.

There has long been a concern in political theory about the actual abuses that companies, churches, and other corporate entities may perpetrate. But much less attention has been given to the problems created by the enormous power of corporations, independently of actual abuses. The assumption seems to have been that when there is no actual abuse, no actual exercise of interference, then all is well. But, unfortunately, this does not follow. The imbalances of power between corporate entities and individuals, and among corporate entities themselves, can threaten relations of respect. They can warp the adjustments of communities to corporations, churches, and other institutional powers, sometimes enabling such bodies to have an influence that operates as silently as gravity. This is power at its most perfect: power that does not need to be actively exercised to have an effect.

We do not think that these problems are beyond solution. As polities have found legal ways of dealing with various imbalances of individual power, they should also be able to draw on legal restrictions to deal with imbalances of corporate power. But our purpose here is not to investigate the details of such responses, which are beyond the scope of this book; it is rather to draw attention to the problems that make them necessary in the first place.

One reason why it is important to recognize the reality of group agents is that this lets us discern the true contours of the moral and political world we inhabit (Coleman 1974). Swaddled in glib conviction that the only social agents are individual human beings, we can look right through the organizational structures that scaffold group agency and not see anything there. We can live in an illusory world in which the comforting mantras of individualist thought make corporate power invisible.

While we have used commercial corporations to illustrate the influence of corporate power, we should stress that this is mainly because less has been done to curtail them than to restrict other group agents. It is not that managers and operatives in commercial firms deserve to be demonized. For all that we suppose, these individuals may operate in a regular, essentially unobjectionable way. They may interact humanely and respectfully with their colleagues and other people and perform under the usual forms of peer expectation and pressure, as they fulfill the role of their job. They may be as oblivious to the full extent of corporate power as anyone else in society. And, like anyone else, they may themselves be shaped by the corporate field of influence in their own individual lives.

9

Identifying With Group Agents

It is now common to connect the idea of belonging to a group with that of assuming a certain identity as its member. This chapter explores the role of identity in the context of group agents, drawing on our account of responsibility and personhood in the previous chapters, and on the theory of group agency developed earlier in the book. We suggest that group agency often requires members to assume a group identity in quite a literal sense of the term.[129]

In the first section of this chapter, we observe that agency requires the subject of any intentional attitudes – beliefs and desires – to identify as the agent moved by those attitudes, and that a more sophisticated agential performance, perhaps as a person, involves self-identification, requiring the use of the first-person pronoun 'I'. In the second section, we apply those observations to group agents, showing how individual members can identify with – and collectively self-identify as – a group agent. And in the third, we consider the sorts of conflicts within and between individuals to which issues of group identity can give rise.

In presenting our argument, it is often necessary to speak of what the first-person singular thinks. We do this by using the first-person pronoun 'I'. But this 'I' should be identified with the narrative voice of this chapter; it should not suggest that we, the authors, aspire to any greater unity than is implied in our group agency.

9.1 Identification and self-identification

The identification gap

Suppose it is evening and I desire that the front door be locked. And suppose I act on this desire myself, rather than relying on someone else. The desire that the front door be locked must engender in me the further desire to lock the door – this is required by instrumental or means-end rationality – whereas this is unnecessary if I rely on another person. How can we represent that further, instrumentally required desire? We have assumed that all desires – like intentional attitudes in general – have propositions as their objects. But my desire to lock the door seems to involve an infinitival expression – 'to lock the door' – not the that-clause that would express a proposition. How can this be so?

One response is that when I, that is, Christian or Philip, desire to lock the door, what I actually desire is that Christian (or Philip) lock the door. This, however, doesn't work. I might desire that Christian (or Philip) lock the door without desiring to lock the door. I might not realize that I am Christian (or that I am Philip). This problem is what we call the 'identification gap': a desire or other attitude involving me under some name or neutral description fails to activate me, because I fail to recognize myself as the referent of the name or description.

Can we construct a propositional object for the desire to lock the door that avoids the identification gap? Happily, we can. The object can be the sentence 'I lock the door', not 'Christian (or Philip) locks the door'. With a proper name like 'Christian' or 'Philip', or with a neutral description, I may fail to know that I am Christian, or that I am Philip, or that I satisfy the description. But I cannot fail to know that I am I. No gap can stop the desire that I lock the door from activating me, because the term 'I' refers to whoever uses it: it is an 'indexical'.[130]

The problem of the identification gap was first clearly stated by John Perry (1979), who argued that we cannot explain an agent's actions without ascribing attitudes that preclude identification failures. I might believe that the person I see in a mirror should get his hair cut, without realizing that I am that person. Or I might believe that the person who wrote a certain memo should apologize for the defamation of another, and not recognize the memo as something I authored myself. If I go to the barber or make the apology, this cannot be explained just by beliefs or desires expressed in third-person terms; an identification gap could still block their connection to action.[131]

Avoiding the gap

How do agents avoid the identification gap, as instrumental rationality requires that they avoid it? One answer is given by the 'cognitive-achievement model'. On this model, agents initially have non-indexical beliefs and desires, formulated in third-person terms, and they are prompted to act only after a further cognitive accomplishment: they identify as the subject within these beliefs and desires. Thus my action to get a haircut or to make an apology is prompted by two things: first, a non-indexical desire that the person in the mirror should get his hair cut, or that the author of the memo should apologize, and second, the subsequent identification as the subject of those propositions. Identification is thus depicted as a cognitive achievement over and above the formation of the relevant beliefs and desires.

This model cannot be right. Recall our little robot, introduced in the first chapter, which moves about a tabletop, setting various cylinders upright when they topple. This agent has beliefs and desires about the positions and orientations of those cylinders, and acts in an instrumentally rational way so as to satisfy its desires – the goal of having upright cylinders – according to its beliefs. Clearly, the robot does not run into any identification gap; otherwise it wouldn't do anything. But equally clearly, its avoidance of the problem is no additional cognitive achievement. It has beliefs that this or that cylinder is on it side, and a desire that it be upright. But these beliefs and desires trigger the robot's action automatically, simply by virtue of how it is constructed.

We might capture this naturally by formulating the robot's instrumentally required desire in infinitival terms; the robot simply desires to raise this or that cylinder. Or we might cast it as a desire in respect of a proposition: 'I raise this cylinder', 'I raise that cylinder'. The propositional mode of attitude-ascription is just as appropriate as the infinitival, provided it does not suggest that the robot is capable of using the indexical 'I'. And it actually has an advantage. We can use that same propositional mode, but not the infinitival one, to ascribe to the robot the beliefs that instrumental rationality also require it to form: say, a belief in respect of the proposition, 'I can raise the cylinder by adjusting it so'.[132]

Whatever mode of ascription we use, the important point is that the robot does not first form beliefs and desires about itself in neutral third-person terms and then recognize itself, through some further cognitive achievement, as that neutrally presented agent. The robot overcomes the identification gap as a by-product of its construction, not in virtue of any additional achievement. Let us call this the 'by-product model' of how that gap is closed.

In the normal run of things, the by-product model applies to human beings and other agents, not just to the little robot. When we human beings interact with our environment, we automatically form beliefs and desires that leave no possibility of an identification gap. We automatically form attitudes that, like the robot's, require ascription in indexical terms or, for the case of desire, in infinitival terms. We do not first form non-indexical beliefs and desires in the third person and then translate them into indexical counterparts. Our construction as intentional subjects usually makes that unnecessary.[133]

From identification to self-identification

On this account, identification is not something reserved for sophisticated agents like human beings. It consists in the formation of beliefs and desires that implicate the agent at crucial points, pinpointing the agent as the one those attitudes activate. It is achieved on the same basis among simple agents like the robot and among normal human beings. But we human beings, unlike the simple robot, also go one step further. We have access to the first-person pronoun 'I' and use it and its cognates explicitly in speaking and thinking about ourselves. We don't just identify with a particular agent in the fashion of the simplest creatures; we self-identify in a very explicit, linguistically mediated mode.

Self-identification has two aspects. We each use the pronoun 'I' to identify ourselves as one person among others, as in 'I am Christian' or 'I am Philip'. But equally, we each use it to identify ourselves in such a way that we cannot fail to know who we are. In our mouths, the first-person pronoun serves to identify the person for whom we speak as just one member of the community of persons and at the same time as a person for whom we speak with a unique authority.

How does such self-identification work? What enables me to identify a particular person as the referent of the first-person pronoun? Extended to this case, the cognitive-achievement model would suggest that I imagine various candidates for the referent of the 'I' and have a general conception of myself that leads me to recognize the true deserver: the person with the correct, me-constituting qualities. But this is clearly an implausible story.

As an indexical term, 'I' is bound to refer rightly to the person who uses it. Thus, in order to use the first-person pronoun, I need not have any general conception of myself of the kind the model postulates. But in any case there need be nothing about this person I am, certainly nothing in the way of recognizable properties, that can give me such a conception of myself. I may connect with the person, as explained in the by-product model, just insofar as it is the person whom my beliefs and desires rationally activate.

Suppose I express a desire that I see a friend, a fear that I will suffer at the dentist's hand, or a hope that I will pass a test. The person I pick out when I refer to myself in this first-personal way need not be conceptualized in any abstract way; I may exist for myself simply as the person those attitudes activate when I am rational in instrumental and related ways. Thus it would be misleading to say that the reason I feel a desire for what that person should do or a fear of what may happen to him at the dentist's is that the person is me: someone, independently conceptualized, for whom I have special concern. It would be misleading to think that those concerns are allocated in my favor, as by the sort of partiality that might lead me to be especially concerned with the welfare of a friend. The person identified by the word 'I' counts as me precisely because he is at the center of such concerns, not the other way around. To put it in a slogan, it is in virtue of my special interest in the person that he counts as me; it is not in virtue of the person being me that I have a special interest in him.

Hume complained that when he looked into himself, there was no substantial self to be found, only a string of psychological states and episodes (Hume 1978, I.4.6), and Sartre observed that all he could find in introspection was a stream of impersonal consciousness, nothing distinctively personal or self-like (Sartre 1957). Such reports are not surprising on our account of self-identification. The agent I am does not count as myself – the one I call 'I' – in virtue of having special, self-like properties that introspection might reveal. That agent counts as myself in virtue of being subject to the special connection to my beliefs and desires that instrumental rationality requires.

Self-identification and functioning as a person

An agent's ability to self-identify plays a central role in his or her functioning as a person. In performing as a person, I enter a system of obligations, making claims on others, authorizing their claims on me, and doing all this as a matter of common awareness. This performance, at least in the normal run, presupposes that I can self-identify as the referent of an 'I'.[134] By using the 'I', as noted earlier, I not only pick myself out as one person among others but also indicate my special relationship as speaker or spokesperson to that referent, implying that this is someone for whom I can authoritatively speak.

The first aspect allows me to understand the reciprocity of obligations and claims. By seeing myself as one person among others, I can recognize the claims of others and see the analogy between their claims and my own. The second aspect matters even more. To make claims on others and to recognize their claims on me, I must have the authority to speak for myself. Suppose I were to acknowledge claims only by using a proper name, saying that Christian, or Philip, promises such and such or admits to having done so and so. Suppose I did not sign off in the first person – even implicitly – on any such acknowledgement. It would then again remain open – at least logically – whether I know that I am Christian, or Philip, and so there could be a gap of authorization, akin to the identification gap discussed earlier. But if I use the first-person pronoun 'I' in formulating my obligations and claims, there is no doubt about who their subject is and who should be moved by them.

This is the bright side of self-identification in the life of individual persons. But there is a darker side too, associated with the sentiment Rousseau famously described as *amour propre* (Dent 1988).[135] It is normally translated as self-love, but this translation fails to mark the contrast Rousseau himself drew with *amour de soi*: literally, the love of self. We may do better to stick to the French terms.

Amour de soi is just the attachment to the particular agent one is that comes by virtue of identification, even identification as understood on the by-product model. It is not an attachment that an agent can fail to have and yet count as instrumentally rational; thus it even has to be ascribed to the little robot in our example. To lack *amour de soi* would be to lack the connection to a particular agent – the agent one is – which ensures that that agent is activated by one's attitudes, as means–end rationality requires.

Amour propre, unlike the simpler attachment, presupposes that the agent has identi-fied himself or herself by the use of an 'I', as one person among many. It appears as the agent compares him or herself with others. It is not the inevitable, innocuous form of self-concern that any rational agency involves but rather a passion for self-promotion, consisting in a preference to shine in comparison with others and prompting a desire to attain a position of superiority, or at least to avoid a position of inferiority.

Amour propre is important in the psychology of the individual person, because it is engaged in many of the most intense emotions. It is only in the presence of *amour propre* that agents can feel shame, pride, or envy, suffer humiliation, or enjoy a sense of triumph. These passions relate to the perceived position of the agents in relation to comparators, not to an absolute level of welfare or prosperity, and they are among the most powerful sentiments. *Amour propre* represents the dark side of self-identification because these passions can drive individuals to extremes to which regular *amour de soi* would never carry them. They give people an intense concern with saving face, even a willingness to do themselves harm in order to prevent others from achieving an advantage.

9.2 Corporate identification and self-identification

Identification in groups

Our observations about identification and self-identification are relevant not only to individual agents but also to group agents. Suppose some of us jointly intend to form a group agent; and suppose we act on that intention, organizing ourselves for agency. As we have noted, we may do this in an egalitarian or hierarchical way; we set the details aside for the moment. The first lesson of our discussion in the previous section is that, to succeed in forming a group agent, we must not let any identification gap open – or, if it opens, we must succeed in closing it. To prevent a gap from opening, we must organize our group attitude-formation such that it leads spontaneously and rationally to action, with the appropriate enactors automatically playing the required roles. To close the gap, if it opens, we must somehow move from viewing the group in a purely third-personal way to thinking in first-personal terms of what it rationally requires us to do.

The argument for this claim runs on the same lines as the argument in the individual case. My attitudes will not necessarily activate me, as rationality requires, unless their expression, in the propositional mode of ascription, involves the indexical 'I'. Equally our attitudes as the members of a group will not necessarily activate us as a group – not necessarily activate those of us who are the designated enactors of the group's attitudes – unless their propositional expression involves the first-person indexical.

How might the identification gap be avoided in the case of a group? One abstract possibility is the following. Although I am a member, I think of the group in third-person terms and track its attitudes and their requirements like an outside observer. I act in the group's name because, on detecting that a relevant member ought to take a certain action, I recognize that I am that member and thereby form the desire that I perform the action. And what is true of me is true of other members too. We may each act in such a way that the group overcomes the identification gap by our each recognizing what is individually required of us to sustain the group agent and by being disposed to act as required. We may be disposed to act as required either because the agency and action of the group is in our individual interest or because we care about the group as we might care about someone we like or love.

This way of closing the identification gap at the group level parallels the mode of identification at the individual level that is described by the cognitive achievement model. This is the mode in which I primarily think of myself in third-person terms, say as Christian or Philip, and let Christian's, or Philip's, attitudes impact on me by means of the further recognition that I am that person.

We think, however, that, as in the case of individuals, identification in a well-functioning group agent is usually achieved more spontaneously. Let each of us be motivated to act for a group, as in the earlier case; this motivation may be individually self-interested or may reflect an independent affection for the group. As members we need not laboriously think of the group in third-personal terms, tracking its attitudes and then working out what is required of us as individual enactors. Rather, we somehow achieve an alignment between what the group's attitudes require of us and our own preferences, and then act without further reflection whenever our response is required. The alignment may be achieved either through explicitly adopting the group's viewpoint – that is, adopting the group's attitudes as our own – or through an incentive structure that guarantees that alignment by appealing to our self-interest, such as when the group agent is internally organized in such a way as to meet the incentive-compatibility desideratum discussed in Chapter 5. In either case, the group effectively connects its beliefs and desires directly to action without letting any identification gap open. This mirrors the by-product model of identification described earlier.

An analogy may help to explain the idea. Consider how pilots relate to cockpit instruments that give information on the plane's altitude, orientation, speed, and so on. Beginner pilots may consult the instruments and let the evidence count in their own reasoning processes. If the horizon is out of sight, they may let panel information weigh against the information from their own senses; the latter may be misleading, since the senses cannot distinguish, for example, between gravity and acceleration (McGeer and Pettit 2002). Rather than sustaining a relationship whereby the instruments are consulted, experienced pilots develop a different, direct connection with them. They let their own bodily cues go off-line, and hitch their intuitions and instincts directly to the instruments. They let the instruments guide them without the intrusion of thoughts about the evidence provided. Or at least they do this when the 'red lights' are off, and nothing indicates that things are amiss.

Just as pilots can connect in this direct way to the instruments on the cockpit panel, so the members of a group may connect themselves directly to the attitudes of the group. They do not treat the group attitudes as mere indicators of what the group is to do, asking themselves explicitly whether they wish to identify with the group, and acting only if they have this wish. Rather, their individual attitudes are under the automatic guidance of the group, so that they can respond as spontaneously as pilots do when they take their cue from the panel before them. Or at least they may do this when there are no 'red lights' that suggest they should hesitate and take stock.

If we reach an alignment between what the group requires of us and our individual attitudes through adopting the group's viewpoint, and not merely through an incentive structure under which individual and group interests coincide, then we, the members, each have attitudes in whose propositional expression the group figures as *we*. We each act on beliefs and desires that call for expression in first-person plural terms. They are desires that we do so and so, or beliefs that we can do such and such, that link up with our responses without the mediation of any belief about our membership in the group. Metaphorically speaking, the group's mind is then instantiated in each of us and leads us to act automatically, as required by the group.[136]

We have distinguished between an indirect, cognitive-achievement-based and a more spontaneous way in which the members of a group agent may think in collective terms, whether on the basis of self-interested motivation or an altruistic attachment to the group. In conclusion to this discussion it is worth stressing that even as members retain a motive for acting as a group, they may fail to think in collective terms and so fail as a group agent. We, the members, may stand to benefit greatly from the actions of a group – a town, university, church, or whatever – and we may even have a common idea of what the group should do. But we may fail to assume an appropriate, group standpoint; we may fail to identify as the group that our collective attitudes should activate. And so we may fail to perform appropriately as a group agent.

This observation is worth making because it highlights the role that one or more activist members can play in sustaining a group agent. They may recall the rest of us to our shared identity and move the group back to a first-personal perspective in which we act more or less spontaneously as group attitudes require. They may reconnect us with those attitudes, transforming our way of thinking in the way in which the thinking of beginner pilots is transformed when the cockpit instruments assume control over their responses. Social activists often describe this shift, in Marxist terms, as one of raising 'group consciousness'.

Not only can the initiative of activists revive group agents whose members are faltering in their identification. It can also produce a corporate unity in those groups that have not yet become fully functioning group agents. Consider groups that are not yet fit to be held responsible, because they are insufficiently 'incorporated', but that can be made fit to be held responsible; in Chapter 7 we called such groups 'responsibiliz-able'. Examples include national, religious, and ethnic populations. Just as there may be developmental grounds for holding such groups responsible – it can promote their development into fully functioning group agents, which are fit to be held responsible – so there may be aspirational grounds for activist members to rally their fellows around the suggestion that the group already has corporate status. Such an intervention can help the group to achieve that status, inducing suitable actions in its members. Or at least it can do this on a particular issue or over a particular period, as when an ethnic minority finds its voice on some matter and acts as a unified agent.

The group agents we have focused on in this book are of the actively incorporated kind, organized to function reliably as agents. But side by side with them we should also recognize the category of aspirational group agents. These are groups that are not yet fully functioning agents but that hover on the verge of agency. Members are routinely disposed to summon their fellows to a sense of solidarity in thinking together as a group agent; and they do so with some effect, however limited or temporary.

Self-identification in groups

Successful group agents are not only characterized by their avoidance or closure of any identification gap. They typically also self-identify as a group, employing the language of 'we' just as the individual, self-identifying agent employs the language of 'I'. This facilitates the performance of a group as a person among persons, just as individual self-identification facilitates the performance of the individual as a person among persons.

It enables those who speak for the group to pick out that group as one personal agent among others: we, the town; we, the university; we, the church. And it enables them at the same time to pick it out as an agent to which they have a special, authoritative relationship, one that allows them to use the indexical 'we'. This is a group that they recognize as one among many – as a group enmeshed in reciprocal obligations – but it is also a group in which they are implicated, a group for which they are entitled to speak, and a group that is moved by certain collectively endorsed intentional attitudes.

It is often said that forming and acting on joint intentions, as agents do when they act together, requires each to think in terms of a 'we' (Gilbert 1989; Tuomela 1995; Bratman 1999; Gold and Sugden 2007). Even when we do something as simple as carrying a piano downstairs together we may need to form appropriate 'we'-intentions. But the 'we' involved in such joint intentions is usually the distributed 'we', not the corporate one that arises when joint intentions lead to a self-identifying group agent. The 'we' of joint intentions refers to us distributively, as the separate agents required to act on these intentions; the 'we' of group agency refers to us corporately, as a single, unified center of attitude and action.

Recall the joint intention we form when we see a swimmer in difficulty and allocate roles in a coordinated effort to save the swimmer. We can naturally describe this by saying that each of us intends that we together save the swimmer. But we could equally say that we each intend that those on the beach together save the swimmer, or that you and she and I save the swimmer. The fact that there is no unified group agent means that the 'we' in each of our intentions is easily reducible to an enumeration of individual pronouns, as in 'you-and-she-and-I'.

No reduction of this kind is possible with the corporate 'we'. The referent here is the group agent as a single entity, not the collection of its members.[137] In the ordinary case of joint action a number of individual agents unite to perform a common action. In the corporate case a number of individual agents unite to constitute a single group agent – an entity that is subject in its own right to the constraints of agency – and then perform one or another action in its name. The 'we' in this corporate case picks out that single agent and enables members to see what is required of them as its representatives and enactors. When those members speak about what *we* owe to other persons, for example, or what others owe to *us*, the group of which they speak is the single person they constitute, not the members, considered one by one.

The corporate 'we' may be used aspirationally, not to express a corporate status already achieved but to encourage members to seek its achievement. Think of the member of the disaffected crowd who stands on a soap-box, calls on the attention of each, and proposes that 'we' will not stand for such and such treatment, that 'we' endorse such and such values and beliefs, and that 'we' are prepared to take such and such action. The aspiration may fail but if it succeeds, it can give life to a corporate 'we' that refers to the emerging group agent. It is this 'we' that figures in the document the Philadelphia founders proposed to their fellows: 'We the people of the United States . . . do ordain and establish this Constitution.'

We mentioned in the case of individuals that self-identification has a dark side as well as a bright side. Not only does it enable an individual person to function as a person among persons, bound in a system of mutual obligation; it also prompts the appearance of *amour propre* and its attendant passions. The same is true of group agents. Collective *amour propre* is prompted by the recognition among individuals that a group agent with which they self-identify exists in competition with others. It is a nation among nations, a church among churches, a university among universities, a team among teams. What the sentiment involves is a desire, recognized and authorized in the group, to perform on a par with competing entities or to outperform them. In a brute form it is the desire to achieve parity and superiority by whatever means; in a more sophisticated form it is the desire to attain such results on the basis of desert.

It is because of collective *amour propre* that the members of a group agent can feel shame or pride in their collective performance, suffer humiliation as a group, or enjoy a sense of group triumph. And the effects of such passions on relations between group agents are well documented. Collective shame or humiliation can lead members into self-destructive rage or total despair; collective pride or triumph can license the most absurd pretensions. These effects are visible across the world and down the ages. They appear in inter-racial and inter-religious conflicts, in struggles between different regions or countries, even in competition between rival sporting clubs.

The members of such active or aspirational group agents squirm in loss and strut in victory, displaying concerns that make little sense on standard conceptions of rational self-interest (but see Brennan and Pettit 2004). On standard conceptions, self-interest is non-positional and individualistic. It focuses on absolute welfare, not relative standing, and on the agent's own, individual welfare, not on that of a larger group. But the reality of *amour propre* goes against the non-positional assumption, and the reality of collective *amour propre* against the individualistic. People are prepared to cut off their nose to spite their face. And, worse – worse, because even more dangerous – they are prepared to do this for the sake of collective standing, not just personal dignity.

9.3 Multiple identities

Investing in group agents

The picture drawn suggests that we form and enact not only the beliefs and desires that mark each of us in our individuality but also those of various group agents we are associated with. These range from schools and universities to churches, from voluntary associations to activist groups, from town meetings to political parties and the states we live in. We may sometimes find it difficult to remain steadily committed to the group agents we are part of; our different commitments may clash. But generally our membership in group agents, active or aspirational, provides us with novel channels of identification and self-identification.

When people act as members of group agents, they affiliate with them in their actions as they affiliate with their own selves in individual action. We describe this process as one of 'investing' in group agents. People not only speak and act for group agents, as for distinct persons; they often invest their affections in them. They treat group agents as entities that make the same intimate claims on them as their individual selves do. Consider, to take some familiar examples, the priest whose life is the church or the revolutionary whose life is the party. Such personalities make vivid for us the image of human beings who give little importance to their individual selves, conducting their lives in the service of the corporate bodies they belong to. Such individuals set aside their individual lives, investing instead in corporate selves that operate on a larger scale.

The possibility of investing in group agents, thereby achieving some kind of 'transcendence' beyond one's individual self, was noted from the earliest days of incorporation. When the notion of the corporate body became established in medieval Europe – particularly when such bodies came to be seen as persons of a novel, artificial kind – the idea of corporate transcendence was embraced with relish (Kantorowicz 1997). At a time when individual lives tended to be short and miserable, membership in a monastic order, trade guild, or city republic may have offered people a certain sense of immortality. Those group agents were not necessarily immortal but neither were they as mortal as their individual members; they gave members a prospect of living on in larger selves they shared with others.[138]

Attaching oneself to a corporate entity is sometimes seen as an intelligible but irrational form of self-neglect. But it is nonetheless a fact of human psychology, as ancient and common experience testifies, that human beings have ample resources for such attachment. Investing in one's own self means privileging an individual agent as the referent of the 'I'; investing in a corporate self means privileging a group agent as the referent of a 'we'. In both cases, the agent picked out by the first-person pronoun, whether singular or plural, is the one whose beliefs and desires prompt the agent to act.

Think of the adage 'Home is where the heart is'. This does not mean that the place we each call 'home' happens, as a contingency of psychology, to be where we invest our affections. Rather it means that we each tend to give the name 'home' to whichever place captures those affections. The affections come first, the constitution of home second. Similarly, we may say 'Self is where the heart is', provided it is clear that we may each be of many hearts, as we may be of many minds. All human beings invest their hearts in what they individually experience and do, letting their attitudes answer to those experiences and dictate those actions. But all human beings, it appears, are equally capable of investing their hearts in the experiences and responses of group agents. They may find a recognizable self not just in the individual persons they are but in any group person they are prepared to serve.

Different group agents, it should be noted, offer different prospects for investment. At the end of the first chapter, we categorized group agents into political, economic, and civic or cultural ones. Clearly, group agents in the political, civic, and cultural categories are more likely to be targets of self-investment than ones in the economic category. Economic group agents – firms and corporations – rely primarily on returns and remuneration to attract and hold members, whether as shareholders or employees. Under such a dispensation members are less likely to consider the group as an entity with which to affiliate robustly. The shareholders' loyalty usually goes no further than prospective returns support, the employees' no further than is justified by the security and salary they receive.

Just as group agents may vary in their capacity to attract the investment of individual affection, so individuals may vary in their readiness to invest in such bodies. One might suspect that the readiness of individuals to do this may depend on how far the investment in their individual lives is consuming and rewarding. But this variation, like the variation on the corporate side, is an issue for empirical inquiry, not something our theory can settle.

Without the capacity for corporate self-investment, we would probably be incapable of organizing in communities and states, or campaigning for charitable causes and public enterprises, or caring about global warming and the future of the world, or even getting involved in spectator sports. But, as we know, this capacity can also lead people to unite in dangerous groupings and rally behind destructive endeavors. Ethnic, cultural, and national animosities may result from this capacity, as may some of the most deadly, self-destructive pursuits of our species (Hardin 1995). We gestured at this topic in our discussion of collective *amour propre*.

Given that we invest in an individual identity, on the one hand, and a number of group identities, on the other, there are serious questions about how we negotiate and reconcile them with one another. In the remainder of this chapter we look at two such issues. One bears on how each of us combines the different identities in which we invest, individual and collective; the other bears on how a number of us can combine to negotiate differences about the identity of a single group agent in which we all invest. One is an intrapersonal issue, the other an interpersonal one.

The intrapersonal issue

On the account offered so far, each of us sometimes acts in his or her individual identity, letting our individual attitudes alone determine what we do; and each of us sometimes acts in a group identity, letting the attitudes of a corporate entity impact on how we act. We sometimes think and act as an individual, sometimes as the member of a larger entity. This then raises an obvious question. What determines – and, if that is distinct, what ought to determine – the identity in which anyone of us acts on a given occasion?

One extreme view would be that this is not a matter in which we – we, in any identity – have a choice. According to that view, we operate, sometimes as individuals, sometimes as the members of a group, and we have no say in the matter of which it shall be; we may not even be aware of the shift from one identity to the other. Which identity is in charge on any occasion is fixed by factors over which we have no control.

On this view each of us relates to our different identities, individual and collective, in the way in which the person suffering from multiple personality disorder (MPD) relates to the personas that come and go in the self-presentation of the patient.

This view is utterly implausible. Almost everyone will agree that identity is subject to choice in a way in which the persona of the MPD patient is not. Which identity we act in is not something imposed from outside, as if we were possessed, now by this identity, now by that. But if identity is subject to choice, then who ought to make the choice? And on the basis of what attitudes – on the basis, in effect, of what identity – should the choice rationally be made?

Elizabeth Anderson (2001) has argued that identity precedes rationality, in which case it seems that this question has no answer (see also Rovane 1997). According to her thesis, 'what principle of choice it is rational to act on depends on a prior determination of personal identity, of who one is'. In other words, before it is possible to explore what an agent should rationally do, the identity in which the agent acts must be established; it must be determined, for example, whether the agent acts as an individual or as a member of some group. Thus it seems that there is no rational way of choosing between identities. In one's individual identity one may rationally choose one identity, in a group identity one may rationally choose another. And there is no neutral identity in which one can rationally decide between the two.

One response to this problem might be to say that the choice of identity should be seen as a collective choice, not an individual one. The idea would be that, in debating about which identity to assume and act in on a given occasion, I as an individual hold a rational discussion with myself – specifically, with myself in a group identity or in a number of group identities – about how to resolve the matter to the joint satisfaction of the different persons I represent. But this position is no more plausible than the view that casts each of us in the image of the MPD patient. It is little short of comic to suggest that we are each an arena in which such different identities have autonomous voices.

Do we have to say, then, as Anderson's principle suggests, that there is no rational basis for adjudicating issues of identity: no neutral identity in which we can resolve those questions? We do not think so. The question as to who ought to make the choice should be kept apart, as our earlier formulation suggests, from the question of the basis on which the choice ought to be made. And when those questions are kept apart, the answer to each becomes more straightforward.

The agent who ought to make the choice as to whether to assume one or another identity, we suggest, is the agent in his or her individual identity. Someone's identity as an individual is special in a number of ways. It is a comprehensive identity, in the sense that there is no natural limit to the domain over which the individual has attitudes. It is an inalienable identity, in the sense that no individual can opt for implementing group identities only. And most importantly, it is a proprietary identity, in the sense that it is not necessarily subject to the control of any other agents in the way group identities are. For a combination of these reasons, it makes perfectly good sense to think that the agent qua individual authorizes the assumption of this or that group identity. By contrast, it makes little or no sense to think that the agent qua member of one or another group agent authorizes the agent's assumption of a certain individual identity.

This means that individual identity, and only individual identity, is prior to rationality, in Anderson's use of that notion. It is always the individual qua individual who decides to assume a group identity, or to sustain an identity more or less automatically assumed. But that does not mean, to turn to the second question, that the choice as to whether to act in a certain group identity should be made, or even has to be made, in a way that is sensitive only to the interests of the individual agent.

An individual agent cannot help but act out of the desires that characterize that agent in his or her individual identity. But that does not imply, as we have noted already, that the agent will act only in accordance with his or her individual interests, or on the grounds that the action chosen will satisfy the agent's desire. If I give money to someone begging on the streets, that is bound to be because I have a desire to do so; but that does not imply that the action is chosen to further my own interests, or on the grounds that the action satisfies my desire to take that action. We do sometimes act on the grounds that doing so will satisfy the very desire at the origin of the act; we do this, for example, with desires that operate like itches, such as the hankering for a smoke or a drink. But this is not an inevitable or even a general pattern (Pettit 2006).

It may be, as we think, that I always choose in my individual identity to assume or at least to sustain this or that group identity. But it does not follow that whether or not I assume or sustain the identity is hostage to whether doing so is in the interest of me in my individual identity. Acting in my identity as an individual, I can recognize the value of this or that group, or I can feel a liking or even a love of the group. And such sentiments may sometimes lead me not just to assume the group identity but even to sacrifice my welfare as an individual to the welfare of the group. Nothing in our discussion implies otherwise.

The sacrifice that group membership may require of individuals is illustrated by a theme that has been central from early in this book. The theme is that, if individuals are prepared to act in the name of a group, then rationality at the group level may require them to act on the basis of judgments and preferences that they do not hold themselves, and that are not necessarily upheld by a majority – in some cases, not even by a minority – of members. To be prepared to put aside one's own judgments and preferences and to act in the name of attitudes one does not personally endorse may be seen as a vivid instance of self-sacrifice.

To sum up, then, the individual identity of every agent is special, since it is up to the agent in that identity to decide whether or not to go along with some group identity; but the agent in that identity may rationally decide to assume a group identity that is at odds with his or her own individual interests. The agent who does the choosing may have to be the individual agent but the basis of the agent's choice may involve the interests of the group, not those of the individual.

We should also emphasize, however, that the sacrifice that group membership can require of individuals may sometimes prove to be too great. Individual agents may not find within themselves the resources needed to remain faithful to the group. Think of our discussion of group 'akrasia' in Chapter 5. Even when individuals opt for acting in a group manner, they may be held back by their own private interests or preferences. They may keep to their private viewpoints and prove unable to get their corporate act together. Such group akrasia is possible precisely because individuals face conflicts between acting for the group and acting for themselves, just as they face conflicts in any difficult choice (Pettit 2003a).

The interpersonal issue

As an individual I am responsible for any action I performed in the past, provided I had no good excuse for what I did. It was I who took that action and I cannot deny the fact. But the desire to cut a good figure can lead me to disown my action. I may say: that was me at the time but it is not me now; I have changed; I am a new man or woman. I may claim that while I am still the same person, I am no longer the same character (Parfit 1984, Part 1). The attitudes and actions disowned are ones I repudiate and, if necessary, apologize for; they should not be taken as indications, so I wish to communicate, of what may be expected of me in the future.

This pattern of disowning some aspects of my past, and owning others, is integral to living in accordance with the consciousness and the concerns that *amour propre* brings on stream. It involves a sculpting of one's self into an image that serves this sentiment. The sculpting need not involve an intentional, narcissistic construction of the self (for a critique, see Strawson 2005). It is an inevitable by-product of the practice of disowning and repudiating some attitudes and actions and owning and acknowledging others (Pettit 2001c). If someone follows that practice, as everyone to some extent does, they will carve out a character for themselves. And in some contexts it is this character, not the person as a whole, that the agent will want to present as the referent of the 'I'.

The self-sculpting that *amour propre* prompts in individuals has a parallel in group agents. Some group agents may operate in a pragmatic space, where there is little or no cause to revisit the past. But this is not the general rule. Many group agents, political, economic, and civic, sometimes distance themselves from attitudes previously avowed or actions formerly taken, thereby carving out the character by which they wish to be known. Just as I may say of my past self that he is no longer me, so the spokespersons for a group agent may say of it in the past: 'That is no longer us', 'We are not the church that condemned Galileo', 'We are not the nation that dispossessed indigenous peoples', 'We are no longer the company that made contracts with the Nazis'.

When agents shape their individual character on the basis of what they own and disown, there can be some ambivalence or dissonance associated with the enterprise. People may display a lack of security about who they are or what they want to be. This pattern replicates itself more intensely with group agents. The practice of owning and disowning in which the character of a group is formed may be controversial, with some members wanting to go one way, others another. There can then be a struggle for the 'soul' of the group. Different members may fight for rival visions of the character of the group in which they are invested.

When this happens, the construction of the group's character will take on a directly narrative form, with rival members telling different histories of where the group is coming from, and what episodes characterize it best. Adherents of the Roman Catholic Church struggle over how much importance to give to traditional teaching on sexual morality. Members of socialist parties struggle over how far traditional socialism commits them to hostility towards the market. Citizens of the United States struggle over how far the republic of their founders was a secular one. And so on in a familiar pattern.

This illustrates how interpersonally difficult the enterprise of forming or sustaining a group agent can be. It can put members at loggerheads with one another, as they divide about matters of value and those divisions generate differences on how to cast a group to which they all belong. If I can think well of the character of a group agent to which I belong, and in which I am heavily invested, then I can feel some pride in its achievements; if I cannot then I must feel a certain shame. But what is true of me is also true of you. And so, if we differ on what is a matter for pride, what a matter for shame, then this can generate intense struggles about how to construe the nature of our group.

Our struggle over the group agent's character is likely to be amplified by a connection with the policies we want the group to pursue. If the Roman Catholic Church has a history of adjusting its code on sexual matters to contemporary practices, then it is easier for liberals to argue for a shift in the Church's policy on contraception. If the United States is a fundamentally secular state, created with a conscious distancing from religious faith, then it is easier for liberals to argue against any favoritism towards the Christian or Judaeo-Christian tradition. It should be no surprise, therefore, that liberals often go one way in such disputes, conservatives another.

These observations show that just as there is an intrapersonal issue for each of us as to how to combine group identities within ourselves, so there is an interpersonal issue as to how we can manage to join with others – particularly others with whom we differ on normative issues – in sculpting an agreed character for a group we all belong to. The life of groups in which this issue arises is bound to involve strife and struggle.

This should not be surprising. We are the group agents we form, as we have argued at length in this book. And when we take a view on the character of any group agent, then we are moved as naturally by pride and shame as when we view ourselves in that light. It is not just that the glory or humiliation of the group agent is reflected onto us, as might be that of a family member. The glory or humiliation is our own; it is ours in the shared identity that group agency involves.

References

Adams, R. M. (1985). 'Involuntary Sins'. *Philosophical Review* 94: 3–31.

Anderson, E. (2001). 'Unstrapping the Straitjacket of "Preference": A Comment on Amartya Sen's Contributions to Philosophy and Economics'. *Economics and Philosophy* 17: 21–38.

Appiah, K. A. (2004). *The Ethics of Identity*. Princeton: Princeton University Press.

Arrow, K. (1951/1963). *Social Choice and Individual Values*. New York: Wiley.

Austen-Smith, D. and J. S. Banks (1996). 'Information Aggregation, Rationality, and the Condorcet Jury Theorem'. *American Political Science Review* 90(1): 34–45.

Austin, J. (1869). *Lectures on Jurisprudence, or the Philosophy of Positive Law*. London.

Ayer, A. J. (1982). *Language, Truth and Logic*. London: Gollanz.

Bacharach, M. (2006). *Beyond Individual Choice: Teams and Frames in Game Theory* (edited by N. Gold and R. Sugden). Princeton: Princeton University Press.

Bakan, J. (2004). *The Corporation: The Pathological Pursuit of Profit and Power*. New York: Free Press.

Barberà, S., F. Gul, et al. (1993). 'Generalized Median Voter Schemes and Committees'. *Journal of Economic Theory* 61: 262–89.

—— J. Massó, et al. (1997). 'Voting under Constraints'. *Journal of Economic Theory* 76: 298–321.

Barker, E. (1915). *Political Thought in England from Herbert Spencer to the Present Day*. London: Williams and Norgate.

—— (1950). 'Introduction'. *Gierke, Natural Law and the Theory of Society*. E. Barker. Cambridge: Cambridge University Press. ix–xci.

Bayes, T. (1763). 'An Essay towards Solving a Problem in the Doctrine of Chances'. *Philosophical Transactions of the Royal Society of London* 53: 370–418.

Ben-Yashar, R. and S. Nitzan (1997). 'The Optimal Decision Rule for Fixed-Size Committees in Dichotomous Choice Situations: The General Result'. *International Economic Review* 38: 175–86.

Bennett, J. (1976). *Linguistic Behaviour*. Cambridge: Cambridge University Press.

Bentham, J. (1970). *An Introduction to the Principles of Morals and Legislation (1823)*. London: Athlone Press.

Berend, D. and J. Paroush (1998). 'When is Condorcet's Jury Theorem Valid?' *Social Choice and Welfare* 15: 481–8.

Berend, D. and L. Sapir (2007). 'Monotonicity in Condorcet's Jury Theorem with Dependent Voters'. *Social Choice and Welfare* 28(3): 507–28.

Berlin, I. (1969). *Four Essays on Liberty*. Oxford: Oxford University Press.

Bikhchandani, S., D. Hirshleifer, et al. (1992). 'A Theory of Fads, Fashions, Custom, and Cultural Change as Informational Cascades'. *Journal of Political Economy* 100: 992–1026.

Black, D. (1948). 'On the Rationale of Group Decision-Making'. *Journal of Political Economy* 56(1): 23–34.

Blackburn, S. (1984). *Spreading the Word*. Oxford: Oxford University Press.

Blackstone, W. (1978). *Commentaries on the Laws of England*. New York: Garland.

Block, N. (1980). 'Troubles with Functionalism?' *Readings in Philosophy of Psychology, Vol 1.* Block. London: Methuen. 268–306.

Boland, P. J. (1989). 'Majority Systems and the Condorcet Jury Theorem'. *The Statistician* 38: 181–9.

Bourdieu, P. (2005). *The Social Structures of the Economy.* Cambridge: Polity Press.

Bovens, L. and W. Rabinowicz (2006). 'Democratic Answers to Complex Questions: An Epistemic Perspective'. *Synthese* 150(1): 131–53.

Bradley, F. H. (1876). *Ethical Studies.* London: Oxford University Press.

Braham, M. and M. J. Holler (2008). 'Distributing Causal Responsibility in Collectivities' *Rational Choice and Normative Philosophy.* T. Boylan and R. Gekker. London: Routledge. 145–63.

Braithwaite, J. and P. Drahos (2000). *Global Business Regulation.* Cambridge: Cambridge University Press.

Bratman, M. (1987). *Intention, Plans, and Practical Reason.* Cambridge, MA: Harvard University Press.

—— (1999). *Faces of Intention: Selected Essays on Intention and Agency.* Cambridge: Cambridge University Press.

Brennan, G. (2001). 'Collective Coherence?' *International Review of Law and Economics* 21: 197–211.

—— (2003). 'In Praise of Inconsistency?' *Paper presented at Como Conference.*

—— and L. Lomasky (1993). *Democracy and Decision: The Pure Theory of Electoral Preference.* Oxford: Oxford University Press.

—— and P. Pettit (2004). *The Economy of Esteem: An Essay on Civil and Political Society.* Oxford: Oxford University Press.

Burge, T. (1998). 'Reason and the First Person'. *Knowing Our Own Minds.* B. S. C. Wright and C. Macdonald. Oxford: Oxford University Press.

Cane, P. (2002). *Responsibility in Law and Morality.* Oxford: Hart.

Canning, J. (1987). *The Political Thought of Baldus de Ubaldis.* Cambridge: Cambridge University Press.

Canning, J. P. (1983). 'Ideas of the State in Thirteenth- and Fourteenth-Century Commentators on the Roman Law'. *Transactiosn of the Royal Historical Society* 33: 1–27.

Carter, I. (1999). *A Measure of Freedom.* Oxford: Oxford University Press.

Castaneda, H. N. (1966). '"He": A Study in the Logic of Self-consciousness'. *Ratio* 8: 130–57.

Chaffee, S. H. (2000). 'George Gallup and Ralph Nafziger: Pioneers of Audience Research'. *Mass Communication and Society* 3(2&3): 317–27.

Chalmers, D. (1996). *The Conscious Mind: In Search of a Fundamental Theory.* New York: Oxford University Press.

Chapman, B. (1998). 'More Easily Done than Said: Rules, Reason and Rational Social Choice'. *Oxford Journal of Legal Studies* 18(2): 293–329.

—— (2002). 'Rational Aggregation'. *Politics, Philosophy and Economics* 1(3): 337–54.

Coleman, J. (1974). *Power and the Structure of Society.* New York: Norton.

—— (1990). *Foundations of Social Theory.* Cambridge, MA: Harvard University Press.

Colvin, E. (1995). 'Corporate Personality and Criminal Liability'. *Criminal Law Foum* 6: 3–44.

Condorcet, M. d. (1785). *Essay sur l'Application de l'Analyse à la Probabilité des Décisions Rendues à la Pluralité des Voix.* Paris.

Conradt, L. and C. List (2009). 'Group Decisions in Humans and Animals: A Survey'. *Philosophical Transactions of the Royal Society B* 364: 719–42.

Copp, D. (1991). 'Responsibility for Collective Inaction'. *Journal of Social Philosophy* 22: 71–80.

—— (2007). 'The Collective Moral Autonomy Thesis'. *Journal of Social Philosophy* 38(3): 369–88.

Cossio, C. (1945). *El Derecho en el Derecho Judicial*. Buenos Aires: Guillermo Kraft.

Cowell, J. (1607). *The Interpreter or Booke Containing the Signification of Words*. Cambridge: John Legate.

Craven, J. (1982). 'Liberalism and Individual Preferences'. *Theory and Decision* 14: 351–60.

Dan-Cohen, M. (1986). *Rights, Persons and Organizations: A Legal Theory for Bureaucratic Society*. Berkeley, CA: University of California Press.

Darwall, S. (2006). *The Second-Person Standpoint: Morality, Respect, and Accountability*. Cambridge, MA: Harvard University Press.

Davidson, D. (1984). *Inquiries into Truth & Interpretation*. Oxford: Oxford University Press.

—— (1985). 'Rational Animals'. *Action and Events*. E. L. Pore and B. McLaughlin. Oxford: Blackwell.

De Schutter, H. and R. Tinnevelt. (2008) (eds). 'David Miller's Theory of Global Justice'. *Critical Review of International Social and Political Philosophy* 11(4).

Dennett, D. (1979). *Brainstorms*. Brighton: Harvester Press.

—— (1981). 'True Believers: The Intentional Strategy and Why it Works'. *Mind Design II: Philosophy, Psychology, and Artificial Intelligence*. J. Haugeland. Cambridge, MA: MIT Press.

—— (1987). *The Intentional Stance*. Cambridge, MA: MIT Press.

Dent, N. J. H. (1988). *Rousseau*. Oxford: Blackwell.

Dietrich, F. (2006). 'Judgment Aggregation: (Im)possibility Theorems'. *Journal of Economic Theory* 126(1): 286–98.

—— (2007). 'A Generalised Model of Judgment Aggregation'. *Social Choice and Welfare* 28(4): 529–65.

—— (2008). 'The Premises of Condorcet's Jury Theorem Are Not Simultaneously Justified'. *Episteme – A Journal of Social Epistemology* 5(1): 56–73.

—— (2010). 'The Possibility of Judgment Aggregation on Agendas with Subjunctive Implications'. *Journal of Economic Theory* 145(2): 603–38.

—— and C. List (2004). 'A Model of Jury Decisions Where All Jurors Have the Same Evidence'. *Synthese* 142: 175–202.

—— —— (2007a). 'Arrow's Theorem in Judgment Aggregation'. *Social Choice and Welfare* 29 (1): 19–33.

—— —— (2007b). 'Judgment Aggregation by Quota Rules: Majority Voting Generalized'. *Journal of Theoretical Politics* 19(4): 391–424.

—— —— (2007c). 'Strategy-Proof Judgment Aggregation'. *Economics and Philosophy* 23(3): 269–300.

—— —— (2008a). 'Judgment Aggregation without Full Rationality'. *Social Choice and Welfare* 31: 15–39.

—— —— (2008b). 'A Liberal Paradox for Judgment Aggregation'. *Social Choice and Welfare* 31: 59–78.

—— —— (2009). 'Propositionwise Judgment Aggregation: The General Case'. *Working paper*. London School of Economics.

—— —— (2010a). 'The Aggregation of Propositional Attitudes: Towards a General Theory'. *Oxford Studies in Epistemology* 3.

Dietrich, F. and C. List (2010b). 'Majority Voting on Restricted Domains'. *Journal of Economic Theory* 145(2): 512–43.

—— —— (forthcoming). 'Opinion Pooling on General Agendas'. *Social Choice and Welfare.*

Dokow, E. and R. Holzman (2009a). 'Aggregation of Binary Evaluations for Truth-Functional Agendas'. *Social Choice and Welfare* 32: 221–41.

—— —— (2009b). 'Aggregation of Non-Binary Evaluations'. *Working paper.* Technion-Israel Institute of Technology.

—— —— (2010a). 'Aggregation of Binary Evaluations'. *Journal of Economic Theory* 145(2): 495–511.

—— —— (2010b). 'Aggregation of Binary Evaluations with Abstentions'. *Journal of Economic Theory* 145(2): 544–61.

Dowding, K. and M. van Hees (2003). 'The Construction of Rights'. *American Political Science Review* 97: 281–93.

Dryzek, J. and C. List (2003). 'Social Choice Theory and Deliberative Democracy: A Reconciliation'. *British Journal of Political Science* 33(1): 1–28.

Duff, P. W. (1938). *Personality in Roman Private Law.* Cambridge: Cambridge University Press.

Dworkin, R. (1986). *Law's Empire.* Cambridge, MA: Harvard University Press.

Erskine, T. (2003) (ed.). *Can Institutions Have Responsibilities? Collective Moral Agency and International Relations.* London: Palgrave.

Eschmann, T. (1946). 'Studies on the Notion of Society in St Thomas Aquinas I. St Thomas and the Decretal of Innocent IV Romana Ecclesia: Ceterum'. *Mediaeval Studies* 8: 1–42.

Estlund, D. (1994). 'Opinion Leaders, Independence, and Condorcet's Jury Theorem'. *Theory and Decision* 36: 131–62.

Feddersen, T. J. and W. Pesendorfer (1998). 'Convicting the Innocent'. *American Political Science Review* 92(1): 23–35.

Feinberg, J. (1968). 'Collective Responsibility'. *Journal of Philosophy* 65(21): 674–88.

Ferejohn, J. (2007). 'Conversability and Deliberation'. *Common Minds: Themes from the Philosophy of Philip Pettit.* Geoffrey Brennan, R.E. Goodin, Frank Jackson, and M. Smith. Oxford: Oxford University Press. 121–42.

Figgis, J. N. (1914). *Churches in the Modern State.* London: Longman.

French, P., J. Nesteruk, et al. (1992). *Corporations in the Moral Community.* New York: Harcourt Brace Jovanovich.

French, P. A. (1984). *Collective and Corporate Responsibility.* New York: Columbia University Press.

Frey, B. and R. Jegen (2001). 'Motivation Crowding Theory: A Survey'. *Journal of Economic Surveys* 15: 589–611.

Fulbrooke, E. (2009) (ed.). *Ontology in Economics: Tony Lawson and his Critics.* London: Routledge.

Gärdenfors, P. (2006). 'An Arrow-like Theorem for Voting with Logical Consequences'. *Economics and Philosophy* 22(2): 181–90.

Garland, D. (2001). *The Culture of Control: Crime and Social Order in Contemporary Society.* Chicago: University of Chicago Press.

Genest, C. and J. V. Zidek (1986). 'Combining Probability Distributions: A Critique and Annotated Bibliography'. *Statistical Science* 1(1): 113–35.

Gibbard, A. (1973). 'Manipulation of Voting Schemes: A General Result'. *Econometrica* 41(July): 587–601.

Gibbard, A. (1974). 'A Pareto-Consistent Libertarian Claim'. *Journal of Economic Theory* 7(4): 388–410.

—— (2003). *Thinking How to Live*. Cambridge, MA: Harvard University Press.

Giddens, A. (1984). *The Constitution of Society: Outline of the Theory of Structuration*. Cambridge: Polity Press.

Giere, R. (2002). 'Distributed Cognition in Epistemic Cultures'. *Philosophy of Science* 69: 637–44.

Gigerenzer, G. (2003). 'Simple Tools for Understanding Risks: From Innumeracy to Insight'. *British Medical Journal* 327: 741–4.

Gigliotti, G. A. (1986). 'Comment on Craven'. *Theory and Decision* 21: 89–95.

Gilbert, M. (1989). *On Social Facts*. Princeton, N.J.: Princeton University Press.

—— (2001). 'Collective Preferences, Obligations, and Rational Choice'. *Economics and Philosophy* 17: 109–120.

—— (2006). *A Theory of Political Obligation: Membership, Commitment, and the Bonds of Society*. Oxford: Oxford University Press.

Gold, N. and R. Sugden (2007). 'Collective Intentions and Team Agency'. *Journal of Philosophy* 104: 109–37.

Goldman, A. I. (1999). *Knowledge in a Social World*. Oxford: Oxford University Press.

—— (2004). 'Group Knowledge versus Group Rationality: Two Approaches to Social Epistemology'. *Episteme: A Journal of Social Epistemology* 1(1): 11–22.

—— (forthcoming). 'Systems-Oriented Social Epistemology'. *Oxford Studies in Epistemology* 3.

Goodin, R. E. and C. List (2006). 'Special Majorities Rationalized'. *British Journal of Political Science* 36(2): 213–41.

Grantham, R. (1998). 'The Doctrinal Basis of the Rights of Company Shareholders'. *Cambridge Law Journal* 57: 554–88.

Grofman, B., G. Owen, and S.L. Feld (1983). 'Thirteen Theorems in Search of the Truth'. *Theory and Decision* 15: 261–78.

Guilbaud, G. T. (1966). 'Theories of the General Interest, and the Logical Problem of Aggregation'. *Readings in Mathematical Social Science*. P. F. Lazarsfeld and N. W. Henry. Cambridge, MA: MIT Press. 262–307.

Gutmann, A. (2003). *Identity in Democracy*. Princeton: Princeton University Press.

Habermas, J. (1984/1989). *A Theory of Communicative Action, Volumes 1 and 2*. Cambridge: Polity Press.

Hager, M. M. (1989). 'Bodies Politic: The Progressive History of Organizational "Real Entity" Theory'. *University of Pittsburgh Law Review* 50: 575–654.

Hanson, R. (forthcoming). 'Shall We Vote on Values, but Bet on Beliefs?' *Journal of Political Philosophy*.

Hardin, R. (1995). *One for All: The Logic of Group Conflict*. Princeton, N.J.: Princeton University Press.

Harman, G. (1986). *Change in View*. Cambridge, MA: MIT Press.

Hauser, M. (2000). *Wild Minds: What Animals Really Think*. New York: Henry Holt and Co.

Hawthorne, J. (2004). *Knowledge and Lotteries*. New York: Oxford University Press.

Hayek, F. A. (1945). 'The Use of Knowledge in Society'. *American Economic Review* 35: 519–30.

Heider, F. and M. Simmel (1944). 'An Experimental Study of Apparent Behavior'. *American Journal of Psychology* Vol. 157: 243–59.

Held, V. (1970). 'Can a Random Collection of Individuals Be Morally Responsible?' *Journal of Philosophy* 67: 471–81.

Helm, B. W. (2008). 'Plural Agents'. *Nous* 42(1): 17–49.

Hindriks, F. (2008). 'The Status Account of Corporate Agents'. *Concepts of Sharedness – New Essays on Collective Intentionality*. B. Schmid, K. Schulte-Ostermann, and N. Psarros. Frankfurt: Ontos Verlag: 119–44.

—— (2009). 'Corporate Responsibility and Judgment Aggregation'. *Economics and Philosophy* 25: 161–77.

Hirschman, A. O. (1970). *Exit, Voice and Loyalty*. Cambridge, MA: Harvard University Press.

Hobbes, T. (1990). *Behemoth or The Long Parliament* (edited by F. Toennies). Chicago: University of Chicago Press.

—— (1994). *Leviathan* (edited by E. Curley). Indianapolis: Hackett.

Hume, D. (1978). *A Treatise of Human Nature*. Oxford: Oxford University Press.

Hylland, A. and R. Zeckhauser (1979). 'The Impossibility of Bayesian Group Decision Making with Separate Aggregation of Beliefs and Values'. *Econometrica* 47: 1321–1336.

Jackson, F. (1987). 'Group Morality'. *Metaphysics and Morality: Essays in Honour of J. J. C. Smart*. P. Pettit, R. Sylvan, and J. Norman. Oxford: Blackwell. 91–110.

—— and P. Pettit (1988). 'Functionalism and Broad Content'. *Mind* 97: 381–400; reprinted in F. Jackson, P. Pettit, and M. Smith, 2004. 95–118.

—— —— (2004). *Mind, Morality, and Explanation: Selected Collaborations*. Oxford: Oxford University Press.

Johnston, M. (2010). *Surviving Death: Religion after Idolatry*. Princeton, NJ: Princeton University Press.

Kantorowicz, E. H. (1997). *The King's Two Bodies: A Study in Mediaeval Political Theology*. Princeton, N.J.: Princeton University Press.

Kelly, E. (2003). 'The Burdens of Collective Liability'. *Ethics and Foreign Intervention*. D. K. Chatterjee and D. E. Scheid. Cambridge: Cambridge University Press. 118–39.

Kelsen, H. (1945). *The General Theory of Law and State*. Cambridge, MA: Harvard University Press.

Kim, J. (1998). *Mind in a Physical World: An Essay on the Mind – Body Problem and Mental Causation*. Cambridge, MA: MIT Press.

Knight, J. and J. Johnson (1994). 'Aggregation and Deliberation: On the Possibility of Democratic Legitimacy'. *Political Theory* 22(2): 277–96.

Knorr Cetina, K. (1999). *Epistemic Cultures: How the Sciences Make Knowledge*. Cambridge, MA: Harvard University Press.

Konieczny, S. and R. Pino-Perez (2002). 'Merging Information under Constraints: A Logical Framework'. *Journal of Logic and Computation* 12: 773–808.

Kornhauser, L. A. (1992). 'Modelling Collegial Courts. II. Legal Doctrine'. *Journal of Law, Economics and Organization* 8: 441–70.

—— and L. G. Sager (1986). 'Unpacking the Court'. *Yale Law Journal* 96: 82–117.

—— —— (1993). 'The One and the Many: Adjudication in Collegial Courts'. *California Law Review* 81: 1–59.

Kornhauser, L. A. and L. G. Sager (2004). 'The Many as One: Integrity and Group Choice in Paradoxical Cases'. *Philosophy and Public Affairs* 32: 249–76.

Korsgaard, C. M. (1999). 'Self-Constitution in the Ethics of Plato and Kant'. *The Journal of Ethics* 3: 1–29.

Kukathas, C. and P. Pettit (1990). *Rawls: A Theory of Justice and its Critics*. Cambridge and Stanford: Polity Press and Stanford University Press.

Kutz, C. (2001). *Complicity: Ethics and Law for a Collective Age*. Cambridge: Cambridge University Press.

Ladha, K. (1992). 'The Condorcet Jury Theorem, Free Speech and Correlated Votes'. *American Journal of Political Science* 36: 617–34.

Laufer, W. S. (1994). 'Corporate Bodies and Guilty Minds'. *Emory Law Journal* (43): 647–730.

Lehrer, K. and C. Wagner (1981). *Rational Consensus in Science and Society: A Philosophical and Mathematical Study*. Dordrecht (D. Reidel Publishing).

Lewis, D. (1969). *Convention*. Cambridge, MA: Harvard University Press.

—— (1976). 'Probabilities of Conditionals and Conditional Probabilities'. *The Philosophical Review* 85(3): 297–315.

—— (1983). *Philosophical Papers Vol 1*. Oxford: Oxford University Press.

—— (1986a). *Philosophical Papers Vol 2*. Oxford: Oxford University Press.

—— (1986b). 'Probabilities of Conditionals and Conditional Probabilities II'. *The Philosophical Review* 95(4): 581–89.

Lindahl, H. and E. Claes (2009) (eds). *Philip Pettit and the Incorporation of Responsibility: Legal, Political, and Ethical Perspectives*. Rechtsfilosophie & Rechtstheorie 38(2). Den Haag: Boom Juridische uitgevers.

List, C. (2001). 'Mission Impossible: The Problem of Democratic Aggregation in the Face of Arrow's Theorem'. DPhil thesis in Politics, Oxford University.

—— (2002). 'Two Concepts of Agreement'. *The Good Society* 11: 72–9.

—— (2003a). 'The Epistemology of Special Majority Voting'. *Working paper, London School of Economics*. London.

—— (2003b). 'A Possibility Theorem on Aggregation over Multiple Interconnected Propositions'. *Mathematical Social Sciences* 45(1): 1–13 (with correction in *Math Soc Sci* 52, 2006: 109–10).

—— (2004a). 'The Impossibility of a Paretian Republican? Some Comments on Pettit and Sen'. *Economics and Philosophy* 20: 1–23.

—— (2004b). 'A Model of Path-Dependence in Decisions over Multiple Propositions'. *American Political Science Review* 98(3): 495–513.

—— (2004c). 'On the Significance of the Absolute Margin'. *British Journal for the Philosophy of Science* 55: 521–44.

—— (2005). 'Group Knowledge and Group Rationality: A Judgment Aggregation Perspective'. *Episteme: A Journal of Social Epistemology* 2(1): 25–38.

—— (2006a). 'The Democratic Trilemma'. *Democracy and Human Values Lectures, Princeton University*. Princeton/NJ.

—— (2006b). 'The Discursive Dilemma and Public Reason'. *Ethics* 116(2): 362–402.

—— (2006c). 'Republican Freedom and the Rule of Law'. *Politics, Philosophy and Economics* 5(2): 201–20.

List, C. (2008). 'Distributed Cognition: A Perspective from Social Choice Theory'. *Scientific Competition: Theory and Policy, Conferences on New Political Economy vol. 24*. M. Albert, D. Schmidtchen, and S. Voigt, Tuebingen: Mohr Siebeck.

—— (forthcoming-a). 'Group Communication and the Transformation of Judgments: An Impossibility Result'. *Journal of Political Philosophy*.

—— (forthcoming-b). 'The Theory of Judgment Aggregation: An Introductory Review'. *Synthese*.

—— (forthcoming-c). 'Collective Wisdom: Lessons from the Theory of Judgment Aggregation'. *Collectiv Wisdom*. J. Elster and H. Landemore.

—— C. Elsholtz, and T.D. Seeley (2009). 'Independence and Interdependence in Collective Decision Making: An Agent-Based Model of Nest-Site Choice by Honeybee Swarms'. *Philosophical Transactions of the Royal Society B* 364: 755–62.

—— and R. E. Goodin (2001). 'Epistemic Democracy: Generalizing the Condorcet Jury Theorem'. *Journal of Political Philosophy* 9: 277–306.

—— R. C. Luskin, et al. (2000/2006). 'Deliberation, Single-Peakedness, and the Possibility of Meaningful Democracy: Evidence from Deliberative Polls'. *London School of Economics*. London: London School of Economics.

—— and P. Menzies (2009). 'Non-Reductive Physicalism and the Limits of the Exclusion Principle'. *Journal of Philosophy* 106(9): 475–502.

—— and P. Pettit (2002). 'Aggregating Sets of Judgments: An Impossibility Result'. *Economics and Philosophy* 18: 89–110.

—— —— (2004a). 'Aggregating Sets of Judgments: Two Impossibility Results Compared'. *Synthese* 140: 207–35.

—— —— (2004b). 'An Epistemic Free Riding Problem?' *Karl Popper: Critical Appraisals*. P. Catton and G. Macdonald. London: Routledge.

—— —— (2005). 'On the Many as One'. *Philosophy and Public Affairs* 33(4): 377–90.

—— (2006). 'Group Agency and Supervenience'. *Southern Journal of Philosophy* 44(Spindel Supplement): 85–105.

—— and B. Polak, (2010) (eds). Symposium on 'Judgment aggregation'. *Journal of Economic Theory* 145(2).

—— and C. Puppe (2009). 'Judgment Aggregation: A Survey'. *Oxford Handbook of Rational and Social Choice*. P. Anand, C. Puppe, and P. Pattanaik. Oxford: Oxford University Press. 457–82.

Locke, J. (1960). *Two Treatises of Government*. Cambridge: Cambridge University Press.

—— (1975). *An Essay Concerning Human Understanding*. Oxford: Oxford University Press.

Lovejoy, A. O. (1961). *Reflections on Human Nature*. Baltimore: Johns Hopkins Press.

Ludwig, K. (2007a). 'The Argument from Normative Autonomy for Collective Agents'. *Journal of Social Philosophy* 38(3): 410–27.

—— (2007b). 'Collective Intentional Behavior from the Standpoint of Semantics'. *Nous* 41(3): 355–93.

Luhmann, N. (1990). *Essays on Self-Reference*. New York: Columbia University Press.

Macdonald, C. and G. Macdonald (2007). 'Mental Causation on the Program Model'. *Common Minds: Themes From the Philosophy of Philip Pettit*. G. Brennan, R. E. Goodin, F. Jackson, and M. Smith. Oxford: Oxford University Press. 1–27.

McAdams, R. H. (1997). 'The Origin, Development and Regulation of Norms'. *Michigan Law Review* 96(2): 338–433.

McConway, K. (1981). 'Marginalization and Linear Opinion Pools'. *Journal of the American Statistical Association* 76: 410–14.

McGeer, V. (2008). 'The Moral Development of First-Person Authority'. *European Journal of Philosophy* forthcoming.

—— and P. Pettit (2002). 'The Self-regulating Mind'. *Language and Communication* 22: 281–99.

McLean, J. (1999). 'Personality and Public Law Doctrine'. *University of Toronto Law Journal* 49: 123–49.

—— (2004). 'Government to State: Globalization, Regulation, and Governments as Legal Persons'. *Indiana Journal of Global Legal Studies* 10: 173–97.

Mäki, U., (2001) (ed.). *The Economic World View: Studies in the Ontology of Economics*. Cambridge: Cambridge University Press.

Malmendier, U. (2005). 'Roman Shares'. *The Origins of Value: The Financial Innovations that Created Modern Capital Markets*. W. Goetzman and G. Rouwenhorst. Oxford: Oxford University Press. 31–42.

May, L. (1987). *The Morality of Groups: Collective Responsibility, Group-Based Harm, and Corporate Rights*. Notre Dame: University of Notre Dame Press.

May, L. and S. Hoffman (1991) (eds). *Collective Responsibility: Five Decades of Debate in Theoretical and Applied Ethics*. Lanham, Md: Rowman & Littlefield.

Miller, D. (1992). 'Deliberative Democracy and Social Choice'. *Political Studies* 40 (special issue): 54–67.

—— (2007). *National Responsibility and Global Justice*. Oxford: Oxford University Press.

Miller, M. and D. Osherson (2009). 'Methods for Distance-Based Judgment Aggregation'. *Social Choice and Welfare* 32(4): 575–601.

Miller, N. R. (1996). 'Information, Individual Errors, and Collective Performance: Empirical Evidence on the Condorcet Jury Theorem'. *Group Decision and Negotiation* 5(3): 211–28.

Miller, S. (2007). 'Against the Collective Moral Autonomy Thesis'. *Journal of Social Philosophy* 38 (3): 389–409.

—— and P. Makela (2005). 'The Collectivist Approach to Collective Moral Responsibility'. *Metaphilosophy* 36(5): 634–51.

Mitchell, E. T. (1946). 'A Theory of Corporate Will'. *Ethics* 56(2): 96–105.

Mongin, P. (1995). 'Consistent Bayesian Aggregation'. *Journal of Economic Theory* 66: 313–51.

—— (2008). 'Factoring Out the Impossibility of Logical Aggregation'. *Journal of Economic Theory* 141(1): 100–13.

Nehring, K. (2003). 'Arrow's Theorem as a Corollary'. *Economics Letters* 80(3): 379–82.

—— (2005). 'The Impossibility of a Paretian Rational'. University of California, Davis.

—— and C. Puppe (2002). 'Strategy-proof Social Choice on Single-Peaked Domains: Possibility, Impossibility and the Space Between'. University of California, Davis.

—— —— (2007). 'The Structure of Strategy-proof Social Choice – Part I: General Characterization and Possibility Results on Median Spaces'. *Journal of Economic Theory* 135(1): 269–305.

—— —— (2008). 'Consistent Judgement Aggregation: The Truth-Functional Case'. *Social Choice and Welfare* 31: 41–57.

—— —— (2010a). 'Abstract Arrovian Aggregation'. *Journal of Economic Theory* 145(2): 467–94.

—— —— (2010b). 'Justifiable Group Choice'. *Journal of Economic Theory* 145(2): 583–602.

Nelson, R. and S. Winter (1982). *An Evolutionary Theory of Economic Change.* Cambridge, MA: Harvard University Press.

Nicholls, D. (1975). *The Pluralist State: The Political Ideas of J. N. Figgis and his Contemporaries.* London: Macmillan.

Nozick, R. (1974). *Anarchy, State, and Utopia.* Oxford: Blackwell.

—— (1981). *Philosophical Explanations.* Oxford: Oxford University Press.

Ober, J. (2008). *Democracy and Knowledge: Innovation and Learning in Classical Athens.* Princeton: Princeton University Press.

Parfit, D. (1984). *Reasons and Persons.* Oxford: Oxford University Press.

Pattanaik, P. (1988). 'On the Consistency of Libertarian Values'. *Economica* 55: 517–24.

Pauly, M. and M. van Hees (2006). 'Logical Constraints on Judgement Aggregation'. *Journal of Philosophical Logic* 35: 569–85.

Perry, J. (1979). 'The Essential Indexical'. *Nous* 13: 3–21.

Pettit, P. (1993). *The Common Mind: An Essay on Psychology, Society and Politics,* paperback edition 1996. New York: Oxford University Press.

—— (1997). *Republicanism: A Theory of Freedom and Government.* Oxford: Oxford University Press.

—— (2001a). 'Capability and Freedom: A Defence of Sen'. *Economics and Philosophy* 17: 1–20.

—— (2001b). 'Deliberative Democracy and the Discursive Dilemma'. *Philosophical Issues (supp. to Nous)* 11: 268–99.

—— (2001c). *A Theory of Freedom: From the Psychology to the Politics of Agency.* Cambridge and New York: Polity and Oxford University Press.

—— (2002). *Rules, Reasons, and Norms: Selected Essays.* Oxford: Oxford University Press.

—— (2003a). 'Akrasia, Collective and Individual'. *Weakness of Will and Practical Irrationality.* S. Stroud and C. Tappolet. Oxford: Oxford University Press. 69–96.

—— (2003b). 'Groups with Minds of their Own'. *Socializing Metaphysics.* F. Schmitt. New York: Rowan and Littlefield. 467–93.

—— (2005). 'The Elements of Responsibility'. *Philosophical Books* 46: 210–19.

—— (2006). 'Preference, Deliberation and Satisfaction'. *Preferences and Well-Being.* S. Olsaretti. Cambridge: Cambridge University Press. 31–53.

—— (2007a). 'Joining The Dots'. *Common Minds: Themes From The Philosophy of Philip Pettit.* G. Brennan, R. Goodin, F. Jackson, and M. Smith. Oxford: Oxford University Press. 215–344.

—— (2007b). 'Rationality, Reasoning and Group Agency'. *Dialectica* 61(4): 495–519.

—— (2007c). 'Responsibility Incorporated'. *Ethics* 117: 171–201.

—— (2008a). 'The Basic Liberties'. *Essays on H. L. A. Hart.* M. Kramer. Oxford: Oxford University Press. 201–24.

—— (2008b). *Made with Words: Hobbes on Language, Mind, and Politics.* Princeton: Princeton University Press.

—— (2008c). 'Republican Liberty: Three Axioms, Four Theorems'. *Republicanism and Political Theory.* C. Laborde and J. Manor. Oxford: Blackwell.

—— (2009). 'Law and Liberty'. *Law and Republicanism.* S. Besson and J. L. Marti. Oxford: Oxford University Press.

—— and D. Schweikard (2006). 'Joint Action and Group Agency'. *Philosophy of the Social Sciences* 36: 18–39.

Pettit, P. and M. Smith (1996). 'Freedom in Belief and Desire'. *Journal of Philosophy* 93: 429–49; reprinted in F. Jackson, P. Pettit, and M. Smith, 2004. 375–96.

Pigozzi, G. (2006). 'Belief Merging and the Discursive Dilemma: An Argument-Based Account to Paradoxes of Judgment Aggregation'. *Synthese* 152: 285–98.

Popper, K. R. (1960). *The Poverty of Historicism*. London: Routledge & Kegan Paul.

Priest, G. (2001). *An Introduction to Non-Classical Logic*. Cambridge: Cambridge University Press.

Rawls, J. (1971). *A Theory of Justice*. Oxford: Oxford University Press.

Riker, W. (1982). *Liberalism against Populism*. San Francisco: W.H. Freeman and Co.

Rosen, G. (2004). 'Scepticism about Moral Responsibility'. *Philosophical Perspectives* 18: 295–313.

Rothstein, P. (1990). 'Order-Restricted Preferences and Majority Rule'. *Social Choice and Welfare* 7: 331–42.

Rousseau, J.-J. (1997). *The Social Contract and Later Political Writings* (edited by Victor Gourevitch). Cambridge: Cambridge University Press.

Rovane, C. (1997). *The Bounds of Agency: An Essay in Revisionary Metaphysics*. Princeton, NJ: Princeton University Press.

Royal-Swedish-Academy-of-Sciences (2007). 'Mechanism Design Theory: Scientific Background on the Sveriges Riksbank Prize in Economic Sciences in Memory of Alfred Nobel 2007', electronically available at: http://nobelprize.org/nobel_prizes/economics/laureates/2007/ecoadv07.pdf.

Rubinstein, A. and P. Fishburn (1986). 'Algebraic Aggregation Theory'. *Journal of Economic Theory* 38: 63–77.

Runciman, D. (1997). *Pluralism and the Personality of the State*. Cambridge: Cambridge University Press.

Ryan, M. (1999). 'Bartolus of Sassoferrato and Free Cities'. *Transactions of the Royal Historical Society* 6: 65–89.

Sartre, J. P. (1957). *The Transcendence of the Ego: An Existentialist Theory of Consciousness*. New York: Farrar, Straus and Giroux.

Satterthwaite, M. (1975). 'Strategy-proofness and Arrow's Conditions: Existence and Correspondences for Voting Procedures and Social Welfare Functions'. *Journal of Economic Theory* 10(April): 187–217.

Schmitt, F. F. (2003) (ed.). *Socializing Metaphysics*. Lanham: Rowman & Littlefield.

Searle, J. (1990). 'Collective Intentions and Actions'. *Intentions in Communication*. P. R. Cohen, J. Morgan, and M. E. Pollack. Cambridge, MA: MIT Press. 401–15.

—— (1995). *The Construction of Social Reality*. New York: Free Press.

—— (2009). *Making the Social World: The Structure of Human Civilization*. Oxford: Oxford University Press.

Seeley, T. D. (2001). 'Decision Making in Superorganisms: How Collective Wisdom Arises from the Poorly Informed Masses'. *Bounded Rationality: The Adaptive Toolbox*. G. Gigerenzer and R. Selten. Cambridge, MA: MIT Press. 249–62.

Sen, A. (1970a). *Collective Choice and Social Welfare*. Edinburgh: Oliver and Boyd.

—— (1970b). 'The Impossibility of a Paretian Liberal'. *Journal of Political Economy* 78: 152–7.

—— (1982). *Choice, Welfare and Measurement*. Oxford: Blackwell.

—— (1983). 'Liberty and Social Choice'. *Journal of Philosophy* 80: 18–20.

—— (2001). 'Reply to Pettit, Anderson and Scanlon'. *Economics and Philosophy* 17: 51–66.

Shapley, L. and B. Grofman (1981). 'Optimizing Group Judgmental Accuracy', University of California, Irvine.

Sheehy, P. (2006). *The Reality of Social Groups*. Aldershot, Ashgate.

Skinner, Q. (1998). *Liberty Before Liberalism*. Cambridge: Cambridge University Press.

Skinner, Q. (2010). *A Genealogy of the Modern State*. London.

Smiley, M. (2005/2008). 'Collective Responsibility'. *Stanford Encyclopedia of Philosophy*. E. N. Zalta. Palo Alto, <http://plato.stanford.edu/archives/fall2008/entries/collective-responsibility>.

Sosa, E. (2007). *A Virtue Epistemology*. Oxford: Oxford University Press.

Spector, H. (2009). 'The Right to A Constitutional Jury'. *Legisprudence* 3(1): 111–23.

Stearns, M. L. (2000). *Constitutional Process: A Social Choice Analysis of Supreme Court Decision Making*. Ann Arbor: Michigan University Press.

Steiner, H. (1994). *An Essay on Rights*. Oxford: Blackwell.

Strawson, G. (2005). *Against Narrativity*. Oxford: Blackwell.

Strawson, P. (2003). 'Freedom and Resentment'. *Free Will*, 2nd edn. G. Watson. Oxford: Oxford University Press.

Sunstein, C. (2006). *Infotopia: How Many Minds Produce Knowledge*. New York: Oxford University Press.

Surowiecki, J. (2004). *The Wisdom of Crowds: Why the Many Are Smarter than the Few*. London: Abacus.

Tollefsen, D. P. (2003). 'Participant Reactive Attitudes and Collective Responsibility'. *Philosophical Explorations* 6: 218–35.

Tsohatzidis, S. L. (2007) (ed.). *Intentional Acts and Institutional Facts: Essays on John Searle's Social Ontology*. Dordrecht: Springer.

Tuomela, R. (1995). *The Importance of Us*. Stanford, CA: Stanford University Press.

—— (2007). *The Philosophy of Sociality: The Shared Point of View*. Oxford: Oxford University Press.

Vacca, R. (1921). 'Opinioni Individuali e Deliberazioni Collettive'. *Rivista Internazionale di Filosofia del Diritto*: 52–9.

van Hees, M. (2007). 'The Limits of Epistemic Democracy'. *Social Choice and Welfare* 28(4): 649–66.

Vincent, A. (1987). *Theories of the State*. Oxford: Blackwell.

Waldron, J. (1999). *Law and Disagreement*. Oxford: Oxford University Press.

Waltz, K. N. (1979). *Theory of International Politics*. Reading, MA: Addison-Wesley.

Wendt, A. (1999). *Social Theory of International Politics*. Cambridge: Cambridge University Press.

—— (2004). 'The State as Person in International Theory'. *Review of International Studies* 30(2): 289–316.

Werhane, P. A. and R. E. Freeman (2003). 'Corporate Responsibility'. *The Oxford Handbook of Practical Ethics*. H. LaFolette. Oxford: Oxford University Press.

Williams, B. (1978). *Descartes*. Harmondsworth: Penguin.

Williamson, T. (2000). *Knowledge and its Limits*. Oxford: Oxford University Press.

Wilson, R. (1975). 'On the Theory of Aggregation'. *Journal of Economic Theory* 10: 89–99.

Woolf, C. N. S. (1913). *Bartolus of Sassoferrato*. Cambridge: Cambridge University Press.

Endnotes

1. On the theory of intentionality, see Davidson (1985) and Dennett (1987), and on social choice theory, see Arrow (1951/1963) and Sen (1970a; 1982). On recent social ontology, see Searle (1995; 2009), a collection of papers edited by Schmitt (2003), and Sheehy (2006); for recent work on ontology in economics, see Mäki (2001) and Fulbrooke (2009). On the sociology of collectives and systems, see Coleman (1974; 1990), Habermas (1984, 1989), Luhmann (1990), Giddens (1984), and Bourdieu (2005). On the constructivist theory of the state, see Wendt (1999; 2004). For thinking on collective responsibility, see French (1984), Kutz (2001), and May (1987), and on legal personhood, Kelsen (1945), Dan-Cohen (1986), and Runciman (1997). We also build on our own earlier work on judgment aggregation (List and Pettit 2002; 2004a; 2005; 2006) as well as on more recent contributions in that area, as reviewed in Chapter 2. See, for example, the papers in a recent journal symposium (List and Polak 2010).

2. We can criticize an agent's actions and appeal to its beliefs, desires, and norms in a way that is impossible with a malfunctioning machine or a thunderstorm. We can regret a machine's defect, or the bad weather, but we can accuse only an agent of being irrational or immoral.

3. Quentin Skinner (2010) takes the Hobbesian view of the state to be a fiction theory: 'To express the point in the terminology introduced at the start of chapter 16 [of Leviathan], the state is thus a person "by fiction". It is never "truly" the case that it performs actions and takes responsibility for them. The only person who ever truly acts in such circumstances is the artificial person of the sovereign, whose specific role is to "personate" the fictional person of the state.' Legal theorists also speak of a fiction theory of group agents (Hager 1989), though they often seem to have a metaphor theory in mind. The real-entity theory they contrast it with is the one we associate here with Gierke and Maitland, but the phrase might also be used to describe our own theory.

4. Contributions include List and Pettit (2002; 2004a), Pauly and van Hees (2006), Dietrich (2006), Dietrich and List (2007a), Nehring and Puppe (2010a), and Dokow and Holzman (2010a).

5. What exactly this entails is developed in Chapter 3.

6. This quote comes from an interview with Margaret Thatcher published in *Woman's Own* magazine in October 1987.

7. Suppose that with every move the computer makes, we look at its electronic configuration, explore the differences various responses would make, and track the effect on its future moves. In that case we will not be able to play chess in the ordinary sense. Thus the very possibility of interacting as chess players seems to require adopting the intentional stance.

8. We may ask, for example, whether the position of the courts vis-à-vis congress parallels their position vis-à-vis the founders in the interpretation of a constitution, or whether these are wholly different positions.

9. We do not take any view here on the precise ontological status of representations and motivations. The approach we take, like functionalist approaches in general, leaves this issue open (Jackson and Pettit 1988).

10. If we identify a proposition with a set of possible worlds, then holding a representational attitude towards that proposition means depicting the actual world as lying within that set of possible worlds; and holding a motivational attitude towards it means being motivated to act in such a way as to 'move' the actual world into that set. There are various generalizations of this account of propositions. For the moment, we set aside complications arising from intentional attitudes involving indexicals. We return to some of these issues in Chapter 9.

11. A variation of this idea would be to represent a proposition as a synonymy class of sentences so that two sentences – say, synonyms or translational counterparts of each other – can express the same proposition. On that approach, the sentences that someone is a bachelor, that he is an unmarried male, and that he is an unmarried member of the species *homo sapiens* bearing a Y-chromosome may or may not express the same proposition, depending on how finely or coarsely we individuate synonyms; we need not take a view on this here.

12. Imagine a significantly upgraded robot. Its physical make-up may be so complex that the best way to make sense of it may be to identify the representations and motivations that mark it out as an agent.

13. Arguably, the only exception is the broadly motivational attitude that consists in a final intention or plan to pick a particular option from a set of options open to the agent; this always has an on-off form.

14. By contrast, re-expressing a credence of x assigned to 'p' simply as a judgment that p is not generally satisfactory, even when x is high, as it may run into so-called 'lottery paradoxes' (e.g. Hawthorne 2004).

15. We may stipulate that a judgment of preferability by an agent is agent-relative only; it does not carry heavy evaluative significance.

16. We can imagine re-expressing an agent's utility of x assigned to 'p' either, though perhaps less plausibly, as a suitable credence for the proposition 'it is preferable that p' or, more plausibly, as a judgment whose content is the proposition '"p" is an attractive scenario to the degree x'.

17. For a related discussion, see Pettit (2007a; 2007b).

18. Crucially, the phenomenon of 'group agency', as discussed here, is distinct from that of 'joint agency' or 'team agency', as discussed in an important literature (e.g. Gilbert 1989; Searle 1990; 1995; Tuomela 1995; Bratman 1999; Gilbert 2001; Bacharach 2006; Gold and Sugden 2007; Ludwig 2007b; Tsohatzidis 2007; Tuomela 2007). Since a joint action can be an isolated act performed jointly by several individuals, it does not necessarily bring into existence a fully fledged group agent in our sense (here we draw on Pettit and Schweikard 2006). In particular, the performance of a single joint action is too thin, on our account, to warrant the ascription of a unified agential status according to our conditions of agency. For example, in the case of fully fledged agents, as mentioned in the Introduction, we can meaningfully hypothesize about how they would behave under a broad range of variations in their desires or beliefs, whereas there is a severe limit on how far we can do this with a casual collection that performs a joint action. Moreover, *any* collection of people, and not just a group with an enduring identity over time, may perform a joint action, for instance when the people in question carry a piano downstairs together or spontaneously join to help a stranger in need. Thus mere collections may be capable of

joint agency, whereas only groups are capable of group agency in the stronger sense we have in mind. However, joint actions, and the joint intentions underlying them, may play a role in the formation of group agents, as we discuss below. Gilbert (1989; 2001; 2006) has argued that every commitment to perform a joint action brings into existence a 'plural subject', but on our account this amounts to an over-ascription of agency. It is important to keep the substantive distinction between group agency in our sense and joint agency in mind, even though some scholars prefer to adopt a different terminology from ours. Tuomela (2007) has developed a detailed map of the conceptual space in this terrain, which includes some of the possibilities discussed here. For a related recent discussion, see also Hindriks (2008). We say more about the kinds of joint intentions involved in joint actions below.

19. Stated like this, the four conditions are mutually related. There are different ways in which these conditions may be further articulated and connected. For a taxonomy of different approaches to defining joint intentions, see Tuomela (2007).

20. The 'and so on' does not require that we each have an impossibly complicated hierarchy of beliefs, but only that we are each disposed, at any level of iteration, to give a positive answer to the question of whether there is still recognition of one another's recognition at that level. On common awareness, see Lewis (1969).

21. Although their joint action may unwittingly lead them to generate such a system, this is no more assured than the appearance of agency based on evolutionary shaping. Recall our earlier note on the distinction between the phenomena of 'joint agency' and 'group agency'. Thus, from the perspective of our account, to say that every performance of a joint action brings into existence a 'plural subject', as suggested by Gilbert's account of joint agency (2001), amounts to an over-ascription of agency.

22. Our theory is deliberately ecumenical on what the precise criteria for licensed authorization and licensed activity are. Different accounts of those criteria thus correspond to slightly different specifications of a group agent's membership.

23. Note, in particular, that we assume the restriction to binary intentional attitudes specifically in the context of jointly intentional group agents. It is conceivable that a non-jointly intentional group agent could hold non-binary attitudes, especially if these result from behavioral as opposed to explicit aggregation, such as through markets. On the aggregation of propositional attitudes more generally, including the non-binary case, see Dietrich and List (2010a) and a later endnote. On behavioral aggregation in prediction markets, see, for example, Hanson (forthcoming).

24. What we are about to introduce is also known as the theory of 'judgment aggregation', but we here use the term 'attitude aggregation' to emphasize a somewhat more general perspective.

25. On the aggregation of probabilistic attitudes, see Dietrich and List (forthcoming) and the classic review article by Genest and Zidek (1986). See also Lehrer and Wagner (1981). Other contributions on the aggregation of non-binary evaluations include Rubinstein and Fishburn (1986) and Dokow and Holzman (2009b). Extensions of the present results on binary propositional attitude aggregation to multi-valued logics were given by Pauly and van Hees (2006) and van Hees (2007).

26. For a discussion of aggregation problems among non-human animals, see Conradt and List (2009).

27. Although an exhaustive and detailed review is beyond the scope of this chapter, we would like to mention a few key contributions. Several authors have proved stronger, or more refined, impossibility results than the one in List and Pettit (2002; 2004a), including Pauly and van Hees (2006), Dietrich (2006; 2007), Dietrich and List (2007a; 2008a; 2010b), Nehring and Puppe (2008; 2010a), Mongin (2008), and Dokow and Holzman (2010a; 2010b). Some of these results provide not only sufficient conditions under which an agenda of propositions gives rise to the impossibility in question but necessary and sufficient conditions, building on ideas introduced by Nehring and Puppe (2002) in the theory of strategy-proof social choice. Many of the current results on judgment aggregation also have precursors in other areas of aggregation theory, particularly in the theory of abstract aggregation (Wilson 1975; Rubinstein and Fishburn 1986), and in axiomatic social choice theory more generally, which goes back to Kenneth Arrow's seminal work (1951/1963). Although much of the recent work on judgment aggregation has focused on proving impossibility results, the literature also contains a number of possibility results, including List and Pettit (2002), List (2003b; 2004b), Dietrich (2006; 2010), Pigozzi (2006), Dietrich and List (2007b; 2010b), and Nehring and Puppe (2010b). The model of judgment aggregation used in List and Pettit (2002) has been extended to multi-valued logics in which propositions can have more than two truth values (Pauly and van Hees 2006; van Hees 2007), and to more expressive logics, including various propositional, predicate, modal, conditional, and deontic logics (Dietrich 2007). Other related bodies of literature are those on the problem of belief merging in computer science (e.g. Konieczny and Pino-Perez 2002) and on Bayesian aggregation as well as probabilistic opinion pooling (e.g. Hylland and Zeckhauser 1979; Lehrer and Wagner 1981; McConway 1981; Genest and Zidek 1986; Mongin 1995). For more detailed introductory and survey articles, see List and Puppe (2009) and List (forthcoming-b). A survey focusing on implications for democratic theory is given in List (2006b). See also a symposium on 'Judgment aggregation' in the *Journal of Economic Theory*, edited and introduced by List and Polak (2010).

28. Below we also comment on what we take to be the conceptual difference between the 'doctrinal paradox' and the 'discursive dilemma'.

29. While the current literature on the 'doctrinal paradox' (including the name) goes back to Kornhauser and Sager's work (see also Kornhauser 1992; Chapman 1998), Horacio Spector has drawn our attention to Vacca's (1921) paper, which presents a surprising early variant of the paradox. Although Vacca uses a different terminology, he correctly identifies the conflict between what are now known as the 'premise-based' and 'conclusion-based' decision procedures in collective decisions on a conclusion based on two or more premises. His main example is isomorphic to the example of the 'doctrinal paradox' given in Table 2.1 below. Implicitly, but without articulating this in logical terms, Vacca also contrasts the standard conjunctive version of the paradox with a disjunctive one. The least compelling aspect of his remarkable paper, however, is his probabilistic argument for using the conclusion-based procedure, where, unfortunately, he does not apply Bayesian reasoning correctly. Spector reports his discovery of Vacca's hitherto overlooked paper in Spector (2009). Apart from a 1945 book by an Argentine legal philosopher (Cossio 1945, pp. 160–4, cited by Spector 2009), we are not aware of any other references to Vacca's paper.

30. As mentioned in an earlier note, some of the recent technical work also draws on important related work on the theory of strategy-proof social choice by Nehring and Puppe (2002), which, in turn, is related to other work in that area (Barberà, Gul, et al. 1993; Barberà, Massó, et al. 1997).

31. Majority inconsistencies can occur as soon as the agenda of propositions, and their negations, on which attitudes are to be formed has a 'minimal inconsistent' subset of three or more propositions, i.e. an inconsistent subset of that size that becomes consistent as soon as any proposition is removed from it (Dietrich and List 2007b; Nehring and Puppe 2007). Examples of such subsets are the set consisting of 'p', 'if p then q', and 'not q', and the set consisting of 'not p', 'not q', and 'p or q'.

32. Although Condorcet's paradox formally applies to the aggregation of preference relations (typically orderings) between multiple options, not to that of intentional attitudes in our sense, it can be seen as a paradox of majoritarian attitude aggregation if preference relations are represented as suitable intentional attitudes towards suitable ranking propositions. There are at least two possible such constructions. Each preference relation in Condorcet's sense can be represented either by a set of judgments on propositions of the form 'x is preferable to y' or by a set of preferences – in our sense of binary motivational attitudes – on propositions of the form 'in a choice between x and y, x is chosen over y'. Under each construction, some additional individually and collectively accepted propositions must be introduced which capture the standard rationality conditions on preference relations. Condorcet's paradox then becomes a paradox of majoritarian attitude aggregation. For details of the construction, see List and Pettit (2004a) and Dietrich and List (2007a). An earlier discussion of this idea was given by Guilbaud (1966), who described the generalization of Condorcet's paradox as the 'Condorcet effect'. Interestingly, Condorcet himself (1785) may have favored a judgmental interpretation of preferences in terms of judgments of betterness.

33. The combined aggregation of beliefs and desires is discussed (albeit in a non-binary framework) in the literature on Bayesian aggregation (e.g. Hylland and Zeckhauser 1979). As mentioned earlier, a more general model of attitude aggregation than the present one, which covers both binary and non-binary attitudes, is developed in Dietrich and List (2010a).

34. Even if an agent doesn't judge that p, this does not automatically imply that the agent judges that not p. After all, the agent could be 'incomplete' in his or her judgment concerning the proposition-negation pair 'p', 'not p'.

35. For simplicity, we identify 'not not p' with 'p'.

36. For the main theorem below, the agenda assumption just stated can actually be weakened to the assumption that (i) the agenda has a minimal inconsistent subset of three or more propositions, and (ii) it is not (nor isomorphic to) a set of propositions whose only logical connectives are 'not' and 'if and only if'. A variant of this result is proved in Dietrich and List (2007a), and for closely related results, see Dokow and Holzman (2010a). Condition (i) is a variant of the so-called 'non-median-space' condition in an abstract aggregation context (Nehring and Puppe 2002). Condition (ii) is a variant of the 'even-number negation condition' in Dietrich and List (2007a) and 'non-affineness' in Dokow and Holzman (2010a). See also the review in List and Puppe (2009).

37. Formally, an individual's attitudes are given by an 'acceptance/rejection function' assigning to each proposition on the agenda the value 'Yes' or 'No', as defined in List (2004b); see also Dietrich and List (2010a). In List and Pettit (2002), we represented each individual's judgments by a 'judgment set', defined as the set of propositions in the agenda accepted by the individual. The two representations are interdefinable: an acceptance/rejection function can be viewed as the index function of a judgment set.

38. Technically, this is also given by an acceptance/rejection function.

39. The logical relationship between the present result and Arrow's theorem is discussed in List and Pettit (2004a) and Dietrich and List (2007a).

40. See the list of references in an earlier note. For derivations of Arrow's theorem as a formal corollary of an impossibility result on judgment aggregation, see Dietrich and List (2007a) and Dokow and Holzman (2010a). Related derivations of slightly weaker Arrow-like results on preference aggregation from results on judgment aggregation and abstract aggregation were given by List and Pettit (2004a) and Nehring (2003), respectively. For further discussion, see also the introduction and some of the contributions in the symposium edited by List and Polak (2010).

41. For earlier discussions of such escape routes, on which we draw in the following section, see List and Pettit (2002) and List (2005; 2006b).

42. In the world of Arrowian aggregation preference relations, unidimensional alignment is similar in spirit to Duncan Black's (1948) well-known condition of 'single-peakedness'. More formally, it corresponds to a condition on profiles of preference relations called, in different variants, 'order-restriction' and 'single crossing' (Rothstein 1990). For more general results, see Dietrich and List (2010b).

43. On supermajority voting, see also Goodin and List (2006). The escape route from the impossibility theorem via relaxing completeness becomes even more limited if we require the group's attitudes to be deductively closed as well as consistent, where 'deductive closure' is the requirement that any proposition on the agenda entailed by other collectively accepted propositions must also be accepted. Deductive closure is implied by collective rationality, but it must be made explicit when completeness is dropped. It turns out that the only aggregation function satisfying universal domain, anonymity, and systematicity and generating consistent and deductively closed group attitudes is the unanimity rule (Dietrich and List 2008a). Under this aggregation function, every group member can veto a positive group attitude on any proposition. Rather than providing an escape route from the impossibility of attitude aggregation, the present route is therefore likely to lead to stalemate, even in a minimally diverse group. For related contributions, see Gärdenfors (2006) and Dokow and Holzman (2010b).

44. Pauly and van Hees (2006) first proved this result for the above assumption about the agenda. For a weaker assumption about the agenda – namely, conditions (i) and (ii) stated in an earlier note – it is shown in Dietrich and List (2007a) that any aggregation function satisfying universal domain, collective rationality, and systematicity is either a dictatorship or an inverse dictatorship.

45. But we also suggest in that chapter that using an aggregation function that relaxes both anonymity and systematicity can sometimes be beneficial, in that it allows an efficient division of labor among group members.

46. For subsequent related results, see also Dokow and Holzman (2009a) and Dietrich and List (2009).

47. Specifically, the agenda must satisfy conditions (i) and (ii), as stated in an earlier note, and (iii) any proposition in the agenda must be deducible from any other proposition in it via a sequence of pairwise conditional entailments. The latter condition was first introduced by Nehring and Puppe (2002) in the context of strategy-proof social choice under the name of 'total blockedness'.

48. This result builds on earlier results by Nehring and Puppe (2002), Pauly and van Hees (2006), and Dietrich (2006). Each of these other results uses somewhat different conditions on the aggregation function and on the agenda. Interestingly, Arrow's theorem (1951/1963) can be derived as a corollary from the result stated here. For further details, see Dietrich and List (2007a) and Dokow and Holzman (2010a) as well as Nehring and Puppe (2010a).

49. Why are the premise- and conclusion-based procedures special cases of a sequential priority procedure? The sequential priority procedure becomes a premise-based procedure when applied to an agenda containing both premises and conclusions, where the premises are given priority over the conclusions, and it becomes a conclusion-based procedure when applied to a restricted agenda containing only one or several conclusions, which are then automatically prioritized.

50. If, as in our example, the distance between two combinations of attitudes is defined simply by counting the number of 'mismatches' (the so-called 'Hamming distance'), then the resulting distance-based aggregation function is a 'consistent extension' of majority voting. This is to say that whenever the majority attitudes are consistent, those attitudes are also the distance-minimizing consistent ones. It is only in cases of inconsistent majority attitudes that the outcome of distance-based aggregation comes apart from the outcome of majority voting.

51. For earlier results on strategy-proof social choice, see also Nehring and Puppe (2002).

52. The sequential priority procedure does so only on the assumption that the agenda is specified sufficiently broadly. If the agenda is specified so as to contain only 'conclusions', the sequential priority procedure becomes equivalent to the conclusion-based one, as noted above.

53. In economics, Kenneth Arrow's 'social welfare function' is an aggregation function in this thin sense, whereas the game-theoretically specified 'mechanisms' explored in the theory of mechanism design are organizational structures in the thicker sense.

54. Within the category of functionally inexplicit organizational structures, we also comment on the role of 'feedback'.

55. As just noted, even when the aggregation function is given, a functionally explicit organizational structure can still take a variety of forms: an aggregation function can usually be implemented in a number of ways, and there are also different possible choices of members or deputies who act on the group's behalf.

56. Specifically, as we have seen, under the premise-based procedure, the group takes majority votes on the propositions designated as premises and lets their outcomes determine its attitudes on other propositions. Under the sequential priority procedure, it considers the propositions in some order of priority and forms its attitude on each proposition as follows: if the attitudes already formed do not constrain the attitude that

can consistently be formed on the new proposition, the group takes a majority vote on the new proposition; but if they do, the group lets those earlier attitudes dictate the new one. Under both structures, the group's attitudes depend on the way propositions are prioritized.

57. If the process involves randomization, then the group attitudes generated in it are the outcomes of a random variable whose parameters may be individual attitudes and other individual contributions. For a related discussion of attitude adjustments in deliberation, see Ferejohn (2007).

58. As we show in Chapter 5, however, such complex voting motives can arise even in organizational structures without feedback.

59. But it is not logically impossible. A group could apply an aggregation function not only to intentional attitudes on object-language propositions but also to attitudes on meta-language propositions. Still, without any feedback between the attitudes formed at the group level and the individual attitudes fed into the aggregation function, the group's capacity to engage in rational self-questioning to enhance its rational performance seems limited.

60. The present discussion extends the one we offered in List and Pettit (2006).

61. This definition entails that necessary facts supervene on contingent facts, since any two possible worlds that are identical in the contingent facts are also identical in the necessary ones. Here the determination is clearly vacuous, but in the cases we are concerned with such vacuous instances of supervenience do not arise.

62. Our thesis holds, regardless of how many or few of the members contribute to what the group says or does, and regardless of the weight given to their contributions. The group's attitudes are superveniently determined by the members' contributions even if some contributions have a greater weight in that determination than others or even if, in the limit, the group's attitudes are determined by a single member, like Hobbes's sovereign. Our thesis also holds when the members defer to some outside authority in producing their individual contributions. That authority may be an ultimate determinant of the group's attitudes but the proximate determinant will still be the members' contributions: their attitudes, actions, or dispositions, influenced though they may be by the outside authority. Although deference to an outside authority is not common, it may occasionally occur, for two reasons. One is epistemic, the other affective. The epistemic reason applies when members of a group ascribe special expertise to an outside authority. They may then let their individual judgments be influenced by that authority. But members may often resist such epistemic deference because there are no suitable outside experts or because they do not wish to abdicate their status as centers of representation. The affective reason for deference applies with preferences rather than judgments. The members may be so affectively attached to a certain authority that they adopt the preferences of the authority. But this possibility is plausible only in special cases, such as in the presence of a charismatic leader or guru.

63. Those interconnections may even be sustained by a joint intention on the part of the members that they together follow the instructions of the Turing-machine program and thereby constitute a group agent.

64. In this chapter we speak of the attitudes of members that fix the group attitudes, without focusing on the fact that it is manifested attitudes that are in question. One issue that arises for any organizational structure under which a group is formed, of course, is whether or

not it induces the sincere manifestation of attitudes. That issue is at the center of discussion in Chapter 5.

65. This functional relation, in turn, can be formally modeled as an aggregation function, as defined in the last chapter.

66. Throughout the formal discussion, we consider groups with two or more members.

67. The relevant results in Chapter 2 are the impossibility theorem (List and Pettit 2002) and the results reviewed in the discussion of relaxing anonymity (Pauly and van Hees 2006; Dietrich and List 2007a).

68. The relevant result in Chapter 2 is the impossibility theorem reviewed in the discussion of relaxing systematicity (Dietrich 2006; Pauly and van Hees 2006; Dietrich and List 2007a; Dokow and Holzman 2010a; related to Nehring and Puppe 2010a).

69. As we have seen, the only exceptions in which proposition-wise supervenience is consistent with robust group rationality are cases such as dictatorships, arrangements that fail to preserve unanimous individual attitudes and cases with only sparse logical connections between propositions.

70. The chapter draws on material in List (2005; 2008; forthcoming-c).

71. This quantitative measure of truth-tracking is rough because there are well-known difficulties in relating conditionals to conditional probabilities. See, e.g. Lewis (1976; 1986b).

72. The present distinction between truth-tracking and truth-indication broadly corresponds to a distinction made in epistemology between the properties of 'sensitivity' and 'safety', as they characterize beliefs (Williamson 2000; Sosa 2007).

73. This question, of course, lies in the terrain of social epistemology (Goldman 1999). In particular, it falls into the area of social epistemology that addresses the ascription of doxastic states to collectives (e.g. Goldman 2004; List 2005; Goldman forthcoming).

74. The most forceful critique has been put forward by Dietrich (2008), who argues that the two conditions are never simultaneously justified. Notice, however, that Dietrich does not claim that the two conditions are mutually inconsistent, that is, that the scenario they pick out is logically impossible. His claim is the weaker epistemological claim that we cannot simultaneously have evidence for the truth of both conditions.

75. Whether not judging that p entails judging that not p depends on whether the group's judgments satisfy the property of completeness, as introduced in Chapter 2.

76. Provided the group size is above a certain minimal number.

77. However, there are some subtle complications (Feddersen and Pesendorfer 1998), as discussed in the next chapter.

78. It is important to emphasize, once again, that these results depend on the truth of Condorcet's competence and independence assumptions. As soon as one of these assumptions is violated, the picture becomes significantly more complicated.

79. The latter happens whenever r is below the kth root of a half.

80. To secure this result, each individual's positive and negative tracking reliability on each premise must exceed the kth root of a half, e.g. 0.71 when $k = 2$, or 0.79 when $k = 3$.

81. While not every decrease in reliability with increasing group size undermines the Condorcet jury theorem, the decrease must not be too fast for the jury theorem to continue to hold. A necessary and sufficient condition to hold even when individual reliability is a function of the group size is given in Berend and Paroush (1998). See also List (2003a).

82. Effects along these lines have been discussed in the literature under the themes of rational ignorance (Brennan and Lomasky 1993), the economy of esteem (Brennan and Pettit 2004), and epistemic freeriding (List and Pettit 2004b), respectively.

83. Though it is in some cases.

84. For further generalizations, see Ben-Yashar and Nitzan (1997).

85. The term 'equilibrium' is sometimes restricted to concepts such as Nash equilibrium, and not applied to the concept of dominance. However, we prefer the present terminology under which all of these different concepts – from dominance, via Nash equilibrium, to various more refined equilibrium concepts – are subsumed under the broad notion of 'equilibrium concept'. This marks the fact that there can be stronger and weaker equilibrium concepts, and that a dominant-strategy equilibrium simply lies at one extreme end of that spectrum; in particular, one can think of a dominant-strategy equilibrium simply as a strengthening of a Nash equilibrium.

86. Similarly, if truthfulness is incentive compatible under a given auction mechanism, we can be confident that bidders will reveal their true valuations for the goods they are bidding for. And if cooperativeness is incentive compatible under a public-goods provision mechanism, we can be confident that individuals will cooperate in contributing to the provision of the public good in question. However, it is important to emphasize that all this assumes an empirically correct specification of preferences and the rationality criterion.

87. This definition is based on the classic definition of 'strategy-proofness' by Gibbard (1973) and Satterthwaite (1975).

88. Thus the precise meaning of the incentive-compatibility condition just stated depends on what individual preferences are deemed empirically possible.

89. The judges in our example clearly fulfill this assumption. The third judge, for example, prefers the group attitudes resulting from untruthfully voting against the proposition about action to those resulting from truthfully voting in favor of it because the former are closer to his or her individual attitudes on the propositions of concern – here the proposition about liability – than the latter.

90. For illustrative purposes, we assume that the total number of jurors is odd.

91. For more technical results, see Austen-Smith and Banks (1996) and Feddersen and Pesendorfer (1998).

92. More generally, an aggregation function such as the conclusion-based procedure supports agency only in a limited sense: it does not allow the group to form intentional attitudes on more than a very thinly specified agenda.

93. Throughout the discussion of the behavioral route, we have assumed that, while individual preferences may change, the relevant criterion of rationality is fixed. We assume that, for the purposes of analyzing the incentive structure in any organization, the appropriate rationality criterion is given by our best descriptive theory of human agency.

94. This notion of decisiveness goes back in social choice theory to Arrow (1951/1963) and Sen (1970b).

95. We have previously discussed some of the ideas in the next two sections in Pettit (2001a) and List (2004a; 2006c).

96. A good introduction to the semantics of conditionals can be found in Priest (2001).

97. At least under certain standard assumptions.

98. It is important to note, however, that how precisely those two questions map onto these two dimensions of decisiveness depends very much on the precise semantics of conditionals that we employ. We set these technicalities aside here. More technical discussions can be found in List (2004a; 2006c).

99. Sen (2001) also makes a point along these lines in his discussion of the difference between the notion of robust freedom in the republican sense and the notion of capability, as applicable, for instance, in welfare economics.

100. We assume that even when someone is successful in overcoming obstacles put in their way, it remains the case that they were deprived of some freedom in the choice made. They chose a penalized option, x, but they had to bear a cost imposed on them intentionally by another. We might say that their control over x was made more costly or that their control over option x-without-a-penalty (the option they originally confronted) was removed: that option was replaced by x-with-a-penalty.

101. We revisit the interpretation of such context-independence in the third section of this chapter.

102. This condition is a proposition-wise variant of unanimity preservation, as introduced in Chapter 2.

103. Related ideas on domain restrictions in the literature on Sen's liberal paradox are discussed in Sen (1983), Craven (1982), and Gigliotti (1986).

104. In the literature on Sen's liberal paradox, this idea has been explored in terms of a framework in which social alternatives are given by vectors of characteristics belonging to the private spheres of different individuals. The desideratum of individual rights then requires that individuals should be decisive over their own private characteristics, but not over those of others. Unfortunately, it turns out that, even in this framework, several variants of Sen's liberal paradox continue to hold (e.g. Gibbard 1974; Pattanaik 1988).

105. It is no objection to this republican way of thinking that someone might be politically deprived of her capacity to choose between x and not-x, were a majority of people in society to turn simultaneously against her or against those in any of the minority categories to which she belongs. After all, the majority that could treat her in that way now is not itself a group agent, at least in the scenario we are envisaging, and the possibility that a majority might form such an agent does not mean that she depends on the goodwill of any actual agent for access to the two options. It does not mean that she is currently unfree, only that it is possible that she becomes unfree, as the majority incorporates and develops a capacity for interference. That possibility may or may not be probable enough to warrant putting factors in place to guard against it. But while it remains a possibility, it is quite consistent with her currently enjoying freedom in the choice.

106. The chapter draws on material in Pettit (2007c). See also a special journal issue edited by Lindahl and Claes (2009), which includes articles by den Hartogh, van den Brink, van Roermund and Vranken, and Tinnevelt. The position defended is related to that of several other authors, most notably Peter French (1984). See also French, Nesteruk, et al. (1992). There is a large literature on issues related to corporate or collective responsibility, including Feinberg (1968), May (1987), and Cane (2002) and the collections edited by May and Hoffman (1991) and Erskine (2003). For an extensive overview of some of this literature, see Smiley (2005/2008). For recent contributions, see, among many others,

Tollefsen (2003), Miller and Makela (2005), Copp (1991; 2007), Ludwig (2007a), Seumas Miller (2007b), and Hindriks (2009). On issues of responsibility in the global context, see David Miller (2007a) and responses in a recent special issue of *Critical Review of International Social and Political Philosophy*, edited (with introduction) by De Schutter and Tinnevelt (2008).

107. Does holding someone responsible in our sense entail holding them responsible in the causal sense? That partly depends on whether we think there are negative causes. We may hold someone responsible for what they didn't do: for not doing anything as distinct from doing nothing, which might be a matter of positive decision. But, not admitting negative causes, we might refuse to say that such a non-event was a cause of that for which we hold the agent responsible.

108. Some of these conditions may be fulfilled without others, leading to familiar scenarios of partial responsibility. For example, partial or diminished responsibility may be assigned if the second or third condition is not realized in the fullest way possible. The present formulation of the conditions is designed to make the conditions independent of one another. The formulation in Pettit (2007c) requires that the normative judgment that figures in the second condition not be epiphenomenal: that it play a causal role in controlling for what the agent does; thus the formulation nests the third condition within the second, and the second within the first.

109. When we treat a group agent as fit to be held responsible then, plausibly, we automatically assume that its attitudes range over a relatively rich agenda. Suppose we fault a group for not treating like cases alike, for example. We then assume that it has a positive attitude on the proposition that it is good to treat like cases alike and fails to act on it. Or we assume that it has the capacity to form such an attitude, having that proposition within its agenda, and that it is fit to be held responsible for omitting to form and act on the right attitude.

110. One of us, Philip Pettit, believes that exercising control in the relevant way requires more than just exercising causal control. It requires in particular that the agent's normative judgments play an appropriate causal role in generating or controlling action and, since he takes this to be linked, that the agent be capable of reasoning. See Pettit (2001c; 2007a; 2007b). As a group agent, we are only committed to the weaker view, that exercising control involves exercising causal control.

111. The argument is reminiscent of the classic 'exclusion argument' against mental causation (e.g. Kim 1998), and we comment on this parallel in a moment.

112. Technically expressed, in the firing-squad case there is a weak sub-optimal equilibrium from which no one can unilaterally depart with moral benefit. In the speeding-car case there is a strong sub-optimal equilibrium from which no one can unilaterally depart without doing moral harm.

113. Braham and Holler (2008) argue that it is always possible to distribute causal responsibility among the members of a collectivity who together bring about some result. That may be so but the concern here is with moral responsibility, not causal.

114. Kelly (2003) suggests that many theorists emphasize corporate responsibility at a cost to individual, enactor responsibility; it should be clear that the line taken here has no such implication.

115. In the early fourteenth century, Oldradus de Ponte wrote against such a view of corporate entities: *Licet non habeant veram personam, tamen habent personam fictam fictione juris . . . Et sic eadem fictione animam habent, et delinquere possunt et puniri* (Eschmann 1946, fn. 34). In English, 'although they do not have a true persona, nevertheless they have a fictive persona, by a fiction of the law. And so by the same fiction they have a soul, and they are able to sin and to be punished'.

116. For Hobbes, this involves the manipulation of symbols in which the semantic connections of words are articulated.

117. Acceptance is important since obligations are only incurred voluntarily on Hobbes's story. But he has a very low threshold for what counts as voluntary acceptance, believing that even actions that are occasioned by fear or intimidation can count as voluntary (Pettit 2008b, Ch. 4). We follow him on the need for voluntary acceptance but not on his account of what counts as voluntary.

118. Persons authorize their words, as spokespersons for themselves. They vouch for their reliability and accept appropriate censure and sanction in cases of failure. For Hobbes it is of prime importance that human beings can serve as spokespersons not only for themselves but also for others, particularly for groups. When agents speak for others, then their principals must own or authorize the words of their spokesperson; when they speak for themselves, they must own or authorize their own words. 'A person, is he, whose words or actions are considered, either as his own, or as representing the words or actions of another man, or of any other thing to whom they are attributed' (Hobbes 1994, 16.1). When the words or actions 'are considered as his own, then is he called a natural person; and when they are considered as representing the words and actions of another, then is he a feigned or artificial person' (Hobbes 1994, 16.2).

119. Hobbes, notoriously, makes much of the fact that giving one's word is binding or obligating only under conditions where one can be assured that one is not putting one's central interests at risk; and he argues on that basis that it can thrive among people only in the presence of 'a common power to keep them all in awe' (Hobbes 1994, 17.4). We ignore that aspect of his views, however. What is important from our perspective is the new departure he makes in developing a performative view of personhood in general.

120. Although this performative view makes the capacity to incur and inherit obligations basic to the idea of a person, it still allows us to say, in commonsense mode, that the reason why certain words uttered earlier obligate the agent later is that it is the same person at both times. There is no vicious circularity here. Let the measles virus be described as whatever virus it is that causes measles spots, so that our conception of the virus depends on our conception of the spots. We may still explain the spots by reference to the virus. Similarly, even though we conceive of personal identity over time as whatever connection it is that sustains the inheritance of incurred obligation, we may still explain why an agent at a later time inherits the obligations contracted by an agent earlier by pointing out that they are the same person.

121. Someone unable to act as his or her own spokesperson may still count as a person on this account. In this case, provisions have to be made for the assignment of a suitable spokesperson, acting on the person's behalf in accordance with the appropriate system of conventions and obligations. The individual will be given the status of a person insofar as it is taken to be appropriate that such provisions are made.

122. Any system of obligations permits certain kinds of influences in its domain and rules out others, identifying claims that one person may make on another as well as ones that are prohibited. It may permit, for example, the influence exercised when one party charms another or presents the other, in a take-it-or-leave-it manner, with reasons for acting thus and so. And it may rule out the kind of influence that makes no pretense of going by common reasons, such as brute force or coercion, and the one that merely pretends to do so, such as deception or manipulation. To resort to such influence, within the domain of the obligations, would breach the spirit of these obligations, if not always their letter.

123. It is conceivable that some non-human animals, such as primates, may be given the status of persons. This is consistent with our account, again assuming that their personification entails the assignment of suitable spokespersons, acting on their behalf in accordance with a suitable system of conventions and obligations.

124. This is quoted in Duff 1938, p. 37, in the Latin: *si quid universitati debetur, singulis non debetur; nec quod debet universitas singuli debent.*

125. The term *corporatio* came into use somewhat later. It appears, for example, in the entry on corporations in John Cowell's renowned legal dictionary, *The Interpreter* (Cowell 1607).

126. One of us, Philip Pettit, subscribes to the thicker view of personhood while the other, Christian List, prefers to keep an open mind on the matter. This divergence illustrates the coexistence of corporate and individual identities that we address in the final chapter.

127. The ideal of respect in the treatment of persons, individual and corporate, should not be confused with the distinct ideal of reverence. According to the intrinsicist tradition, persons are constituted out of special stuff or have some intrinsically special properties. And so in this tradition persons are often said to have a more or less sacred status and to deserve a special sort of reverence. Conceiving of persons in the performative way, we do not think that they are deserving of reverence just in virtue of their personhood; if that ideal has application in some cases, it will be in virtue of other properties like life or consciousness or humanity. A regime of mutual respect commands attention as an ideal, not because of the stuff out of which persons are constituted but because of the capacities that they display. That is why it has relevance to group agents, whereas the ideal of reverence probably has none.

128. We take it as a working assumption that group persons do not have whatever functional characteristic it is that makes individual human beings distinctively valuable, such as sentience of the right kind or other distinctively human qualities.

129. For an overview and critique of 'identity politics', see Gutmann (2003). For a discussion of the range of ethical issues connected with group identity, see Appiah (2004). We discuss neither topic in this chapter, although the considerations we raise are relevant to both.

130. Not only is the desire whose object is the sentence 'I lock the door' indistinguishable from my desire to lock the door. That same desire may be ascribed in a third-person fashion too. 'Christian (or Philip) desires that he lock the door' ascribes the same desire to me as I express in saying 'I desire that I lock the door', since 'he' in this usage implies that the mode in which I, Christian or Philip, would express the object of the desire requires an 'I'.

131. Perry's path-breaking paper built, as he says, on earlier work by Castaneda (1966). There is now an enormous literature on the topic of self-involving beliefs and desires. The paper that spawned this literature in the wake of Perry's contribution is David Lewis's

'Attitudes De Dicto and De Se', reprinted in Lewis (1983). We abstract from many details in this literature, since they are not pertinent to our concerns. Since we model propositions as sentences, there is no problem for us in saying that the indexical sentence 'I lock the door' is appropriate to express the object of my desire. If we were to model propositions as sets of possible worlds, we would have to express indexicals using sets of centered possible worlds.

132. Did it support that suggestion, it would violate a ceiling constraint on attitude-ascription of the kind that we discussed in Chapter 1; it would convey a false message as to the sophistication of the robot.

133. We say that it usually makes that unnecessary, not that it always does so, because it is logically possible that I or anyone else might close the identification gap on the pattern described in the cognitive-achievement model. I might suffer from some pathology, for example, whereby I think of myself primarily in third-personal terms, say as Christian or Philip, and only manage to let Christian's or Philip's attitudes activate me by recourse to the sophisticated thought that I am that person. Simpler agents like the robot can only avoid the identification gap in the manner of the by-product model. And normal agents like you and me may avoid it in the same way. But it is still an open possibility that it be avoided in artificial, pathological ways as well. We return to this thought in speaking later of how group agents overcome the identification gap.

134. The claim that self-identification is required for functioning as a person raises the question as to whether it is required for reasoning generally, including theoretical reasoning on the basis of logical properties like consistency. We do not think that it is. I may reason from premises that implicate but do not mention a self, as in 'p' is true; 'if p, then q' is true; so 'q' is true as well. That a single, continuing self is implicated in such reasoning is emphasized by a number of authors, on the grounds that there is reason for someone to draw the conclusion only if the premises are held by that very person. See Bernard Williams's discussion of the Cogito in Williams (1978); see also Burge (1998). But the fact that a continuing self is implicated in reasoning does not imply that the person has to self-identify. However, the special reasoning that invokes the very concept of a reason, registering that the truth of some propositions provides a reason *for me* to hold by another proposition, may require self-identification.

135. For an argument that the distinction is already recognized by Thomas Hobbes, though not in so many words, see (Pettit 2008b).

136. Alternatively, group agency may materialize as a by-product of individuals desiring some neutral but common goal that rationally leads them, in their own words, to desire as a means that *we* do such and such (see, for example, Bacharach 2006). This scenario is logically possible and nothing we have said rules it out. If it materializes, then while means-end rationality may lead individuals sometimes to want to do something individually, it may lead them at other times to want to do something collectively. It may lead them each to want, not that *I* do so and so, but that *we* do so and so. This can happen, in particular, without any independent recognition that acting with others in this way can further one's own individual interests or without any independent attitude of affection towards that group. But even if this possibility is realized, it remains the case that the group will only command the continuing allegiance of its members if such allegiance is

consistent with the members' motivation. Thus the concerns raised in our discussion in Chapter 5 remain fully pertinent.

137. There are cases where a corporate 'we' is essential, even though there is no question of joint or corporate agency; an example might be where we are a marginalized minority that constitutes the object of majority attitudes in the community.

138. The approach was even more deeply theologized with the representation of the church or *ecclesia* as a mystical corporate body, a *corpus mysticum*, and with the insistence that outside the church there was no salvation: *extra ecclesiam nulla salus*. Another, related possibility of surviving is emphasized by Johnston (2010).

General Index*

---

*This general index also contains the names of authors discussed in the text; a full index of names, which includes cited authors, appears below.

Name Index